Palgrave Studies in Classical Liberalism

This series offers a forum to writers concerned that the central presuppositions of the liberal tradition have been severely corroded, neglected, or misappropriated by overly rationalistic and constructivist approaches.

The hardest-won achievement of the liberal tradition has been the wrestling of epistemic independence from overwhelming concentrations of power, monopolies and capricious zealotries. The very precondition of knowledge is the exploitation of the epistemic virtues accorded by society's situated and distributed manifold of spontaneous orders, the DNA of the modern civil condition.

With the confluence of interest in situated and distributed liberalism emanating from the Scottish tradition, Austrian and behavioral economics, non-Cartesian philosophy and moral psychology, the editors are soliciting proposals that speak to this multidisciplinary constituency. Sole or joint authorship submissions are welcome as are edited collections, broadly theoretical or topical in nature.

More information about this series at
http://www.palgrave.com/gp/series/15722

Matúš Pošvanc

The Evolutionary Invisible Hand

The Problem of Rational Decision-Making and Social Ordering over Time

palgrave
macmillan

Matúš Pošvanc
F. A. Hayek Foundation
Bratislava, Slovakia

ISSN 2662-6470 ISSN 2662-6489 (electronic)
Palgrave Studies in Classical Liberalism
ISBN 978-3-030-71799-5 ISBN 978-3-030-71800-8 (eBook)
https://doi.org/10.1007/978-3-030-71800-8

This Palgrave Macmillan imprint is published by the registered company Springer Nature Switzerland AG
The registered company address is: Gewerbestrasse 11, 6330 Cham, Switzerland

Dedicated to my family. Thank you for your support.

Contents

1
Introduction

This book presents a new theoretical approach to the description of economic phenomena over time. A realistic and meaningful description over time is one of the basic preconditions for the success of any economic theory. The presented theoretical solution or proposal has two main characteristics. The first is a modification of the theory of subjective value in the form of the claim that one perceives the satisfaction of one's needs in the context of one's overall individual portfolio of goods. The causal relationship of the "old" theory in the form of "need is satisfied by good" is modified in terms of "sum of needs is satisfied by portfolio of goods (sum of goods)." This is a small modification, which, however, brings several important elements to the description of economic phenomena over time. The old theoretical approach did not enable us to operate over time because of different value context of goods which changes over time. However, the portfolio of goods is, in fact, a formally logical homogeneous construction of the mind, which is applicable over time. The portfolio is constructed by individual goods and is always different from this point of view, however, it provides, at the

M. Pošvanc, *The Evolutionary Invisible Hand*,
Palgrave Studies in Classical Liberalism,
https://doi.org/10.1007/978-3-030-71800-8_1

same time, a homogenous concept applicable; the portfolio per se. This brings qualitatively new possibilities to describe economic phenomena over time. The second characteristic is the anchoring of this modification of the theory of subjective value in evolutionary (intersubjective) apriorism. The anchoring of the concept in evolutionary apriorism allows a description of development; not empirical, so to speak accurate description, but the construction of the so-called conjunctural history or logical-historical method of describing the evolution of phenomena where exact empirical data are missing (the method has already been used by Adam Smith, Friedrich Hegel, F. A. Hayek, and other evolutionary thinkers). The vitality of this new theoretical approach is shown in the fundamental problem that the book solves: "How do we do that which we can correctly estimate for the future, so that we can learn from realized mistakes and be economically successful?" To deal with the problem, the text is divided into the three logical parts. The first part provides basic argumentation for the main question "How do we deal with economic problems in time?" The vitality of the presented concept is then shown in the following two parts of the book—the application of the presented concept onto the problem of equilibrium and in the problem of indifference.

The first part of the book is presented in the following way: "*Why Are We Economically Successful? The Theory of Economic Error and Learning.*" It addresses two basic issues: "Why are we economically successful?" and "How do we know that we have made an economic error?" From the point of view of the practical life of any individual, these are trivial issues. We know when we are economically successful and when we are not. We know when we have made an economic error, and possibly, we know how to correct it. These questions are much more challenging to a social scientist, who should explain this very "trivial" knowledge. The problem is inevitably related to our outlook for the future. It is problematic to explain how we compare two points in time: The moment when the decision that led us to the future was implemented and a comparison of the moment that actually came. Only this comparison allows us to answer the question of whether we were successful or whether we have made a mistake. The triviality of the problem is immediately lost, once we realize that we do not know what the future will be like when we make a decision. How do we estimate it? And how is it possible that we can somehow manage to prepare good estimates? And if we make a mistake, how do we actually learn when we are merely estimating the future in the context of current information? Isn't every moment of our life so unique that there is no such thing as learning from the past? Is our decision-making rational at all? Or is everything just a work of chance, which we (incorrectly) call rationality? So how do we grasp the future? These are not trivial questions. They are related to the estimation of the future, the question of the rationality of our action, the problem of economic profit/loss and costs, the problem of coordination of several individuals in the community and the problem of the individual, and the market economic equilibrium.

We will focus on a more detailed description relating to the problem of economic estimation of the future and explore how such great minds as Frank Knight, Ludwig von Mises, Hans Herman Hoppe, G. L. S. Shackle Ludwig Lachmann, or F. A. Hayek approach the problem. We will try to identify the vital parts of their systems that will allow us to design a new solution proposal. This will be methodologically anchored in Hayek-Pavlík's evolutionary (intersubjective) apriorism. I will show how we estimate the future, why we are relatively successful in estimating the future, and why we are economically successful overall, i.e., why we experience economic progress. I will show how the so-called "invisible hand"—the most famous metaphor in economics—helps us in this matter while defining the modus operandi behind the principles and forces which govern it. I will demonstrate that people can also coordinate with each other through the economic-normative criteria that have evolved. I will explain the principle of coordination exclusively in the context of the future, i.e., in the context of individuals' expectations and plans. We will show that concepts of error, profit, loss, and cost have a subjective and intersubjective character as well. The division will allow us to explain several issues related to the coordination of individuals—with the specifying of criteria for identifying economic error and success.

The second part of the book is called "*In Defense of the Invisible Hand Concept: Modification of the Austrian Theory of Equilibration and Social Ordering.*" Tiebien (2012, p. 614) concludes that the concept of equilibrium has persisted on the scientific scene for such a long time because

"Equilibrium is indispensable." He argues that at the end of the day, each replacement of the Walrasian doctrine introduced its static version of the concept of equilibrium. Even those theories that are considered a description of the equilibrium as a process are, after all, just end-state theories in disguise. The reason for this conclusion is the high degree of complexity of the described problem, which cannot be realized without appropriate simplification and assumptions. From the point of view of the Austrian School of Economics, equilibration theories are often considered redundant or that they do not describe real phenomena. However, there have been some attempts to describe a realistic concept of equilibrium. This can be seen in the works of Mises, Hayek, O'Driscoll, Rizzo, or Hülsmann. Tiebien (2012) states that the Austrian school has provided a useful insight into theories of equilibration. This chapter follows the program of the Austrian school in the field of equilibrium theory, or more precisely equilibration. The ambition of this chapter is to briefly introduce a fully dynamic theory of equilibration, which is not a masked static version of equilibrium. However, Tiebien's (2012) remark that every equilibrium theory has its static side is correct. In this chapter, it is necessary to present a potential solution to this seemingly logical paradox—the static-dynamic character of equilibrium and to present a theory that has both a static (thymological) and dynamic (praxeological) component. A useful phenomenon for solving this paradox is the portfolio of goods by which man satisfies a combination of his needs. The portfolio as a static-dynamic phenomenon allows us to present a realistic concept of equilibrium, both at the level of the individual in the form of defining their individual state of equilibrium and an individual process of equilibration, and a subsequent description of the problem of equilibration at the level of society. At the same time, another ambition of this chapter is to connect several approaches to the problem of equilibrium which are present within the program of the Austrian school. It will draw on and connect vital parts of Mises's (1998) approach of the Evenly Rotating Economy, as well as Hayek's (post-1937) program of social ordering. The chapter will focus on the transition from the equilibrium to the disequilibrium state, explaining why there is a tendency to an equilibration (invisible hand of the market), and describing the phenomena of competition and business discovery as consequences of individual transition between equilibrium and disequilibrium. At the same time, the presented concept is not based on the description of the circulation of goods, nor is it based on price equilibrium or demand/supply equilibrium, which, as the reader will see, are the result of equilibration tendencies of individual interactions. It is based on a description of plans and expectations of individuals who interact economically with each other. The concept is not presented based as a mathematical construct, but it implies future possibilities for its mathematization.

The last part of the book is called "*The Problem of Indifference and Choice: An Answer to Nozick's Challenge to Austrians.*" The aim of this part of the book is to link the Austrian School's approach to indifference with the mainstream approach. It looks critically at an interesting ongoing discussion about the problem of indifference and choice within the Austrian School. The discussion was conducted in response to Nozick's (1977) address to representatives of the Austrian school on the problem of indifference, implying the invalidity of the law of diminishing marginal utility in the absence of a presupposition of indifference. It briefly introduces the discussion and its main problems. Stated reservations will be replaced by suggested solutions based on the minor modification of the theory of subjective value and on the premise that needs are satisfied by a portfolio of goods over time. The discussion will allow the preservation of elements of Indifference analysis as interpreted by the neoclassical mainstream. However, it will also allow interpretation of the problem of choice based on *strict preferences* and creates room for Indifference, also from the point of view of the Austrian School of Economics. This is quite a controversial conclusion, but it is a logical consequence of the proposed minor modification in the theory of subjective value.

The book is anchored quite strongly into the realm of the so-called Austrian School of Economics. It is intended to address this group of scientists directly. However, it could be of interest also for many mainstream economists. Why? The presented theory tries to connect the mainstream with the Austrians. It is intended to show the importance of the Austrian School for economic science. The book is presented as a novel theoretical approach, however, anchored in other theoretical writings. It is possible to consider this book as some kind of "economic philosophy." It deals with the very core problems of economics; it is focused on the so-called essences of the phenomena. The book does not contain empirical data. However, the text contains various kinds of illustrative examples that describe the problem in terms of the so-called conjunctural history method. I hope that questions, topics, and proposed solutions will motivate readers to open the book and to dive into an exploration of them.

Matúš Pošvanc

References

Hayek, A. Friedrich. 1937. Economics and Knowledge. *Economica.* New Series 4 (13): 33–54. Online version on WWW. DOCUMENT. https://mises.org/library/economics-and-knowledge Accessed 22 Jan 2021.

Mises, Ludwig. 1949, 1998. Human Action. Scholar Edition. Auburn, Ala*: Ludwig Von Mises Institute*. WWW DOCUMENT. https://mises.org/library/human-action-0/html/pp/663.

Nozick, Robert. 1977. On Austrian Methodology. *Synthese. Vol. 36, No. 3, Mathematical Methods of the Social Sciences, Part II (Nov. 1977), pp. 353–392.* WWW DOCUMENT. https://www.jstor.org/stable/20115233.

Tiebien, Bert. 2012. *The Concept of Equilibrium in Different Economic Traditions.* Edward Elgar Publishing.

2

Why Are We Economically Successful?

The concept of success/error related to economic activity is not a special concept for an individual. The individual knows when an error has been made and knows when he/she is successful. In asking the question, "*How do you know that you have made a mistake*?"; in most cases, the general public would remain in silent wonder as to why anyone would ask such a question at all. From a scientific point of view, it is not entirely easy to explain this mundane perception that people have. This is because we tend to compare two moments in time in connection with the mistake:

(a) the moment of implementation of the decision that led us to the result,
(b) the moment of whether or not the result was fulfilled.

However, at the time the decision is implemented, we do not yet know what will happen. After all, we cannot predict the future. If something happens that we did not know would happen, how can we even say that we made a mistake at the time our decision was made?

M. Pošvanc, *The Evolutionary Invisible Hand*, Palgrave Studies in Classical Liberalism, https://doi.org/10.1007/978-3-030-71800-8_2

At the same time, our actions and activities are constantly focused only on the future. We cannot change the past. We do not know the future in terms of whether and what natural deterministic phenomenon will occur, i.e., how nature and the surrounding reality will behave. A much bigger problem is that we do not know the future reactions of other members of society. We cannot look into the minds of people, nor can we analyze their thoughts, or plans. The bigger the society, the higher the so-called uncertainty resulting from possible combinations of actions of all people. Given this massive degree of darkness connected with risk and uncertainty, how is it even possible for us to survive? How is it even possible that we can deal with the future and do it even relatively successfully? Is it all just a coincidence? Is it just our illusion that we are behaving rationally? How is it possible for an entrepreneur to successfully bring to the market a product whose planning, production, and subsequent successful sales are sometimes several years apart, yet they are successful? Explaining or grasping the future is a challenge.

If we knew the future, we could be objectively certain, when we have made a mistake. If we knew the future and acted unfavorably toward it, we would be *objectively* wrong. However, if we do not know the future, how can we ever say later that what we did was an error? As the reader will see below, an *ex post* evaluation, when we say: "had I known then what I know now, I would have behaved differently" will not help either. How do we know we would have behaved differently from today's point of view? Because we do not know the alternative development of our past, we are unable to say objectively, *ex post*, that by making a decision at *time t*, we have made an objective error. Had we decided differently, in a way we now consider appropriate, today we could claim once again, that the decision was wrong because we do not know the alternative consequences of our alternative decision.

If it is difficult to compare the plans (the plan drawn up at time *t*) with the reality of what will happen (*at time t + 1*), how do we know that we have even made a profit or a loss? This is still not the final problem if we realize that profit/loss is a subjective phenomenon that can be perceived as utterly different by everyone. It is also questionable whether achieving profit means the entrepreneur achieved any result expressed e.g., if money received is higher than zero or if the achieved result is higher than the original plan that the entrepreneur had?

We face some interesting questions that seem to become more interesting once the reader realizes that people do not have an issue dealing with these kinds of problems. People solve these types of problems practically every day. The answer to the problem is more likely to come from economic science, i.e., to provide a proper description of how to respond to these questions. In this essay, we will, therefore, focus on the problem of how we grasp the future, how we anticipate it, and how we compare it with the past and present. We will then introduce the concept of economic error, profit/loss, and costs. The presented solution to the problem will allow us to define the problem of entrepreneurship and the functions of the entrepreneur more precisely.

We will proceed as follows. We will begin by defining the problem of grasping and anticipating the future and describe the concepts of risk and uncertainty. We will look at some proposed solutions used today to solve the problems in question. We will examine works from authors such as professors Knight, Mises, Hoppe, Shackle, Lachmann, and Hayek,[1] who deal with similar issues; especially how, according to them, human subjects grasp the future. After introducing these ideas, we will introduce our chosen path and methodological background in the form of Hayek–Pavlík's evolutionary apriorism.

As the reader will see, the chosen methodological background will allow us to discover the answers to the questions which we set out. Subsequently, we will describe how we are able to predict the future and why entrepreneurs and the rest of us are relatively successful in estimating it. However, this will not end our journey. Another very important problem will confront us; the problem of the mutual coordination of human actions, which was of particular interest to professor F.A. Hayek. We will argue that economic coordination does not only take place against the background of normative concepts manifested in the socio-legal environment around which Hayek had developed his

[1]The authors often supplement each other. The reader should not get the impression that if this essay cites, e.g., Mises or Hoppe, that Shackle–Lachmann's interpretations of a phenomenon related to the future are completely different and less relevant. I originally wanted to focus on three lines of approach: The Knight–Mises–Hoppe–Hülsmann line, the Shackle–Lachmann line, and the Hayek–Kirzner line. However, after a more detailed examination of the selected authors, I had great difficulty in classifying them in this way.

theory of cultural evolution. We will show that there are normative-economic coordinates of human action, upon which people *rationally* "tune" their mutual and individually determined goals to satisfy their individual needs. We will try to identify the basic background of the problem of economic error. We will demonstrate that the problem of economic error has several levels—technical, individual-subjective, and intersubjective. Based on our findings, we will then modify the approach to the profit/loss and cost problem, which, like the concept of error, will be individual-subjective and intersubjective in nature. As you can see, we are facing some interesting questions.

2.1 Defining the Problem: A Comparison Over Time

The problem we face is primarily related to human choice and the related issue of uncertainty. The reality (world of things) in which one lives is to some extent predictable. As we will see below, the reality (world of things) is related to the problem of risk which one can deal with in principle. However, as explained by Shackle (1992, pp. 122–126) the choice is always about what "*we imagine and what we want.*" One does not even have time to choose the present; it is too late for the present. The present is already happening. Therefore, the choice is only about the future. We imagine and think about the future; it is the future that is the subject matter of human action. At the same time, it is the most complicated phenomenon that we must explain. Shackle writes: the depth of the problem is related (1992, pp. 122–123):

> *To call it future is to concede the presumption that it is already "existent" and merely waiting to appear. If that is so, if the world is determinist, then it seems idle to speak of choice. Choice, if it means what our instinct and workday attitude assume, is originative, it is the start of a new train of influences. If so, we cannot know what choices will be made at moments still to come. And this essential and vast gap in the "relevant knowledge" required for rational choice cannot be overcome, if world is what all our talk implicitly supposes.*

In Shackle's view, the future is empty. Although the present shows us that the choices made in the past have filled it with some content that manifests itself in the present. Shackle's view is that we cannot speak of any kind of rational action and decision-making in the context of the future, because we live in a world that we influence through the choices we make and that our choices have a unique and always anticipatory character. We are simply not equipped with enough information to make a "*fully informed decision*" and Shackle believes that only such a decision could be considered a rational one.[2] From Shackle's point of view, there are simply no objective criteria for a rational decision that would make it possible to assess what was rational and what was not. The future is referred to as kaleidic. This inevitably follows Shackle's claims that everyone else faces the same problem. This means that by not knowing what the other person will do, I cannot even anticipate my own correct and rational decision made in the context of the other. Selgin (1990, p. 34) perfectly describes the problem:

> *Now let us pass briefly to Shackle's strong thesis: the matter of the kaleidic future. Here what may be claimed against praxeology is not that it fails to recognize the categories of uncertainty, time, and expectations, but rather that it fails to reckon with some of the more crucial implications of these. What praxeology fails to account for … is how actors may effectively anticipate the future and, in particular, how they may anticipate future actions of other people, given that the future is "unknowable." If people cannot foretell the future, then even the broader, praxeological idea of "rationalism" (which assumes some-more than incidental-capacity for actors in the social world to select means appropriate to their chosen ends) is unfounded. Economics is obliged, in this case, not merely to account for the use and dissemination of*

[2] Shackle approaches the possibility of economic analysis only in terms of objectively given facts of neoclassical equilibrist analysis which eliminates the time factor from economic analysis. According to neoclassical economics, it is the only applicable economic analysis. In principle, it is an honest awareness of the problem of time and change, and the application of economic analysis only in the context of certain theoretical assumptions, e.g., Selgin (1990, p. 30) quotes Shackle in this context: "*If there is a fundamental conflict between the appeal to rationality and the consideration of the consequences of time as it imprisons us in actuality, the theoretician is confronted with a stark choice. He can reject rationality or time.*" However, one of our tasks is to identify the possibilities of implementing economic analysis in the context of the passage of time.

existing knowledge (as Hayek would have it), but to explain the possibility of entrepreneurial prediction.

Clearly, if Shackle were right, there would be no such thing as a rational economic decision.[3] As soon as time enters the scene, according to Shackle, all our actions are only speculative and the result of this speculation (manifested, for example, in profit) should be random.[4] Of course, the problem would also be how human action then affects the achieved results of satisfaction, which is to appear at a later date. As Selgin (1990) points out, the following statement by Mises (1957, 1985, p. 269, bold added by the author of this book) could not apply either:

Man acts is tantamount to the proposition: Man is eager to substitute a state of affairs that suits him better for a state of affairs that suits him less. In order to achieve this, he must employ suitable means. ***It is the reason that enables him to find out what is a suitable means for attaining his chosen end and what is not.***

Thus, if Shackle's interpretation were to apply, nothing like the rational choice of appropriate means to achieve one's goals over time could exist, and any success/failure is a matter of chance. As Selgin (1990) further

[3]From this point of view, it is completely understandable, that when examining economics why e.g., Shackle resorts to describing static equilibrium. For him, it is the only scientifically honest (!) method of studying economic phenomena. At the same time, Shackle is well aware that the elimination of several variables is a simplification, but in the context of the description of real reality, this is the only option for him.

From the classical Austrian analysis of the problem of economic phenomena, where it is argued that the neoclassical way of examining the problem of equilibrium is unrealistic, it is questionable to what extent the analysis based on the examination of human action is equally realistic. If we can even talk about any realism of the Austrian way of studying economics, it is only at the level of general and abstract knowledge, which is the modus operandi of human action. An equally interesting and related question arises as to how much this kind of abstraction of the description of human action differs from the neoclassical description based on the elimination of some variables.

[4]Shackle–Lachmann solves this problem by describing speculative markets, where one part of the speculative market belongs to the so-called bulls (speculators on price growth) and the second part of the market is called bears (speculators on falling prices). At one point in time, one or the other simply hits the bull's eye and actually guesses the "result" correctly. However, it does not explain how our predecessors made decisions, they did not know these types of bull-bear markets and, if we go even further into history, did not even calculate in monetary units.

states, Shackle's system and the interesting questions that arise from it do not remain the only challenge to explain the problems associated with the rational grasp of the future. Other proposed solutions bring challenges and questions when Selgin points to Alfred Schutz and Ludwig Lachmann. Schutz (1959), in the Husserl's tradition, explains that we have some knowledge about the future and that we use it successfully. Schutz does not accept that the future is completely empty as is implied if we paraphrase Shackle. We can think about the future and anticipate it in the context of abstract assumptions. Schutz (1959, p. 81) writes:

> *First, our anticipations and expectations refer not to the future occurrences in their uniqueness and their unique settings within the unique context, but occurrences of such and such a type typically placed in a typical constellation. The structurization of our stock of knowledge at hand in terms of types is at the foundation of the aforementioned idealization. Yet because of their very typicality, our anticipations are necessarily more or less empty, and this emptiness will be filled in by exactly those features of the event, once it is actualized, that make it a unique individual occurrence. Secondly, … not only the range but also the structurization of our stock of knowledge at hand changes continually. … It is this system of relevance, however, that determines the structurization of the stock of knowledge at hand and divides it into zones of various degrees of clarity and distinctness. Any shift in the system of relevance dislocates these layers and redistributes knowledge.*

Schutz also says that we use this knowledge as "*common sense*" while having the character of social knowledge. Schutz's solution is somewhat similar to Mises's solution to the problem through *Verstehen*, but at the same time, it has the features of Hayek's system of dispersed knowledge and its coordination. However, Schutz is also aware that the fundamental problem one faces is in human action in the context of others. And he, too, remains somewhat skeptical, but much less so than Shackle. Schutz (1959, pp. 86, 87) writes:

> *As long as we succeed, within this unified and delimited realm of the specious present, in keeping our projects consistent and compatible both with one another and with the stock of knowledge at hand, there exists a reasonable chance that our future action will conform, at least in type, to our projects as*

> *anticipated modo future exacti. Such a chance will, however, be a subjective one, that is, it will exist merely for me, the actor, in the form of reasonable likelihood, and there is no warranty whatever that this subjective chance – a chance for me – will coincide with objective probability, calculable in mathematical terms.*

Schutz realizes that the use of knowledge is only possible in its abstract and general form; only in this way is knowledge applicable over time. It is in this sense that he uses his dictum of common sense and the system of mutual knowledge sharing solve the problem of the future relatively "successfully." However, he does not answer one important and related question: How is this possible? How is it possible that our knowledge, not only about the reality (world of things) but also about the world of action (praxeology), can be used successfully and rationally? What are our "objectified" criteria[5] for success/failure in anticipating the future, and how are they objectified (Hayek 1937), that we all understand them in the same way? And we have to note that they have this kind of character in order to be operational in time and from the subjective perspective of any individual. The second problem is Schutz's weak pessimism, which speaks only of a "reasonable chance" which implies that his solution is only practical; this means that it is good that it works. However, this does not address the question of why this is so; isn't the result just random in nature? In the context of Schutz's first quote, this should not be a coincidence or just a meaningful chance.

Selgin (1990) further presents the problem through the work of Ludwig Lachmann who uses Schutz's solution to grasp the future but combines it with Hayek's (albeit modified) solution of knowledge coordination. Here Lachmann introduces and applies to the problem of so-called "*divergent expectations.*" In Shackle's tradition, Lachmann is well aware that we live in an ever-changing world. It does not only change in the context of the situation, i.e., the surrounding reality, but mainly in the context of human value changes. Lachmann (2005, pp. 225–226) writes:

[5]As the reader will see later, these are not objective criteria, but intersubjective criteria. These people perceive them as tacit knowledge, they do not question it in any way, and in this respect, they are objectified criteria for them, based on which they make decisions.

> *The world of the market economy is thus a kaleidic world, a world of flux in which the ceaseless flow of news daily impinges on human choice and the making of decisions.*

Lachmann was attempting to solve the problem of this constant change through a concept of "*divergent expectations*," which is our tool for attempting to grasp the unknowns associated with the future. In principle, the more diverse these expectations are (in the form of dispersed knowledge), the more likely it is that someone's expectations will be met. This is fully reflected in the speculative markets where the so-called bulls vs. bears act. According to Selgin (1990), the problem that can be implied from Lachmann's concept of divergent expectations is fundamental, in the form of the absence of any criteria that could inform entrepreneurs ex ante about the plans and expectations of consumers.

From these few mentioned and selected works and quotations, it should be clear that the greatest challenge to explain the problem of grasping the future *is paradoxically caused by the problem of choice. Paradoxically, because it is precisely the choice that allows us to influence the future and change it potentially in our favor.* It is also a choice that causes an identical problem when comparing today with the past. This is due to the differing values of economic context (caused by other choices) at the time the choice in question was made. In other words, the question arises as to how we value two states in a time continuum, provided that we accept that people's preferences and evaluations *can change.* At the same time, how is it possible that we are economically successful despite the fact that people's preferences and evaluations can change? Does this mean that value changes do not happen that often? Or that there is some component of stability of evaluation, or potentially some kind of natural determinism, contained within the choice with which we are allowed to anticipate the future? So how do we grasp the future? How do we know if we have made a mistake? And how is it even possible to learn from the mistakes and learn from the past if we are faced with an absolutely veiled (kaleidic) future that is inherently unique? Capturing and anticipating the future is related to understanding how the world around us and other people behave. This division is related to the problem of risk and the problem of uncertainty.

2.1.1 Risk and Uncertainty

The division of the above-mentioned problem into issues of risk and uncertainty is connected in economic theory, usually by the works of Frank Knight. Knight (1964) shows that risk and uncertainty are different concepts. While the concept of risk is related to the *possibility* of predicting some phenomena (for example, Knight states, the probability of how many bottles needed to produce champagne will break during its production per e.g., 1000 bottles produced), the concept of uncertainty relates to choice, subjective evaluation and people's subjective preferences. Hoppe (1997, 2007) explains that what Knight perceives as risky and uncertain, Mises (1998) describes in the context of the so-called *class* and *case probability*. While a *class probability* is related to the frequency of some phenomena, i.e., the probability that in a class of phenomena known to us, a phenomenon related to a given member of this class will occur; in a *case probability*, we are only aware of some of the reasons why something happened, whereas other determining factors are unknown to us. In principle, class probability can be linked to how the world around us is "managed" and how it relates to statistical risk assessment, i.e., with what probability a given natural phenomenon occurs. Whereas case probability connects precisely with human (unpredictable, dependent on free will) action,[6] it is related to an estimate related to uncertainty, i.e., we estimate how other members of the community will behave.

According to Hoppe, whether Knight or Mises divide the problem into risk and uncertainty in connection with the question, "*why does a competitive business not eliminate the existence of profit*," or the problem is related to the question of why there is a profit at all, both authors answer the question in the sense that it is precisely because of the existence

[6]Shackle is also aware of this problem; within this context, Lachmann (2005, p. 228) compares Shackle to Mises: *Both authors emphatically reject the calculus of probability as a tool for dealing with human conduct in a world of uncertainty. Shackle devotes his chapter 34 ('Languages for Expectation') to this matter. He sums up his view in the heading of section 34.40: 'Probability concerns groups of events, not single critical choices'* (1972, p. 400). *Mises makes the same point by distinguishing between class and case probability.*

of uncertainty (not risk). The uncertainty we have with the connection of another's behavior does not allow us to determine the likelihood of whether a phenomenon derived from human action will occur. The conduct of others is too unique in the context of the future for us to apply statistical methods to it. The distinctiveness associated with human action and choice has a unique and unrepeatable context. Although a phenomenon may belong to a group of phenomena (which is a condition for the use of the concept of probability), it lacks the character of randomness. According to these authors, it is not possible to use tools related to statistical methods of probability, which are based on a statistical determination for this type of phenomenon. On the contrary, the reality (nature) is about the extent to which we can use our knowledge to determine what will happen and what will not. The probability literally shows us the degree of our ignorance. The probability is therefore related to whether or not a phenomenon, a defined group of phenomena related to reality (the world of things) will (or will not) occur with a certain probability.

Profit, on the other hand, is the entrepreneur's reward for the correct detection of unique economic phenomena (case probability), e.g., what the other person wants. Of course, the entrepreneur also handles the elements of reality that is needed to make the best use in the context of case probability. The case probability is a major problem for entrepreneurs. To satisfy the consumer's wishes, they must first detect subjective preferences (domain of case probability) and only then use the elements of reality. Dealing with reality as such is a domain of risk and phenomena related to *class probability*, but we still use them in our (human) context of *case probability—meaning we use parts of reality to meet someone's needs.*

As Hoppe (1997, 2007) shows, in the case of knowledge of the surrounding reality, we focus on the description of its causal functioning, where we look for time-invariant regularities, i.e., homogenized elements of phenomena that are related to the described reality. Based on this, we acquire certain knowledge about a given class of phenomena which we apply in time, and, if the knowledge is correct, it provides us with a certain degree of certainty about the behavior of the reality in the future. Of course, entrepreneurs try to increase the level of certainty, but it can never be complete due to the unlikelihood of fully understanding the functioning of nature per se. Given that a person is interested in influencing reality, they can also formulate hypotheses about the phenomena in question regarding the relative occurrence of a phenomenon within a class of phenomena. The hypothesis about the probability of the occurrence of a given phenomenon can also be the subject of business in the field of insurance (insurance payment), i.e., special entrepreneurs preparing for the eventuality of the possible circumstances by increasingly accumulating savings. The insurance companies or entrepreneurs themselves accumulate a higher rate of savings, which economically mitigates the risk of the occurrence of that given event, whereas the given event will occur with a statistical probability.[7]

Hoppe further argues that the above-mentioned tools cannot be applied to the estimation of the future associated with human action. Hoppe (2007) also points out that Mises (1998) has not given a very satisfactory answer on how to deal with the problem of uncertainty. Furthermore, Hoppe (2007) argues that Mises left a sufficient line of arguments to formulate an answer. Hoppe shows that while in the case of reality we deal with time-invariant i.e., homogeneous phenomena, this is not so in the case of human actions. Time-invariant, i.e., the only homogeneous element here, is the action itself, which we know is based on the preference of the higher to lower satisfaction of perceived needs. We know that it is always focused on the future and we know that it always takes into account the new value context of the individual. According to

---

[7]Using Knight's example with bottles of champagne, an entrepreneur buys 1001 bottles for every 1000 bottles used because he anticipates that 1 out of 1000 bottles will be broken. This way, the entrepreneur increases the degree of certainty related to the phenomena in question in order to achieve their intentions towards customers. However, this does not mean that purchasing 1001 bottles increase their level of knowledge about the surrounding reality. Nor does it mean that they are not interested in increasing their knowledge of the surrounding reality, which subsequently enables them to reduce the need for insurance; e.g., by investing in inventing a better method of bottle production, which will reduce the volume of breakage. Naturally, investing in a higher degree of knowledge of how reality works must be economically feasible. Using the bottles example means that the degree of certainty associated with lower average bottle breakage and the level of investment into a possible solution must bring economically meaningful results, otherwise, it is more advantageous to use either insurance or accumulating savings and not investing. In other words, it sometimes makes more sense to accept one bottle out of a thousand bottles being broken, than to invest in a solution that will reduce the bottle breakage.

Hoppe, who followed Mises's theory, when grasping the future, we use the so-called *Verstehen (understanding)* through various forms of communication. Based on *Verstehen and communication*, we have access to the thoughts and insights of others as opposed to accessing the objects of reality. In other words, we understand, and based on communication, we know what other people do and want. Although another person may have better knowledge related to the surrounding reality and the related problem of risk, we can also gain and share knowledge about reality through communication.

However, it is also true that the specific anticipation of the future related to a particular person and a particular value context remains unknown to the anticipator (me or anybody); it is given only to the person who can best estimate his/her future in the context of what he/she perceives for themselves. The field of human action, therefore, creates a special category and method of insight based on individualization, which is, to some extent, synchronous and diachronic. By the synchronous character, Hoppe advocates a modus operandi which is an action; its characteristics do not change over time. We can say that in this way, we grasp the human abstract, essence, or essence of the other's view of reality as well as other members of the community. By the diachronic character, Hoppe recognizes the specific context and disposition of man, which implies a strictly individualized, very specific, diverse, and over time, changing character of one particular person, the mutatis mutandis of each person.

The point of view of this essay is that it is primarily problematic to estimate the future in the context of human action, i.e., uncertainties, which Mises calls *case probability* (Klein 2009 explains the term as "case judgments without probabilities").[8] Here, we face a real unknown. How do we estimate the future associated with other people's actions from an individual point of view, if we know that others principally behave

---

[8]It is very interesting how Klein (2009, Footnote 6) approaches the problem. He notes that the very notion of "case probability" is misleading. According to him, Mises should have called the phenomenon "case non-probability," or maybe "case judgments without probabilities." According to Klein, it is not possible to apply deterministic principles of homogenized and time-invariant phenomena of reality to the phenomenon of human action. We will return to this remark later in the text because it is important to us.

exactly the same (i.e., they also act)? And if everyone anticipates the future in the context of their specific goals while also trying to anticipate what others are doing, given that we live in a society, how is it possible that we do not face absolute chaos? Does this mean that our concreteness is the same for every human? The problem can be characterized by the question: *If the phenomena related to case judgments without probabilities are absolutely unique and specific, how is it possible that an entrepreneur or anyone else can still predict the future connected with the action of others?* How is it possible that we are economically successful? Is it just a coincidence? Or is it some form of supernatural quality that is related to the entrepreneur's good judgment? Or is Lachmann's remark that the more diverse an entrepreneurial activity, the more likely it is that an entrepreneur will be correct? So, is it an accident? How is it possible to make progress and improve the state of affairs at all, if we are contemplating an absolutely veiled future in its concrete form and we move only on the level of general understanding (Verstehen) of the action of other human beings? And it's not just the problem of the judgment of some kinds of professional entrepreneurs per se; it is quite the opposite. We use the term (entrepreneur) in the sense of the so-called ideal type, so the problem is connected with any judgment of any man.[9]

It should also be recalled that the problem of uncertainty associated with human behavior is linked to the problem of risk (class probability). It is still the tangible items that we transform, and they are the subject of our interest because they serve us in the context of *case judgments without probabilities*. This means that when dealing with the estimation of the future (case probability), an entrepreneur also uses the possibilities of reducing the risk associated with the world in order to improve their estimation of how the elements of reality will behave in the future. This is based on the use of better technologies or better knowledge related to insurance. Knight (1964, p. 213) e.g., describes the example used by Mangoldt, that the risk is compounded by overheads (an example

[9]It should be noted that we use the term "entrepreneur" in economic theory in the form of an ideal type. In reality, each of us is to some extent an entrepreneur, worker, or owner of capital goods, land, or are consumers (Mises 1949; 1998, pp. 252–256). In other words, each of us somehow makes an entrepreneurial estimate of the future. And as we see around us, if politicians don't stop us using political force, we're relatively successful.

of the probability of champagne bottle breakages during production), i.e., improvements in this area (e.g., a combination of production factors that cause a lower bottle breakdown rate) are important for the business in the context of estimating consumer behavior in terms of reducing its costs. Naturally, it must be an economically meaningful improvement. Given that human action (related to *case probability*) is purposeful in the sense of estimating the future, the use of *class probability* must also be purposeful in this sense. In this respect Huerta de Soto (2012, pp. 46–52) is instructive, describing that any knowledge related to *case probability* is equally implicit and unexpressed, referring to Michael Polanyi who argues that tacit types of knowledge (Huerta de Soto ranks them among Mises's *case probability*) are in fact the dominant principle of all knowledge.

However, even the area of knowledge about risk (*class probability*) is not without controversy. In this area, it is possible to talk about two basic problems and whether *class probability* has an objective or subjective character, i.e., whether the phenomenon of probability is a feature of reality per se, which we observe and derive empirically[10]; or, whether it has a "propensity" character, that is to say, probability describes a certain interpretation of reality,[11] while the causal and strictly deterministic part of reality is obscured. It also provokes controversy as to whether there is a so-called a priori concept of probability.[12] However, we will not develop our essay in this direction; we will address this question at another time and in a different context. The theme of this essay will deal exclusively with the problem of *case probability* which is related to human action and with estimating the future in the context of another individual.

---

[10]Position held e.g., by Richard von Mises; defended e.g., by Hoppe (2007); the given concept is also promoted by authors such as Venn or Reichenbach.

[11]The term "certain interpretation of reality" is manifested in the fact that there is controversy, whether it is a classical (Laplace), subjective (de Finetti, Savage), epistemic and inductive interpretation (Ramsey, Cox), logical interpretation (Keynes, Carnap), or the newly proposed intersubjective interpretation (Gillies) of probability. See in more detail in Gillies (2006).

[12]For closer look see e.g., van den Hauwe (2011).

2.1.2 Estimating of the Future as the Economics Problem

Shackle's warning about the non-existence of the future, i.e., that the future is empty, is relative. As Schutz points out, the future is full of plans, thoughts, and people's insights. From a human point of view, it is not a specific situation. Nevertheless, we are heading into the future state of affairs where some ideas are based on some degree of knowledge, and some form of mutual coordination of these plans. Let us illustrate some existing solutions to the problem *of grasping the future related to unpredictable human action*, which are described by Frank Knight, Ludwig von Mises and Hans Hermann Hoppe, but also by G.L.S Shackle and Ludwig Lachmann himself, as well as by Friedrich Hayek.

2.1.2.1 Knight (Grouping, Specialization, and Cooperation)

Knight (1964) devoted several individual chapters of his famous book to this problem. He writes that when dealing with uncertainty, we cannot group phenomena into any group due to their uniqueness, and we cannot apply the rules of statistical probability to the world of reality. Knight also approaches the problem of the future from the decision-makers' happiness point of view. He claims that even if the decision made is based on some faith or inspiration, it must be accepted as rational (Knight 1964, p. 236). If we were to set Knight against Shackle, who in principle argues that a rational decision cannot exist, then Knight would certainly oppose Shackle. He would argue that even if one decides based on some faith, it is a rational decision. Knight does not need objective criteria for rationality. In his view, rationality springs from the subjective point of view of a person. Knight further writes that decision-making can be influenced not only by estimating the future in terms of uncertainty (case probability/uncertainty, which is immeasurable) but also in combination with objective probability[13] related to the world of things (class probability/risk, measurable and removable through various types of insurance and savings). He argues that decision-making is linked to a choice that takes place between what brings us a lower return with higher certainty (probability) and what brings us a higher return and a lower degree of certainty. The action is, of course, focused on the future, which means that the entrepreneur must deal with both the physical state of affairs, i.e., the goods produced (facing a problem in connection with *class probability*), as well as an estimate of demand and future results of its activity (*case probability*). Knight further defines six types of ways of dealing with uncertainty. First, he argues that there is *less* uncertainty (certainty is not removed completely) in some groups as opposed to individual cases (pp. 238–239). He states that the entrepreneur does not produce for a specific consumer, but they produce *for a market.* Knight argues that even absolute uncertainty tends to have some kind of regularity when grouped, based on some similarity or common element.[14] Knight's statement about regularity is interesting; however, it is logically inconsistent with the claim about the uniqueness associated with human action. The second method is about the diversity of people and how they deal with uncertainty. This argument is related to the fact that different people specialize in different ways and they consolidate the group activities they perform in different ways as well. Specialization directly implies some form of grouping.[15] Knight speaks of this as a method of specializing in some specific problems, while speculation is seen as the most important phenomenon of specialization. Knight argues that it is obvious

[13]On this basis, we could classify Knight among those who claim that class probability has an objective character. Knight is also a proponent of the a priori nature of the probability problem in the context of the mathematical expression of probability.

[14]Knight goes further within this context. He claims that the creation of these groups results in the creation of different sizes of entrepreneurial units. The size of the company makes it more likely that correct estimates will prevail over incorrect ones. Knight clearly suggests that one way of dealing with an uncertain future is through different types of organizational units, business entities, based on some form of cooperation between individuals.

[15]"*Specialization itself is primarily an application of the insurance principle; but, like large-scale enterprise, it grows up to meet uncertainty situations where, on account of the impossibility of objective definition and external control of the individual ventures or uncertainties, a "moral hazard" prevents insurance by an external agency or a loose association of venturers for this single purpose*" (Knight 1964, p. 256).

that a specialist in a certain field can make a better judgment for the future than someone unfamiliar with the field (p. 258). Knight complements these two methods of dealing with uncertainty in two other ways. Thirdly, by controlling the future in terms of building capital structures and, in a fourth sense, by increasing the prediction of the functioning of reality, which are interrelated strategies relating to the progress of human civilization. Knight does not stop there and names the other two potential strategies, which he calls "diffusion" and "monitoring the minimum degree of uncertainty." Diffusion, for Knight, means that it is better, for example, for 100 people to lose $100 each rather than for one person to lose $10,000, i.e., it is better that a technology injures more workers rather than kills several. "Monitoring the minimum level of uncertainty" is associated with some business activities that achieve much more certain results over time than other business projects. It is clear that given the fact that it is not possible to compare the loss of $100 to a loss of $10,000 subjectively, the diffusion strategy should be rejected from the typical Austrian school's point of view, as it is impossible from a subjective point of view to compare what is better/worse for this or that individual. Knight's view of the consumer who relies on the producer to predict the future is interesting. He writes:

> *The main reason is that he does not know what he will want, and how much, and how badly; consequently, he leaves it to producers to create goods and hold them ready for his decision when the time comes. The clue to the apparent paradox is, of course, in the "law of large numbers," the consolidation of risks (or uncertainties). The consumer is, to himself, only one; to the producer, he is a mere multitude in which individuality is lost. It turns out that an outsider can foresee the wants of a multitude with more ease and accuracy than an individual can attain with respect to his own. This phenomenon gives us the most fundamental feature of the economic system, production for a market.* (p. 241)

From an individual perspective, Knight then identifies at least five more ways in which individuals deal with the future. The first is our different perception, grasp, and anticipation of future events. The second is the different ways in which resources are used to achieve future goals. The third is the different ways of implementing plans and our ability to adapt to change.[16] The fourth is the collective trust between the individuals making decisions. And finally, the fifth is the degree of certainty with which the decision is made, when some individuals, who demand certainty, prefer not to engage in any threatening activities and, vice versa, some individuals follow their hypotheses rigidly. Knight summarizes the problem of grasping the future as follows:

> *The problem of meeting uncertainty thus passes inevitably into the general problem of management, of economic control. The fundamental uncertainties of economic life are the errors in predicting the future and in making present adjustments to fit future conditions. .... „ We are thus brought naturally around to a discussion of the most thoroughgoing methods of dealing with uncertainty, i.e., by securing better knowledge of and control over the future.* (pp. 259, 260)

Knight does not explicitly address the issue of error. He takes the error as a given quantity with which he works. To him, the error is an objectified quantity, otherwise, he could not claim that the error is merely a bad prediction of the future set against the organizing of resources that are currently adjusted, and which should correspond with the future. Shackle should never agree with Knight because he does not believe in the notion of a "*general problem of management of economic control,*" which implies the Misesian rationality of an entrepreneur's behavior. It is also clear that, in principle, Knight approaches the solution of uncertainty and risk based on grouping, which has a different character in the risk area (probability of occurrence of a phenomenon within the defined group) and a different character in the area of uncertainty (production for the market—a wider group of people). Knight does not think very deeply about how people are solving the problem of the future through the tools described. However, Knight's description of tools is instructive for the purposes of this essay.

[16] As we can see, the first three strategies are similar to Lachmann's divergent expectations.

2.1.2.2 Mises, Hoppe (Verstehen)

Mises (1998) divides knowledge in terms of *class probability* and *case probability*. Mises describes *class probability* as the kind of knowledge we apply to the surrounding reality, pointing out the degree of our ignorance associated with the exact causal nature of the surrounding reality. The degree of ignorance is manifested in the degree of probability of occurrence of this or that phenomenon. We do not know that something will happen one hundred percent because we do not know all the causal phenomena of reality. Mises's successor, Hoppe (1997), adds additional remarks to Mises in the context of assumptions about the surrounding reality. In the context of the future, according to Hoppe, we are *practically* more certain about some reality-related phenomena compared to other phenomena. We know that for e.g., a house will remain standing tomorrow unless something happens to its foundations, or we know that a machine will work if the conditions under which it was constructed are maintained. We can also be certain of the results of our activities in terms of the production of certain goods. We know how to produce them, and if the production conditions do not change, the result of that activity is, *practically* speaking, certain. Of course, this area is also subject to change and we cannot be 100% sure. We can potentially face the surprise factor. That's why Hoppe talks about *practical certainty*. And if we face some kind of surprise, which is of a *relative nature*, we use different types of insurance or we increase the rate of savings. We are also expanding our knowledge of the surrounding reality that allows us to reduce the insurance rate and the need for higher savings. This means that if we have an *economically meaningful* opportunity to build a better house and secure it against collapse or if we build a machine from better materials and increase its durability, we will do so, and in doing so, we increase the certainty associated with our environment.

However, when interpreting *case probability*, we have a much bigger problem. On the one hand, Mises still calls it *probability*, which is strange given the nature of his interpretation of this phenomenon. As we have already mentioned above, in the context of Mises' work, it might be more appropriate to talk about the improbability or, as Klein (2009) points out, *case judgments without probabilities*. In my opinion, however, as we will demonstrate below, Mises had his reasons. Mises clings to the concept of *Verstehen* while explaining how we grasp these phenomena.[17] The term *Verstehen* means one person's view of another in the sense that we understand each other and our actions i.e., we understand the reasons behind our actions. It is not about empathy (*Einfühlung*) and speculation about the motives of someone's actions. It is the very understanding and identification of the action of the other person. On this basis, we can explain the concept of voluntary exchange, we are able to grasp that all of us prefer one thing over another, or we can define the concept of marginal utility, etc. However, Mises is not as explicit in *case probability* as he is in the case of *class probability*. When mentioning the reasons for the existence of the *Verstehen* concept, he refers to identical structures of the human mind (see e.g., Mises 1962, p. 16; or Mentzel 2018).

If we were to characterize Mises' solution to the problem of *case probability*, then it is possible to say that Mises claims that people know something about the future. Contrary to Shackle's belief, the future is not completely empty. When referring to *Verstehen*, Mises identifies time-invariant principles, i.e., the abstracts of human behavior. Therefore, they can be applied over time and to each individual. But how do we apply our understanding of *Verstehen* to grasp the future? How do we anticipate the actions of the other person? We will not find a relevant answer in Mises's works. Hoppe (1997) can, therefore, be instructive for Mises' interpretation. He argues that Mises left us a relevant analytical apparatus to be able to answer this question.

When explaining *case probability*, Hoppe clearly deviates from the possibility of applying statistical methods. One of the reasons is learning and the diversity of knowledge we have. According to him, the difference between knowledge and our individual predictions of the future precludes any possibility of defining all potential states of human action. This prevents the existence of knowledge about the relative frequency of their occurrence, which we can identify in knowledge related to *class probability*. However, Hoppe rejects Shackle–Lachmann's interpretation that we know nothing about future action. Hoppe explains that we can

[17] Here, Mises follows Weber and the historical school. He also differentiates himself against some of the historical school's conclusions, but that is a different discussion.

make several statements about the future. We know that it is possible to change behavior through learning; recognize error and success (however, Hoppe does not present the concept of error), know when an individual's hypotheses about reality are confirmed or falsified. In other words, according to Hoppe, we know the modus operandi of human action; Hoppe calls this *uniform and constant logic of human action and learning*. Hoppe basically describes the abstract, time-invariant knowledge of human action. It does not matter what specific expression it has. However, it will always be subject to a given abstraction, i.e., we cannot exactly predict our future goals, which we've set ourselves while in the mode of concreteness. Nonetheless, we can say that goals exist, that we must use subjectively assessed means to achieve them, face costs, and make decisions in some future context. We have this certainty associated with human action. In other words, we are not able to predict only those aspects of human action that are subject to learning, i.e., what we call a specific action influenced not only by my particular content of action but also by the particular content of other peoples' actions.

Although these specific aspects of human action are fundamentally unpredictable, we still have to deal with the future in some way. We must somehow estimate our future as well as anticipate the actions of others. We have to understand them. How we do it? Hoppe (1997, p. 71) writes:

> *In contrast, in the field of past and future human history, we are capable of distinguishing between every singular event (each event can be treated as heterogeneous); and to improve our grasp of the past, and our anticipations of the future actions of our fellows, we know and are capable of learning something about the individual causes-the personal knowledge-uniquely affecting the outcome of each and every singular human event (with each event deserving of its own special attention).*

Following Mises, Hoppe further explains that we do this based on an understanding of human character. The character of a person is formed based on past actions and past behavior. However, at the same time, one must also make a prediction regarding the stability or instability of parts of one's individual system, i.e., a person must anticipate the circumstances based on which their conduct remains unchanged or their behavior changes. The following passage where Hoppe (1997) quotes Mises (1962) is interesting:

> *As Mises explains, we must "assume that, by and large, the future conduct of people will, other things being equal, not deviate without special reason from their past conduct, because we assume that what determined their past conduct will also determine their future conduct. However different we may know ourselves to be from other people, we try to guess how they will react to changes in their environment. Out of what we know about a man's past behavior, we construct a scheme about what we call his character. We assume that this character will not change if no special reasons interfere, and, going a step farther, we even try to foretell how definite changes in conditions will affect his reactions".* (Hoppe 1997, p. 72; Mises 1962, pp. 49–50)

It follows that if we want to talk about the future behavior of some people, we must place them into groups according to their character, i.e., we determine some kind of ideal type, meaning a group of individuals or institutions (made up of several people based on their character). Based on these ideal types (characteristics) we know or anticipate how they will behave, what will cause changes in their behavior, or what causes will contribute to their behavior remaining the same. From this point of view, the term "*case probability*" makes perfect sense.

While Knight (1964) omitted the explanation of the phrase "*produced for the market*" with the exact definition of what it means "*for the market*" and how it is possible to combine the prediction of the future with production "*for the market*," following Mises, Hoppe offers an interesting explanation. Any estimates related to the problem of *case probability* are realized, based upon the definition of ideal types. Basically, this is, in Knight's terminology, "*for the market*." Based on our understanding of the past, a definition of the ideal type of group (of people) or a man-made institution, we can make a hypothetical or, in Hoppe's words, a *provisional*, prediction that helps us anticipate the pattern of behavior for the individual or for a group of people. We are able to define in this way what it means "for the market." Hoppe says, that unlike the natural sciences, it is not entirely possible to identify the success or failure of our prediction in this case.[18] Hoppe (1997, p. 73):

> *Maybe our prediction was wrong because some people, as can happen sometimes, acted out of character. In this case, we would want to use our hypothesis again even though it had been apparently falsified. Or maybe our prediction was successful, but the individual in question has meanwhile undergone a change in his character. In this case, we would not want to use our hypothesis again even though it had just been seemingly confirmed. Or maybe the actor in question knew our prediction and deliberately acted so as to confirm or falsify our hypothesis, in which case we might or might not want to change our future prediction. Every success and every failure, then, bears only inconclusive results and necessitates another tentative judgment, a new and updated understanding of the actors concerned and a renewed assessment of their characters in light of their most recent actions, and so on.*

In the context of Mises, Hoppe believes that an understanding of the other person is always an understanding of their personality, based on their past actions. This creates the character of the individual, which is applied in his future activities. As Hoppe emphasizes, this is not a question of determining the future based on past proceedings, *but rather in the sense that the past values and know-how of an individual (which determined his past actions) shape and constrain his future values and know-how (which determine his future actions).*

For Mises, the past associated with the existence of personality is important. Because it is clearly the past from which we can identify the individual patterns of behavior and anticipate these patterns with respect to the future. Therefore, there is no kaleidic flow or flow with no discontinuity, according to Mises/Hoppe. People's lives have a pattern of behavior that is intertwined with social change (*patterned social change*).

---

[18] "*Moreover, whether we evaluate our predictions as successful or not, the meaning of success and failure is necessarily ambiguous*" (Hoppe 1997, p. 73). However, Hoppe contradicts himself here in the sense that either we can learn from errors and success, and then the meaning of success and failure is not ambiguous or the concept of error and success is only a chimera without any objectified criteria.

There is no human personality without the past. And then it is the individual personality per se that predicts a person's behavior toward the future.

To support his argument, Hoppe contends that the existence of capital goods—as an empirical fact capital goods is involved in the economic process across several production periods of time—have a continuous temporal character. Hoppe also refers to the existence of plans which imply that a person makes decisions and acts in a time continuum, i.e., the person realizes what they intend to do throughout the time. Hoppe also points out that if the Shackle–Lachmann absolute kaleidic approach to explaining how we grasp the future were to apply without any connection between the past and the future, we would be faced with the problem of explaining why some of us are more successful than others in predicting the future. If knowing and understanding others and the ability to predict their behavior did not matter and vice versa, if the past and the future were not connected in any way, our predictions about the future should statistically be distributed identically among people. In other words, if anything is a question of luck then statistically people would alternate in being successful in predicting the future.

Although Hoppe refers to a *commonsense* interpretation of Mises's analysis of grasping the future, it should be noted that the interpretation is not without problems. In building his system, Mises points out that, inevitably our actions are focused on the future. The past is lost. The past is the sum of circumstances that man has no way of changing. The character of a person who is dependent on what they have experienced in the past can change at any time, depending on the nature of the action. The action is what ultimately determines the direction. Regardless of the past and only depending on what and how a person wants. Mises finds himself in a strange middle ground. On the one hand, he is fully in line with the Shackle–Lachmann system, which is also based on the dominance of the will and its necessary direction to the future. To paraphrase Shackle,[19] it's too late for the past and present. On the other hand, the past is meant for Mises to be the decisive factor for understanding

[19]As Lewis (2017) shows, Shackle has another kind of mistake in his system when he claims that free will is called "uncaused cause." See also Footnote 24 below.

and perception of the other person, which, in the context of personal value judgments, is the decisive factor for the anticipation of the future associated with their actions. Mises' argument is simply inconsistent.[20]

The anticipation of the future is realized on the basis of what Mises calls the character of a person, about whom we realize assumptions in the context of their value judgments ("*definite assumptions about the actor's future value judgments*," see Mises 1962, p. 50). At the same time, Mises claims that we make assumptions most of the time (*by and large*!) unless some conditions change, e.g., an entrepreneur anticipates that others will behave in a similar way as they did unless some conditions change. Hoppe adds that this is an estimate of the relative stability or a change in the different parts of the value system of other individuals. Both Mises and Hoppe thus explicitly claim that there should be certain forms of regularity in our actions, not only at the abstract level (which must be agreed upon) but also at the level of specific behavior. Does this really mean that if the environmental or internal conditions of one person do not change, they will behave in the same way? And why should they? Why couldn't they change their behavior? And why should we even assume that if the exact same conditions occurred, e.g., the same conditions as a week, an hour, a minute, or a second ago, why couldn't the other person make a completely different decision than they did a second, a minute, an hour or a week ago? What's stopping them? After all, the person has free will and is not a robot. They are not obliged to act a certain way but can choose.

This is an unfortunate implication by Mises and Hoppe that there is a possibility of defining the future state of our actions, which would enable us to determine the relative frequency of these actions. If we anticipate the future more or less based on the idea that one does not *change one's nature too often* and only changes it from time to time, then to what extent is it a Shackle–Lachmann coincidence that a person behaves as

[20]It is a modus operandi, a characteristic feature, Mises uses across his argumentation system. It is not so much the fact that there is no human character formed by his past, but that free will can reverse and reject any past human experience and, conversely, create a new character trait. For a critique of the dichotomy of Mises' approach, see Pošvanc (2019b).

expected and to what extent is this a fully rational Mises–Hoppe judgment? So how is it? And why should statistical methods not be used for these cases?

While at the level of abstract behavioral characteristics, such as subjective assessment, preference for a higher over a lower degree of satisfaction, a voluntary exchange, etc., Mises–Hoppe's argument is applicable over time, given that these are time-invariant concepts, the concreteness of someone's action should make it impossible to anticipate the future associated with the outcome of an individual's action. Unless we would assume a certain stability of their reactions and behavior which does not change often. But this contradicts the claims that we are not able to identify a specific state of future actions.

Other claims are also problematic. If we cannot unambiguously evaluate our prediction about the future behavior of another, can we actually call our prediction a prediction? At the same time, Hoppe is skating on very thin ice, claiming on the one hand that the outcome of our prediction related to the other's actions is always ambiguous ("*the meaning of success and failure is necessarily ambiguous … Every success and every failure, then, bears only inconclusive results and necessitates another tentative judgment*. For more details see Hoppe 1997, pp. 72–73). However, later Hoppe refers to *set of objective criteria for success-profit and loss, continued operation and bankruptcy, and growth, stagnation, or decline of capital values*" (Hoppe 1997, p. 77). So how is it? Do we have objective and unambiguous success/error criteria or is the meaning of success/error ambiguous?

2.1.2.3 Shackle and Lachmann (Orientation, Divergent, Expectations, and Institutions)

Shackle (1992, pp. 364–408) solves the problem of grasping the future in two principal ways. The first is the concept of expectations, and the second is the concept of orientation. Shackle argues that the choice per se implies that there are some competing and at the same time coexisting states that we consider while we are choosing. It follows that the coexistence of these mutually competing states is only possible on a level of ideas never at the level of reality. The reality, i.e., the state of reality we choose, cannot coexist. It always has some specific form. This results from the existence of choice. Choice will always and under all circumstances cause "this" *or* "that" to happen; never "this" *and* "that" at once.

The fact that one can exercise free choice also implies that it is not possible to know the sequence of specific events. This is because it is the choice that dictates this potential sequence. Shackle further argues that our expectations must be the area where we search for answers. However, expectations are not the answers to what will happen. Shackle also clings to the practicality of the expected sequence of events. Practicality stems from the fact that there is nothing like considering all possible and intended alternatives. It is simply not possible to realize expectations in all their possible combinations because there is no time limit for the future. This means that in the absence of a time limit for the future, it is never possible to consider all potentially possible alternatives to our expectations. The time limit of our lives also plays a role here. In other words, we must always decide; and it must be a practical decision where something happens. According to Shackle, expectations are not passive, resolved, or static. According to him, expectations are a process with a systematic basis. In principle, we seek the answer to the question "*What happens if I do this or that?*" (Shackle 1992, p. 367). According to Shackle, we make a decision systematically between expectations based on their so-called *desiredness*, i.e., how much is this or that action required. At the same time, expectations must meet the aspect of how close they are to the certainty that they will occur (*nearness to the truth*), which Shackle calls *standing*—the status of the given expectation. The formulated hypothesis about the future circumstances will, therefore, have two basic components—desiredness and standing, which according to Shackle creates a system. However, a system implies some coherence. The system then consists of competing thought descriptions of the future, which have an individually determined time horizon that interests a person. Shackle argues that each of these conceptual descriptions of the future has its own time horizon and content, which prevents the existence of something like the repetition of some attempted action. To choose between hypotheses and to start acting means to influence the wholeness of the chosen direction up to the individual time horizon of the chosen hypothesis.[21] Hypotheses related to our actions are therefore always in a rival mode.

Shackle then explains aspects of applying expectations related to the physical world. The given problem is outside the interest of our work and consists of a discussion of probability in terms of *class probability*. However, Shackle does not avoid the area, or as he puts it a system, he calls epistemic. A characteristic feature of such a system, as we have already shown in Mises, is the choice that makes each event a separate phenomenon. Shackle shows that, unlike the physical world where hypotheses generally offer some kind of probability, i.e., the physical world hypotheses are each true to a certain extent and within parameters. Therefore, the hypotheses related to human action are mutually exclusive and cannot be attributed to the probability of what will happen. Shackle (1992, p. 408) writes on human action:

> *If all the rival hypotheses which, at some moment, have been formed in answer to a question concerning the sequel of given conduct, are regarded as equally possible; if the evidence which disables one is exactly paralleled by evidence disabling the others; and in particular, if all of them are regarded as perfectly possible, with no positive obstacle seen lying in the path of any one of them; then it will be natural and sensible to pay attention only to the best and worst of these hypotheses, formulated up to the moment in question, according to desiredness.*

However, as he noted, rational expectations are, to some extent, an unknown concept for Shackle.[22] While expectations are a plan, i.e., something we imagine, what we hope for, what we create in our minds, what we believe in, what we assume, and what we associate with something else. Shackle uses the term *orientation* for everything we own and use to implement our plans. We consider the technical, organizational,

---

[21] Here, like Lachmann, Shackle denies the existence of something like the "trial and mistake" principle, which stems from the nature of the choice, which is unique. The choice is what Shackle calls an *uncaused cause*.

[22] "*'Rational expectations' remains for me a sort of monster living in a cave. I have never ventured into the cave to see what he is like, but I am always uneasily aware that he may come out and eat me*" Littlechild (2003).

and utility properties of things. From his point of view, orientation is also a product of the mind. Everything that changes expectations changes the evaluation of all things we use in terms of orientation.[23] Given that Shackle places a significant emphasis on the concept of choice, which is unique and on which what he calls *future history* depends, and given that all people make some choices, this reasoning inevitably leads to the fact that it is neither possible, by definition, to consider all the related eventualities nor the choice per se. The fact that it is not possible to plan and imagine all the contexts relative to free choice explains why surprise is a part of our lives.

Lewis (2017) explains Shackle's theory of how people make decisions based on what Shackle calls, *Field*, *Scheme*, and *Constrains*. In principle, it is about how people realize the supposition of the future based on their reactions to related current circumstances, which they assess against similar experiences in the past. Field brings people information about what is happening in the external world. The scheme is created based on the sharing of individual beliefs about reality and provides a basis for the interpretation of real-time data. The tool that makes this possible is a language that, according to Shackle is an "*outward shape of thought the form which is inseparable from the content*" (Lewis 2017, p. 5). It is precisely the language conventions or rules that allow a person to react correctly to a certain perceived situation. In principle, restrictions for a person, determine the limits enforced on the possibilities of what to strive for, whether in terms of the possibilities that reality allows, i.e., not everything that is desired and is feasible, or/at the same time a limitation that other people impose on a person's actions, which is reflected in the rules and institutions. A characteristic feature of the process that Shackle describes by combining these three variables is a novelty that is constantly generated and that provides us with feedback and thus influences the context and the past. Therefore, according to Shackle, the reality is not only full of surprises and novelties, but it also provides a degree of regularity (at least in that we can be absolutely certain that there is uncertainty associated with human action). Cantillo (2010) writes that,

---

[23] *Orientation* will be one of the cornerstones of how we believe we are grasping the future. See below.

according to Shackle, the perception of order in the past does not imply that there is any kind of order in economic matters. In the context of the Shackle system, it is not possible to know the future objectively. This is prevented by free will, which constantly creates new features of reality. According to Shackle, the only way to face the future is with imagination, which is not necessarily based on the past; in other words, Shackle rejects determinism[24] in the field of human action. Cantillo (2010) writes that "*well, this is exactly*" Shackle's point:

> *If no knowledge about the future can be assumed, if the epistemic gap must be filled with imagination and anticipation, and if we still need to form some expectation about the future value of scalar quantities, we cannot claim general and objective knowledge, but we can state individual belief. We cannot say to what extent the individual is certain, but we can state to what extent he feels uncertain. And uncertainty is a completely open and indefinite set of possible outcomes. So, it is with the future, and so it is with money.*

As Cantillo goes on to say, Shackle is actually writing about the only certainty we have,[25] which is permanent uncertainty. However, it is positive in this respect, not negative. While a probability is a measure of knowledge, uncertainty and related novelty is an acceptance of lack of knowledge, which in turn in all circumstances gives individuals the

[24] However, this kind of explanation of the in-determinism of the will pushes Shackle to argue that the will, as a reason for action, has no cause (the will would be an uncaused cause). The critique and quite successful modification of Shackle dualism related to the problem of "uncaused cause," or the in-determination of the will, is realized by Lewis (2017), who shows that if we apply to Shackle vital parts of Hayek's theory of mind which is introduced as a system composed of parts (neurons), however, where neuronal interconnection creates a system with separate, new, emerged properties, i.e., the mutual organization of neuron-parts of the mind creates very new properties in the mind (the concept of the will) which do not apply to those parts as such (separate neurons do not have these properties), it is possible to avoid the given dualism and eliminate in Shackle the problematic claims associated with the existence of the will as an "uncaused cause."

[25] As the reader will see below, the following presented solution will contain precisely this kind of certainty, which I will combine, among other things, with another certainty that is mentioned by Mises, meaning here, an abstract knowledge about human action, which, as the Hayek-Pavlik method shows, is *created* in an evolutionary (I would add *intersubjective*) way based on the differentiation of *mind/s* concepts (mind concepts are Shackle's concept of Scheme) based on the Hegelian "crossing" of boundaries of created mind/s concepts; boundaries as (Shackle's concept of Constrains) must be crossed by differentiation and creates, in that way, a new kind of a priori knowledge, providing us with some new certainty.

opportunity to act according to their own goals and the ability to adapt to new conditions.

Despite the fact that immersing oneself in the problem of uncertainty and the description of the characteristics of uncertainty is remarkable for Shackle, it must be stated that he was unable to answer the question we ask ourselves in this essay. Why we are successful in estimating the future in terms of *case probability?* And is there any meaningfulness in learning if we are constantly faced with novelty? What are the systematic principles of learning and how is learning possible? Or, in other words, what is a definition of systematic behavior? "*Because how can we know what is systematic and what is not if there is novelty?*" (Cantillo 2010, p. 23). If we accept Shackle's thesis that the future cannot be known objectively, how are we able to perceive it? The fact that we are trying to learn is also implied by Shackle himself in the context of his description of how < field—scheme—constrains> work, in the context of desiredness and standing. This enables us to imagine the future, from which we create rational expectations, and which are reflected in building the orientation system (the sum of mutually organized goods).

Ludwig Lachmann, who follows Shackle from the Austrian School's perspective, perceives the socio-economic world as the so-called open system, which results from the fact that people have free will, which is not determined by the past and which, in this context, provides genuine original decisions or choices. Lewis and Runde (2005, pp. 5–6) explain this as follows:

> *... if in any given circumstances (x) a person chose to do y, then s(he) could always have chosen some other course of action (not-y), perhaps as a consequence of interpreting the situation differently (reflecting the subjectivism of interpretation), or by forming different expectations of possible future eventualities (reflecting the subjectivism of expectations), or simply by acting differently on the basis of those same interpretations and expectations (perhaps reflecting changes in preferences).*

Lachmann's suggestion on how we grasp the future by the concept of divergent expectations is not only based on a high degree of diversity in its estimation, meaning that the more diverse the rate of estimates of different individuals, the greater the likelihood that someone will successfully estimate the future. Lachmann's conception of divergent expectations is possibly linked to Huerta de Soto (Huerta de Soto 2012, p. 70), who, referring to Hayek, explains that we are unable to know or know more in a particular area of our lives without increasing the number of human beings (the reader can see a very interesting inter-subjective feature here).[26] It is the higher number of people that, in the context of Lachmann, allows for a higher rate of accurate estimation of the future based on the diversity of expectations. According to Lachmann, these estimates of the future are most evident in developed markets, where the so-called bulls and bears, which, according to current information, are constantly discovering the market price of commodities. This corresponds to the current estimate of the future in a certain, condensed form. However, divergent expectations are not the only way to look at the future. In this area, Lachmann (2005, p. 277) also refers to the activities of the institutions:

> *Institutions reduce uncertainty by circumscribing the range of action of different groups of actors, buyers and sellers, creditors and debtors, employers and employees. We understand how they work by grasping the meaning of the orientation of these groups towards them. For us, orientation is a fundamental hermeneutic concept. Orientation, of course, changes in time, but it cannot be regarded as a 'function' of anything else. It does not fit into a world of 'function-maximizing' agents.*

For Lachmann, the work of institutions is not just an exogenous factor with regard to human behavior, i.e., some kind of limiting factor (or factor of certainty) of their behavior toward the future. Institutions consisting of rules, beliefs, norms, and standards[27] are at the same time produced, reproduced, and transformed by the very behavior of those individuals who follow them. According to Kuchař and Dekker (2019),

---

[26] Huerta de Soto (2012, p.70), in a footnote in this context, states that in this way we are able to actually understand the biblical commandment from Genesis: "Be fruitful and multiply, and fill the earth subdue it" (Biblia, Pismo Svate Starej A Novej Zmluvy- Bible Old & New testaments-1978 Slovak language Edition Publisher: Tranoscius, Liptovsky Mikulas).

[27] As the reader will see below, it is precisely inter-subjective standards that we can consider as normative coordinates in the economic sense of the word. See below.

who analyzed the correspondence between Lachmann and Shackle, Lachmann had been trying to convince Shackle of the importance of institutions. In his letters, Lachmann points out to him that the organization and market coordination of people is based on rules, primarily property rights and compliance rules, and it is the institutions that limit the absolute uncertainty about the future that Shackle (primarily) mentions. It is clear from the correspondence that Shackle partly agrees with Lachmann, although he adds "*They are (institutions), indeed, the chambers in which civilized and social life is housed. The individual, of course, is constrained by them and finds in them vital resources. But* ***he is still their architect, he shapes and reforms them continually***" (Kuchař and Dekker 2019, p. 7, bold added by the author; we will use this emphasis later in the context of intersubjectively defined norms and criteria as coordination standards).

Lachmann's work, however, does not answer the question of why we are successful. If divergent expectations cause someone to get bogged down in what the future should be like, all in the context of the certainty provided by social institutions, it is still not clear how it is possible that some of us simply guessed the future conditions correctly. Hoppe (1997, p. 62) states the following:

> *Lachmann and his followers conclude precisely this: (1) that there can be no such thing as an economic theory capable of prediction at all, that all of the social sciences are nothing but history and "economists must confine their generalizations to the knowable past"; and (2), that all of our predictions concerning human actions, which we must venture day in and day out, are nothing but haphazard guesses, that "man in his true humanity," as Lachmann approvingly cites Shackle, "can neither predict nor be predicted."*

As we have shown above, Hoppe (1997) criticizes the Shackle–Lachmann version of grasping the future in the context of knowing something about the future—at least we know that man acts, with Shackle's certainty that, in principle, we have no certainty about the future in a concrete form, only the certainty of uncertainty. We begin to form quite interesting characteristics of the future, of which we know something; it could be shaped this way for now:

(a) we know that we act,
(b) we are certain of uncertainty,
(c) we act to change our future.

But firstly, let's look at the work of our last chosen author—Friedrich August von Hayek.

2.1.2.4 Hayek (Dispersed Knowledge and Social Order)

Friedrich Hayek did not deal directly with the problem of grasping the future per se. However, in principle, his entire intellectual story does not solve anything else. Hayek was involved in coordinating the activities of individuals in society. And since the past can no longer be reversed, and Shackle's remark that it is too late to influence the present is true, so the coordination of individuals in society can be nothing more than the coordination of their plans. Plans are not being implemented without assumptions about the future. In this context, Hayek creates his work, which consists of several sub-areas: economic, social, psychological, or political. His entire work is, in principle, aimed at explaining how it is possible that, as individuals, we can coordinate within the community, and what is the right, and appropriate condition for the coordination to be as harmonious as possible concerning the various "parts" of the society/individuals. Hayek (1937) begins his famous essay by stating that before economic analysis focuses on why we make economic errors, it is good to define when those *errors* do not materialize.[28] Hayek then turns his attention to the question of preconditions for the correct coordination of human activities. He asks how individuals obtain correct information about others' actions. This is what leads them to the correct coordination of their plans and thus to the correct allocation of scarce resources. According to Lewis (2014), Hayek leaves economics as an equilibrist analysis and begins to study economics as a social science based on different kinds of *orders*. Thus, he started creating a socio-economic ontology. Hayek (1937) is fully aware of the problem of coordinating economic plans over time. He claims that it is not so much

[28]As can be seen, Hayek begins with remarkably similar questions as stated in this work.

a problem of an individual or a group managed by one of its members, where the plan does not require any special criteria to be implemented.

According to Hayek, given the subjective nature of the decision, i.e., subjective assessment of objective circumstances at the time when a person makes a decision, a person is in permanent equilibrium. This means that the decision to carry out an activity in a particular time and under given data, which from the subjective point of view of a given person is rational, implies that the given action carried out under given information causes the desired state of affairs, i.e., (direction to) equilibrium. The fact that a person subsequently faces new information that changes the person's perception of the desired condition and thus causes an adjustment to their plan, does not mean that we have objectively got into disequilibrium. The reason for this claim is that it is not possible to compare the previously performed activity with the new one. The circumstances in question, before and after, are perceived from a subjective point of view, when we always make a rational decision. Unfortunately, Hayek does not see the problem here.[29] The problem of Hayek's explanation arises when there are more plans, or they are planned by several and independent individuals (or groups) because each of the individuals has a different perception of the surrounding reality, the plans are based on the expectations of the individuals. If the plans are to be coordinated in any way, each of the individuals must have access to the input data of the others so that the plans can be coordinated. In the context of this essay, the following reasoning of Hayek (1937, bold added by author; I refer here to online version of the article) on the problem of input data is important:

[29] Hayek must be criticized for such a defined position. He is not consistent. His position implies the impossibility of learning, respectively it would be necessary to declare that learning or a higher degree of coordination of our activities over time is only a *cliché* and is not possible at all. This follows from the claim that every single situation to which a person responds by changing a plan is unique concerning its subjective interpretation. However, this contradicts his claims about the mutual coordination of our activities based precisely on learning; learning implies that we know where we have made a mistake and how to correct it or how to avoid it. However, this would require mutually objective, respectively, as we will see below an intersubjective comparison of the two situations over time.

> *In the traditional treatment of equilibrium analysis part of this difficulty is apparently avoided by the assumption that the data, in the form of demand schedules representing individual tastes and technical facts, are equally given to all individuals ... this does not really overcome the difficulty created by the fact that one person's actions are the other person's data, and that it involves to some degree circular reasoning.*
>
> *... The data which here are supposed to be* ***objective facts*** *and the same for all people* ***are evidently no longer the same thing as the data which formed the starting point for the tautological transformations of the Pure Logic of Choice****. There "data" meant those facts, and only those facts, which were present in the mind of the acting person, and only this subjective interpretation of the term "datum" made those propositions necessary truths. "Datum" meant given, known, to the person under consideration.* ***But in the transition from the analysis of the action of an individual to the analysis of the situation in society the concept has undergone an insidious change of meaning****.*
>
> *... this does not answer the question whether the facts referred to are supposed to be given to the observing economist or to the persons whose actions he wants to explain and, if to the latter, whether it is assumed that the same facts are known to all the different persons in the system or whether the "data" for the different persons may be different.*
>
> *...* ***the question of why the data in the subjective sense of the term should ever come to correspond to the objective data is one of the main problems we have to answer****.*

As we can see, the very problem for coordinating the actions of individuals (and moving toward equilibrium), according to Hayek, is to identify the process of how subjective information about my specific plan becomes in principle a piece of objective information (valid over time) for other market players so that they can use it in the context of their plans, and vice versa. At the same time, it is important to realize that *objective information* which will become a part of the plans of others, is *dispersed* among other market participants (society) so that no one has it (the objective information) in its entirety. Hayek (1937, 1945) indicates that one of the solutions for the coordination of such dispersed knowledge is the price system and the institutions that are formed around the price system (media, stock exchanges…). However, Hayek (1937, bold added by the author) also claims the following:

> *… price expectations and even the knowledge of current prices are only a very small section of the problem of knowledge as I see it.* ***The wider aspect of the problem of knowledge with which I am concerned is the knowledge of the basic fact of how the different commodities can be obtained and used, and under what conditions they are actually obtained and used, that is, the general question of why the subjective data to the different persons correspond to the objective facts.***
>
> *… we have to explain if we want to show why the propositions, which are necessarily true about the attitude of a person toward things which he believes to have certain properties, should come to be true of the actions of society with regard to things which either do possess these properties, or which, for some reason which we shall have to explain, are commonly believed by the members of society to possess these properties.*

Hayek already implies the complexity of the problem he has defined. A problem he will focus on for the rest of his professional career (Lewis 2014). Hayek's Sensory Order is where he tries to solve a mind-body problem which basically focuses on the solution. Lewis (2014, p. 8) writes that according to Hayek:

> *.. the mind just is a classificatory system, a complex neural process whereby stimuli from the physical world are transformed into the phenomenal world of our perceptions. In this view, perception is always an interpretation, so that the phenomenal, or sensory, order which characterizes our experiences is the product of the creative activity of our minds rather than something given to us by the world itself.*
>
> *…. Consequently, while the classificatory apparatus possessed by any two individuals will share many common features so that their sensory experiences will be ordered in similar ways, they will not be identical. Different people will experience the world in different ways. Thus, Hayek's claim that knowledge is subjective and dispersed reflects his beliefs about human nature.*

The point is that Hayek uses the same modus operandi, which is valid both at the level of the individual mind and, subsequently, at the level of society. This provides (as we will partially see below) an ontological explanation of the given phenomena, i.e., an ontological explanation of the mutual coordination of individual activities in the market (see also Lewis 2014). In other words, he shows the connection between the fact that the mind is "subject" to certain rules, and that same principle is implemented at the social level. It is not only the price system and prices that, according to Hayek (1937, 1945), allow individuals to coordinate with each other in the community.[30] The problem which Hayek is facing is much more fundamental. It is remarkably similar to the one we write about in this essay. It is a question of how it is possible that an individual who subjectively attributes certain qualities and evaluations to goods so that those very qualities and evaluations are not only perceived individually but *at the same time*, they are equally communicated and interpreted at the social level by others. This is what allows the coordination of the individuals. This is nothing more than our question of how entrepreneurs can be successful in estimating the future. Success depends on whether we correctly estimate how other people will attribute characteristics. Hayek turns his explanation of coordination to a description of the evolutionary development of institutions and normative systems, thus creating, according to Pavlík (2004, p. 19), the most important and generally valid metaphysical theory of spontaneous order.[31] Hayek tries to solve the above-mentioned problem with his change of focus from equilibrist analysis to normative systems. He noted that standards not only give people certain guidelines for their behavior but that also these guidelines provide certainty in the context of the future. Because these elements allow a person to realize expectations in the context of other

---

[30]Lewis (2014, p. 11) shows that according to Lachmann, prices are not unambiguous coordination elements, because each price can be interpreted from an individual point of view in different ways, i.e., although prices show a relative perception of the scarcity of goods in question and a perception of scarcity by individuals, however, this does not mean that the subjective perception of the prices does not cause a high degree of diversity in the perception of scarcity in question, which in turn makes it impossible to attribute coordinative characteristics to prices.

[31]This remark is not a cliché. Hayek's system is built on a very solid ontology of individual phenomena, which proves e.g., Pavlík or several followers of Hayek such as Caldwell or Lewis.

people, both functions are important elements of the coordination of individuals' activities.

Lewis (2014, p. 13) also points out that from Hayek's point of view, the problem is even deeper. Namely that it is not just the use of dispersed knowledge, but rather the use of knowledge that is rooted not only in our skills, habits, and formal rules (e.g. property rights), but also in informal rules (e.g. keeping promises), which are a kind of historically accumulated knowledge—our "guide" to grasping the future and the actions of others. Because each of us has an identical "guide," it allows us to respond correctly to new stimuli and correctly interpret the expectations of others and coordinate our actions. Thus, it is a kind of system order, which on one hand was laid out for today's generations by previous generations whereby previous generations followed these abstract rules. While today's generation creates a concept with its specific actions (but within the context of abstract standards), from which future generations will benefit. The existence of rules in the future thus depends on today's human activity (Lewis 2014, p. 16). Turning attention to the system of order allows Hayek to talk about the spontaneous nature of a given coordination, which results from the fact that the interactions of parts of one's system create new *emergent properties* of the system that would not otherwise exist; i.e., they are not reducible to the parts of the system itself—it is the particular connections of the parts of the system that allow these new properties to arise and manifest themselves in the form of new phenomena.

Although Hayek is criticized from many quarters for his views, it must be acknowledged that he puts forward a very interesting interpretation of how people can coordinate their actions individually. However, his interpretation also has some problems. On the one hand, Hayek claims something like "let's submit to the spontaneous genesis of the rules," but on the other hand, there are always some people (intellectual beings) who formulate the rules.[32] Equally valid is Hoppe's (1994) critique of

[32] See e.g., *Lachmann, recognizing the organic evolution of institutional structures, seems to have also stressed the importance of design in the emergence of institutions. In the following paragraphs of the letter from May 2, 1985, he writes: "I distrust Hayek's attempt to reduce the fundamental institutions of the market economy, such as the family and property, to products of the process of cultural evolution. If they are indeed such products, so are the Soviet Union and the British*

Hayek and his application of the principle of purposeless unconscious production of abstract catallactic rules if they are applied in the context of societies with a developed system of division of labor, which implies the existence of purposeful rationality.[33,34] Criticism of Hayek's approach to prices and economic calculation is criticized in Pošvanc (2019a).[35] In terms of the work presented here, it is necessary to criticize Hayek for his lack of specificity. Hayek talks about the existence of some kind of mutually shared rules of the interpretation of reality. But what are these rules? He does not describe them. Lewis (2014, p. 14) only explains the problem as follows:

> *The fact that people are social beings who draw on shared traditions, customs, and rules in order to act helps us to understand how the dangers of the solipsism raised by the subjectivity of interpretation can be avoided. When it comes to judging the significance of disequilibrium prices, say, people are able to transcend the confines of their own subjective point of view by drawing on shared interpretive frameworks. The use of the latter helps to ensure that people reach similar interpretations of the meaning and significance of price signals, making it easier for them to predict one another's actions and thereby increasing the likelihood of their developing mutually compatible plans.*

But what is our economic interpretive framework, which is likewise shared? How did this interpretive framework come about (apart from being evolutionary)? What are its basic elements, and how did these elements evolve in the historical context? To some extent, Hayek is

welfare state. Since the dawn of history, political rulers have tried to interfere with markets and to manipulate them in their interests. Was all this merely a matter of "fatal conceit"? No constellation of social forces behind them?" in Kuchař and Dekker (2019, p. 2, footnote 2).

[33]Pavlík (2004, pp. 550–552) agrees with Hoppe and proposes an adjustment of Hayek's statements.

[34]See also Hayek's criticism of some Rand's objectivists, e.g., in Kinkor (2000). If we look away from the style, which sometimes goes beyond the necessary criticism of Hayek (Kinkor declares Hayek, for example, a statistician or an advocate of collectivism or socialism), then Kinkor's remarks on the absence of a mode of purposeful action in Hayek's work, i.e., the action of reason, by which the thinking being is equally governed, must be considered as valid.

[35]A critique of Hayek's approach to the problem of economic calculation, which Hayek bases on the work of his teacher Mises, but also a proposal to modify Hayek's concept, which will be consistent with the approach presented here, can be found in Pošvanc (2019a).

simply describing the results, not the process by which we (as individuals and as humanity) arrived at the results. In principle, he does not answer the question he asked himself in 1937 and to which he tried to find an answer throughout his entire professional life. Meaning: "***the general question of why the subjective data to the different persons correspond to the objective facts.***" It must be stated that Hayek does not find a satisfactory answer. He even circumvents it by introducing the concept of *catallactics* and he is satisfied with stating that coordination in the free market is happening. Lewis and Lewin (2015) try to explain Hayek, whose interpretation of the coordination system does not contain an explicit answer to how and on what basis people coordinate, whether or not they face the novelty and uniqueness of the upcoming event (Shackle), again only in the context of social rules:

> *The answer to how people cope with such uncertainty is found, once again, in social rules.* (p. 28) … *Put (this) slightly differently, those rules constitute a generative mechanism that, when set in motion by the behavior of the people whose (inter)actions they shape and structure, gives rise to the emergent causal power to coordinate people's plans even in the absence of centralized direction. The fact that the mechanism underpinning the overall order of action is animated only by human agency is significant because it implies that outcomes in the market are the product of the interplay between two ontologically distinct and relatively autonomous causal powers, namely the overall order of actions and the power of people in engaging in purposeful, creative decision-making. It is for this reason, of course, that Hayek describes the working of the market system as involving the interplay of causal powers—or 'regularities', as Hayek terms them—'on … two levels' and involving the 'interaction between the regularity of the conduct of the elements [people] and the regularity of the resulting structure.* (p. 30)

The repetition of people's behavior and the feedback received from the system's regularity enables coordination which is the creation of the interconnectedness of people's actions that make up the social order. The reciprocal social ties between the elements of the system (people), which are "held" by the rules (formal and informal), ensure mutual coordination of expectations based on the arrangement of the system per se, i.e., based on the fact that the system itself provides feedback on the elements of the system. This would not be possible without the given element (a human being) in the system. It is, therefore, the arrangement of the system per se that allows the arrangement. As we see, apart from the fact of the circular argument, there is no explanation of how a given orderliness takes place and what the basic elements are—the coordinates of a given process in terms of normative standards that allows for interpreting subjective data to be interpreted in a different manner other than subjectively, i.e., either intersubjectively or objectively. In other words, how the interplay of two different systems ontologically—the human mind and the economic society—takes place, of course, on an abstract and general level. As Shackle and Lachmann note, it is always a person who implements the given standards (even if he/she did it unconsciously within the background of his/her activity in the distant past). However, the interaction of the elements and the whole is, as the reader will see below, a very instructive guide to the direction in which to implement our interpretation and which will also make it possible to eliminate this shortcoming of Hayek's system.

The same related problem is, in principle, that Hayek writes primarily about general abstract formal and informal rules such as property rights, or agreements, which are the basic coordinates of society. These are "located" in the area of normative order, i.e., a normative sphere of knowledge. However, Hayek does not write about identifying normative principles in the economic sense. These are "located" in the teleological order, i.e., in the teleological sphere of knowledge, which has an equally purposeful—rational character.[36] In other words, Hayek did not identify *time-invariant* a priori *evolutionary principles* related to the economic order that is related to the question of how it is possible that we are economically successful in estimating the future needs of *others*. If we use Mises' terminology, Hayek's theory does not explain the background and how *Verstehen* in an economic sense works, based on which entrepreneurs

[36]The division of the Kantian world "as it should be" into the normative and teleological sphere of knowledge can be identified in Engliš (1930). Engliš divides knowledge about the world into the formal-logical knowledge, which is the basis for other types of knowledge, namely empirical (natural sciences), teleological (we can include here economics) and normative (we can include here legal sciences). Teleological and normative knowledge is at the same time knowledge in the context of man's normative idea of the world—"how it should be." See Engliš (1930) for more details.

make the right decisions. As we mentioned above, he cannot. By emphasizing traditions, Hayek discourages the active influence of reason and thinking in this area. As stated by Pavlík (2004, pp. 21–22):

> *The neglect of the positive aspects of the Smith-Hegelian heritage-led Hayek, within his cultural evolutionism, to an overestimation of the role of unconscious production /of rules/, which was understandable and excusable in his time, due to Marxism's demands for conscious management of society as a whole; this revaluation also brought him into conflict with other approaches to grasping spontaneous order, such as the approach of Menger or his own teacher Ludwig von Mises.*

This is also evident in the context of the interpretation of Lewis and Lewin (2015, p. 30), who point out Hayek's empirical nature of the explanation. This follows precisely from the fact that Hayek is satisfied with the mutual influence of the elements of the system (people) and the system as an ontologically different entity. It is mutual learning and mutual feedback that generates coordination. Hayek thus explicitly refuses to identify and describe the principles of formation of given bonds and their time-invariant characteristics, which e.g., Mises or Hoppe try to identify.[37]

One of the tasks of this work is to modify Hayek and use the vital parts of his work. Our task is to identify time-invariant principles of economic coordination of subjectively perceived expectations of individuals in society, that enable their mutual coordination. We will show, in a logical abstract mode, how a person grasps the future and how it is possible for them to be successful. We will demonstrate how the mutual coordination of people's plans work and on what basis the intersubjectively created economic coordinates work, which include *intersubjectively perceived* concepts of profit, cost, calculation unit (monetary) and implies the need to define an intersubjective concept of economic error and success. At the same time, we will show that a person is guided by reason, abstract

[37]"*As Hayek remarked in 1983, "while the analysis of individual planning is in a way an* a priori *system of logic, the empirical element enters in people learning about what other people do … [Y]ou can't claim, as Mises does, that the whole theory of the market is an* a priori *system, because of the empirical factor which comes in that one person learns about what another person does.*" In Lewis and Lewin (2015, p. 31).

rules, and the so-called economic-normative principles and, at the same time, we will show how, in the absence of full awareness, the coordinates could have been created within the background of the not-fully conscious activities of our prehistorical ancestors.

2.2 Intersubjectivism: The Path (Leading) to the Solution

This part of the book aims to explain some of the problems set out above, through what I call intersubjectivism. I would like to emphasize by using the term "intersubjective" that we are dealing here with some new phenomena per se which emerge over the subjective nature of man, however the subjective nature of man is also the necessary base for these new phenomena. This part aims to *outline* the *possibilities* of some *solutions*. The reader should be aware of the fact that it cannot be considered as something which provides a solution once and for all; it is more an invitation to search for solutions than a solution per se. We will proceed as follows. First, we set out some assumptions (we will draw from the above-mentioned authors' works). However, before we focus on solving the problem, it will be necessary to describe certain methodological starting points, which will then allow us to formulate a fully fledged solution. It means that we will focus on Hayek–Pavlík's method of evolutionary apriorism which will provide a vital concept that we will apply mutatis mutandis to the problems we have determined and we will introduce the basic characteristics of the modified theory of subjective value, which was first presented in Pošvanc (2019a) as a new concept. I think that it is a *connection* of Hayek–Pavlík's method of evolutionary apriorism and a presented modification of the theory of subjective value which enables us to provide a basic description of how we estimate the future, thereby answering the question of why we are successful in estimating the future.

We will demonstrate that the suggested solution is interconnected with an explanation of the elimination of uncertainty provided by Knight through the production *for the market* and we will show why Knight's approach is valid and not just an intuitive solution to the problem. We will show that the proposed solution is applicable in the kaleidic world that Shackle writes about. We will highlight how consumers identify successful business ideas and their characteristics and describe the evolution of entrepreneurship over time. We will also incorporate the role of normative systems and institutions according to Hayek and Lachmann. However, we will demonstrate that in the context of normative systems it is not only the normative rules that are relevant. We will also identify economic-normative concepts that allow people to coordinate their activities, and what the characteristic features are, with regard to economic concepts of success/error, profit/loss, economic learning, and economic rational decision-making, thus eliminating Shackle's skepticism. We will provide the interpretation primarily in the context of a subjective evaluation, plans, and the imagination, which Shackle demands. The interpretation will, of course, be described in accordance with Hayek's remark on the impossibility of a specific description of economic phenomena. We will present the interpretation at the level of abstract principles. The interpretation should be valid for both the nonmonetary economy and the monetary economy. It will describe the modus operandi of the given phenomena. In this way, we hope to provide relatively satisfactory answers to the questions on how we estimate the future and why we are economically successful.

2.2.1 Some Assumptions and Claims

The proposed solution is based on the following assumptions, which are relevant in terms of the works of the above-mentioned authors.

2.2.1.1 Kaleidic Future and Time-Invariant Certainties (Regularities) Related to the Cognition in the Mode of Case Probability

The solution will be fully applicable in a time continuum. We will consider the future to be fully kaleidic in its concrete form. Shackle is convincing in this matter. It is simply not possible to *objectively* know the future in terms of *case probability* in its *concrete form.* This is prevented by free will, which constantly creates new *concrete features* of reality. The only way we can face the future in this context is through our imagination. However, what needs to be adjusted in the context of Shackle is the existence of time-invariant certainties that are applied yesterday, today, and tomorrow, and will be valid at any time in the future. We explore the future through abstract knowledge relating to human action.

We can declare several certainties about the future in terms of human action. The certainty we have is the existing uncertainty, whether described by Knight, Mises, or Shackle. We know that there is no future we can determine with certainty. It is a fluid concept. It is a certainty that can provoke skepticism but also a degree of certainty, with which a person can work as a given characteristic of their life. While *class probability* related to the functioning of reality and its causal context is a measure of the extent of our knowledge of the functioning of reality, uncertainty, and related novelty based on the actions of other individuals is an acceptance of the impossibility of knowing the future in its concrete form. However, this allows the individual to act according to their own goals. It also offers the possibility to continuously adapt to new conditions in all circumstances. The second kind of certainty we have is that our actions and thinking are based on certain abstract, and mutually shared and time-invariant concepts as described e.g., in Mises and his followers. We simply act, we subjectively prefer a higher to lower satisfaction of needs, we use the so-called *Verstehen* (logical understanding of the other), etc. The third certainty we will work with is society. We are sociable beings and only within society can we respond to some of the problems we face.

2.2.1.2 Dealing with Reality: Probability and Elimination of Risk

A person is a part of reality and their physical body is also a part of it. A person recognizes the surrounding reality. Our knowledge of reality keeps increasing. We rightly assume that unless an exceptional event happens, our house will remain standing, and human-designed technologies will keep working. An exceptional event may, of course, occur, i.e., adverse weather could cause a house to fall and technology could stop working. However, an exceptional event related to the surrounding reality may also be associated with the purposeful action of others. The house or technology can be purposefully destroyed by another person. We always perceive reality in the context of us—the people. The certainty that relates to reality, while demonstrating at the same time, that not everything intended is possible. On the one hand, it is deducted from the very and still limited knowledge of reality that we comprehend in the context of ourselves. And on the other hand, it is also inferred by the very character of human life in society. This means that not everything is possible because we own reality (we use institutions of ownership or compliance with agreements) and the fact that something belongs to others limits our individual possibilities to deal with reality. It is a characteristic related to life in a society which at the same time enables individual development. As Knight, Mises, Shackle, or Hoppe show, the practical certainty associated with knowing reality and at the same time expanding knowledge significantly, helps people to anticipate and grasp the future. Likewise, the human tools associated with the use of statistical methods, insurance, increase the certainty associated with the practical nature of our lives in a time continuum toward an uncertain future, i.e., practically possible human life in a kaleidic uncertain world.

2.2.1.3 Institutions and Normative Systems: The Legal and Economic Nature of Grasping the Future

Legal institutions and normative systems form a very important part of how we approach the future. Hayek's or Lachmann's explanation of the influence of institutions and normative systems is more than vital. The norms that limit the actions of others toward the future and which direct them as if within an ice hockey rink barrier, cause the grasping of the future related to *case probability* and creates a certain degree of human-created future and thus abstract time-invariant certainty. This manifests itself in a concrete form of the content of agreements (in the form of *if—so*) and their enforcement. However, as we pointed out in the explanation above, it will be necessary to identify the coordinates that determine the teleological (economic) nature associated with grasping the future and determining what is meant by economic error/success. It will, therefore, be necessary to identify abstract time-invariant *economic-normative standards* and their use. These will allow us to explain and eliminate Shackle's skepticism about the problem of the learning process, given that, according to Shackle, we constantly face new situations that, in principle, cannot be compared or studied from. We will eliminate this problem by identifying time-invariant and thus comparable economic criteria. Not objectively, however, but intersubjectively. This will also remove the skepticism with the above-mentioned problem of rationality, or the problem related to the definition of systematic behavior.

2.2.2 Evolutionary Apriorism: A Methodological Introduction

For this essay to succeed, it is necessary to identify a kind of modus operandi that we consider to be correct, which will be applied to the problem defined by us before proceeding to describe the solution. In principle, it is about identifying the basic characteristics of how our cognition works. This is a fairly strong statement: "*Well, let's see how cognition works.*" We must approach this subject theoretically and not with absolute certainty or the statement "*this is how it is.*" The reason for this is based on Hayek's humility for what we know and what we can know. For this very reason, his work constantly emphasizes the fact that the solutions proposed are an identification of the path rather than a clear and unchanging solution.

Our modus operandi will be presented in the context of theory, i.e., what can be considered as a valid concept in this area of study today. The presented concept has a philosophical and historical basis, which, as the Slovak philosopher Ján Pavlík shows, can be traced back to many thinkers. This approach to the problem of cognition presented here I would like to refer to as *Hayek–Pavlík's evolutionary apriorism*. The reader must be reminded that this approach is not based solely on Hayek's work on *spontaneous orders*. In Pavlik's interpretation of Hayek's work, Pavlík (2004) traces the background of the theory of spontaneous orders from

Giambattista Vico, Adam Smith, through Kant, Hegel, phenomenologists Husserl or Heidegger, to the works of Hayek. I dare to say that in a unique and original way, this indicates Pavlík's depth of understanding of the problem. Pavlík selects and combines valid sections of works from several important thinkers and philosophers and builds a very interesting *new* puzzle of insight into the problem of an individual, their knowledge, and social cooperation. This insight even combines the work of thinkers with whom he may not agree, such as Marx or Comte, or thinkers who choose other methodological paths like Mises, Engliš, or Barry Smith, and creates another insight, based on a combination of their knowledge. One can say that this is a unique and very personal philosophical view that results in what I would like to refer to as Hayek–Pavlík's evolutionary apriorism. We will now introduce this approach, as it will form a vital basis for answers to the problems we have stated.

2.2.2.1 Hayek–Pavlík's Method of Evolutionary Apriorism

Pavlík (2006) repeats the well-known thesis that within any system of knowledge, one of the main problems of the system created is the existence of the so-called *vicious circle* or *pettito principi error* because any (scientific) knowledge is based on some (a priori) assumptions.[38] This problem can be eliminated through Hegel's so-called spiral movement of the "*experience of consciousness*", i.e., encountering the internal inconsistency of the system of knowledge as a whole—and exceeding this limit by synthesizing a more general and widespread version of the interpretation of reality, which will incorporate the currently valid knowledge.[39]

[38] Pavlík (2006, pp. 25–26): "*Indeed, the vicious circle seems to follow not only from the fact that the process of nature's becoming self-reflected (both at the sensory and conceptual level) appears to be, at first sight, a purely circular movement but also from Hegel's explicit formulation of the basic methodological principle of the monistic approach. It reads as follows: The results of any truly scientific or scientifically-philosophical inquiry must show that what served as an immediately and unconditionally valid starting point of the inquiry (e.g., the* a priori *principle of constantly operating causes) is in fact necessarily mediated (conditioned) by what has been discovered during the inquiry.*"

[39] In this way, according to Pavlík, the so-called fallibilistic apriorism of Barry Smith is circumvented, which, on the contrary, is based on the fact that empirical facts can sometimes bring a priori knowledge to their margins and thus falsify them, which, according to Pavlík, would cause the blurring of the boundaries between empirical and a priori knowledge. Smith must

To explain the basic characteristics of this method, let's start with Pavlík's remark that a priori does not mean something predetermined, something innate in the form of an idea (Pavlík 2004, p. 623, translated from the Czech language by the author):

> *The most common mistake that occurs in connection with an apriorism is the vulgar notion that a priori knowledge is something originating from innate ideas that are present in our minds as given forms before the acts of sensory perception occur. Although this misinterpretation has been refuted countless times by Kant himself, as well as many neo-Kantians, it must be refuted again and again in every treatise on apriorism. In fact, a priori correlations between the contents of the mind (whether those occurring in the field of sensory perception, emotional experience, or in the field of conceptual thinking) are found - and this finding has the character of discovery - only within the experience itself, namely as the necessary formal aspect of it, which enables and conditions every experience of a given type. It is obvious that the knowledge of what the experience provides us with now proves itself to be an eternally necessary form of every experience. The experience does not depend on the validity of other acts of experience, because the (newly discovered) necessary form is in already them - and in this necessity, a timelessly identical form of experience – only filled with new content. Therefore, other acts of experience cannot replace our knowledge of the necessary forms of experience (formulated in the form of a priori judgments concerning various ways of reconciling empirical contents) neither can they verify or falsify it.*

One of the tasks of apriorism is to explain where these necessary forms from which we interpret our experience are taken, how they originated, and how they were created. This task stems from the fact that apriorism itself encounters its assumptions based on which it interprets reality and that the newly perceived content is categorized based on a priori forms of thought. These had to arise somehow, or they must be explained in some way, i.e., in an identical way as the grasping of the content of our experience through these forms of thinking is explained. It is, therefore, not at all surprising that in order for Pavlík to satisfactorily clarify this role, he must connect the ontogenesis of knowledge, thinking, and language in

be influenced by Popper in this version of a priori, according to Pavlik. For more details, see Pavlík (2004, pp. 656–661).

his method. Nonetheless, the explanation of the details of this program is beyond the scope of this work.[40] We will remain focused on those essential features of his theory that we can use in the context of the goal of our essay.

The important thing is that Pavlík calls for a return to the vital foundations of the method used by Adam Smith, for the so-called theoretical history (*conjectural history*). Theoretical history or the consistency of logical and historical, or the logical imagination of history at the level of abstract and time-invariant principles or the principle of the procedure of interpretation from simple to complex or from the abstract to the concrete is a way of replacing empirical and concrete descriptions of phenomena, in case we lack relevant empirical data for the given description.[41] It should be clear that the application of this method is appropriate to the area of issues related, on the one hand, to the emergence of social cooperation and descriptions of how this cooperation could have started, and, on the other hand, to the functioning of highly complex phenomena. It is not a coincidence that this method can also be used to describe the inception of any knowledge where we are also unable to identify any empirical facts or where these empirical facts would be uninterpretable phenomena without this kind of knowledge. In the context of describing the dawn of the given phenomena, we try to identify the basic abstract principles, without empirical concretization of the phenomenon, which allows, for example, for the description of the beginning of what we call the market system or the system of the mind.

[40]To clarify this program, it is necessary to see Pavlík (2004), a brief introduction is given by Pavlík (2006) and a detailed continuation of the program is present in Pavlík (2010). It is necessary to warn the reader in advance of the fact that it is a very extensive and in-depth, but inspiring, work, reading of which "rewards" the reader with an endless number of new and interesting questions. I put rewards into the quotation marks because Pavlík does not offer (just like Hayek in his theories) definitive solutions. On the contrary, his work opens the door to further exploration, which in my opinion should excite and not disappoint, because knowledge has these very features.

[41]Pavlík (2004, p. 579), by referring to Dugald Stewart, Smith's first biographer, argues that Smith was not the first to use the method; before him, they were e.g., Montesquieua, Hume, or d'Alembert.

In other words, it is a description of the abstract and generally valid principles of the operation of some *orders*.[42] This makes it possible to reconstruct a beginning that we do not know empirically, and also to subsequently describe a complex structure, which in turn is so complicated that even if we had some relevant empirical data, it would not be possible to capture it in its entirety. So, it's not some fantasy; it is a description of logical principles, time-invariant forms,[43] which we apply to the surrounding reality, i.e., in the words of Pavlík (2004, pp. 661–662, translated from Czech by the author) research must:

> *… focus on the finding of the true meaning, the differentiation of which established all a priori correlation between the elements of the researched area, and which now functions as one of a large number of semantic elements of interconnected networks of logical correlations. … Finding an abstract meaning then means that one can begin to reconstruct the essential moments of the process of semantic differentiation, which led to the establishment of the investigated semantic concreteness. This will then make it possible to reveal implicit logical correlations between their individual elements.*

---

[42]Pavlík (2004, p. 885, translated from Czech by author) writes: "*Given the intrinsic relationship between phenomenology and the original version of Gestaltism, it is possible to treat Smith's imagination method as an active Gestalt, which, through the production of a unifying principle, inserts the aforementioned structure of unity in plurality into the incoherent phenomenal matter.*"

[43]Pavlík (2004, pp. 590–591, translated from Czech by the author) writes: "*It is more than obvious that Smith (and even before him Hume) reach, especially in their conception of feeling, the threshold of the phenomenological method, i.e., apply phenomenological procedures without being aware of them. What they present as empirical knowledge of the individual features of immutable and universal human nature (inclination and emotion, which already have the* de facto *character of intentional acts), is only lacking its inner contradiction and inconsistency. Only by translating it primarily into Husserl's "sensible intuition," i.e., to the cognitive act, which sees the phenomenon occurring in the individual exemplification of the general essence or relational structure. This "sensible intuition" then, through the method of variations, by which the sensible intuition "cleanses" itself from accidence (lat.; meaning a variable non-essential feature or property), results in an intuitive view of the general and necessary essence of the phenomenon under study, i.e., in a categorical view, which grasps the general relational structure (gestalt). Only the phenomenological reinterpretation of Smith's method allows, for example, his "laws of sympathy," i.e., the rules of justice (which, according to Smith, arise from empirical generalization). These can be understood as true priori laws (or eidetic laws) independent of the relative conditions of the experiential empirical process, and that his fundamental statements such as "people necessarily approve or disapprove of certain types of behavior" from his Theory of Moral Sentiments, could be preserved as valid parts of philosophical discourse.*"

It should be equally clear to the reader why we have opened the subject of apriorism at this point in this essay, as the subject is nothing but a description of the application of a logical form to the reality (content). This is because even in the goals we set for this essay, there are issues that must be traced to the past and, these must be described in an abstract formal mode. As we have demonstrated in the case of estimating what we call the future, we have only the certainty of absolute uncertainty but at the same time, the absolute certainty that we can only grasp the future in the abstract form of our actions. It should also be clear to the reader that, even in this case, we must face the vicious argumentative circles within the description of the given system, which in principle always manifests itself in the question related to the description of the starting point of the application of the given principles; description of a sedimentary history of our knowledge and its origin.

Pavlík's program (presented in Pavlík 2004) tries to apply the Smith–Hegel method (if we can refer to it in this way) to incorporate into the most general theory of spontaneous orders so far. The most general in terms of its application, i.e., to Hayek's theory of cultural evolution.[44] The generality and universality of Hayek's approach lie in focusing his theory on the emergence of institutions and normative systems, as well as the description of the mind—in Hayek's Sensory Order—as a

[44]However, Pavlík (2004, p. 21, translated from Czech by the author) is justifiably critical of Hayek, when he writes: "*In addition, in his conception of spontaneous order, Hayek did not include what is inherent in both the spontaneous order of the market and the spontaneous order of the living organism and life in general. That is, the structure of the circular return to the beginning; he did not include there the corresponding structure of spontaneous genesis, i.e., the process of concretizing the differentiation of the undeveloped form of the self-relationship, which is the "germ cell." In fact, he gave up not only Hegel's legacy but also on A. Smith's legacy … The reason is, of course, well known—Hayek quite rightly rejected the part of Hegel's (later Marx and Comte's) conception, under which the historical process is predetermined by the social human essence (including a circular self-relationship), which in the form of an embryo develops from itself the individual phases of the historical process in the same way as a plant develops from a seed in the course of its growth phases. However, Hayek was too zealous—in addition to the above-mentioned positives of Smith and Hegel's approach, which consisted of the possibility of applying the structure of spontaneous genesis by concretizing differentiation to explain the development of the human mind in the inter-individual relationships of men (as in Smith's Theory of Moral Feelings), and also the possibility of explaining the origin of language and establishing universal grammar, etc., Hayek thus closed the way to Hegel's interpretation of the development of* a priori *structures of the human mind, which, according to Hegel, also takes place in the form of concretizing differentiation, but explicitly and emphatically in subject-object relations and also through a trial and error process.*"

self-organizing emergent and multilayered system, which Pavlík (2006, 2011) uses, for example, when explaining the so-called bridge between mind and body (*the mind-body problem*) in the sense of psycho-physical parallelism.[45]

According to Pavlík, it is necessary to perceive the description of such a system (in the concrete form of the market description) as a quasi-organic system, the *basis* of which is a circular reciprocity between the system as a whole and parts of that system[46] (so-called germ cells[47]), the given circular reciprocity passes in a *spiral way*. According to Pavlík, Smith already realized that such a quasi-organic market system can only work on condition that certain abstract formal rules are observed in the form of property rights or in the fulfillment of promises and contracts. The more general theory of this concept is within the works of Hayek. As Lewis (2016) also explains, a system cannot be reduced to its parts. There are *links* between the given parts of the system that create a new phenomenon—the system per se, which must, therefore, be viewed ontologically as a separate entity. Mutual influencing, mutual harmony between the system and its parts is then possible. It is also true that the relationships between the parts of the system determine a certain elasticity of the whole system, which subsequently has the possibility

---

[45]Pavlík (2006, pp. 24–25) writes: "*… the Hayekian psycho-physical parallelism merely endeavors to show that causality as it really exists in nature outside our brain can be reflected in the causal relations within the neuronal network, i.e., within what is the external (spatial) side of mental processes; at the same time, it is also thought, in a reflectionist manner, that the causal relations within the brain which reflect the causality outside the brain are structurally isomorphic with the* a priori *causal relations as imposed within our mind. In addition, in the frame of the Hayekian parallelism, it is shown that some complicated entanglements of causal processes in neuronal networks are able to produce such relational order which is structurally isomorphic with the* a priori *teleological and normological orders which are imposed on sensory phenomena within our minds; it is also shown that there exists a structural isomorphism between some other types of entanglements of causal relations within the neuronal network and the classification of events on the basis of their sensory similarities and dissimilarities.*"

[46]Pavlík (2004) "traces" the circular principle in Smith, later in Kant, which comes with the principle of inner self-relationship, which Hegel then interprets as an inherent feature, the primordial basis of all spontaneously realizing processes.

[47]The germ cell is understood by Pavlík (2004, pp. 600–601, translated from Czech by the author) as: "*The germ cell of the system can also be characterized as an elementary relational concreteness, whose designations are abstract in relation to the designations of the developed complex system (systemic macrocosm), whereas it is true, that the relational structure of the elementary concreteness of the germ cell determines the structure of the relationship in its full concreteness, i.e., in the developed system, which has been established by the process of differentiation.*"

of (spontaneous) development based on modifications and transformations of the given bonds. Pavlík (2004) identified the same characteristics in Smith, who speaks of the well-known *invisible hand of the market*, which seems to guide the system itself and, at the same time, points out the links and interconnection of individual parts of the system, while the whole system structure always leads into some kind of order. Let us return to the essential part of Pavlík's description, which he draws from Hegel, namely the "*spiral nature of the system of cognition*," which serves within the theory to "overcome" discovered circular arguments (pettito principi error) of any kind. Pavlík (2006) explains that Hegel (inspired by Smith and Fichte) considers encountering the limits of our knowledge, i.e., the limitations of our apriori knowledge related to the interpretation of the world, as being exceeded, because it allows us to see beyond the boundaries set by the previously accepted apriori knowledge. Based on this, we can identify a much more vital and generally applied knowledge of the world. At the same time, it shows that, given that our knowledge has expanded and enriched, we do not fall into a vicious circle of arguments.[48] The given explanation also implies that it is a never-ending process of cognition.

If we organize such a briefly presented concept into the main points, then based on the works of A. Smith and F. Hegel, the basic concepts of Hayek–Pavlík's theory of spontaneous order are:

- A quasi-organic system based on semantic "conceptual" differentiation, i.e. elementary specific parts of the system, which are interrelated, while it is true that the system cannot be broken down into its elements, i.e., be perceived as a mere sum of the given elements.
- Reciprocity of the system and parts, which has a spiral structure as it grows; i.e., we can also use the parallel of creating a new layer of more abstract relationships; in principle, it is a matter of moving from the abstract (simple) to the concrete (more complex) concepts and so the process continues. This means that simpler phenomena manifest themselves in their concrete form and begin to form new interrelationships. The resulting complexity will cause the knowledge to run into

[48] For more details see e.g., in Pavlík (2006, pp. 26–33).

> the limits of the given specific relations. The mind-system begins to look for more abstract expressions. However, in this way it exceeds the given limits, i.e., by creating new abstract phenomena that are grasped more easily at the newly created "higher" level of the cognition, while at the same time, this abstraction includes and explains the interconnection of specific phenomena in the lower layer of cognition. However, these new abstract phenomena on the new layer of cognition are further reflected in the new concrete system of phenomena. The process starts once again.

In this way, Pavlík presents the concept of evolutionary apriorism, a constantly evolving system of knowledge, which always encounters a mismatch between the premise and current knowledge, i.e., encounters a problem, "triggers" a spontaneous process of searching for qualitatively better and more abstract interpretations related to the limits of our knowledge.[49] And in terms of humility to knowledge or lack of knowledge, the theory, of course, predicts that absolute knowledge, in the sense of knowing the whole, will remain obscured for us forever.[50] So, let us

---

[49] Pavlík (2006) demonstrates this e.g., on the example of knowledge in physics and mathematics on pp. 38–50.

[50] However, within the intersubjective view that we're using in this work, it is questionable to what extent for us, for example, knowledge to explain ourselves, is/will be blurred. In this respect, I consider the term blurred to be more correct than the term fully unknown. Exceeding the limits of our knowledge is always realized by a scientist (e.g., by Pavlík) in the form of a new theory, but as we can see, the presented knowledge does not have exclusively his (Pavlík's) "brand" of thinking. The thinker, of course, encounters a problem defined by him. However, it "appears" to him due to the combination of other individual ways of looking at the same problem (by other thinkers), respectively, related issues. It is the combination of many concepts that enables the identification, respectively, the appearance of that thinker's problem. Given knowledge (his and others), therefore, does not have an *exclusively* individual character. It is the very combination of concreteness made up of several individuals that makes it possible to simultaneously reveal newer and newer sediments of thought, which are revealed and discovered by the thinker/s. Here, too, the intersubjective character of our knowledge is manifested. From this point of view, I am also inclined to terminology in the sense of naming the theory presented here as Hayek–Pavlík's *intersubjective* evolutionary apriorism. As the reader will see below, the explicit acknowledgment of intersubjectivity "helps" to solve several dilemmas, even those set out here. At the same time, it is not an intersubjective "truth," but an intersubjective process of seeking it. The intersubjective process of searching suggests that the limits of our mind, to which Hayek points, may be systematically exceeded by the systematic thinking of several individuals, thus creating a new system of knowledge that is not solely dependent on the influence of the individual scientist. It seems that Hayek's description of the theory of cultural

try to apply the principles of this theory to the problems we set. We will see how successful we are.

2.2.3 Modified Theory of Subjective Value

Pošvanc (2019a) shows that the generally used premise of the theory of subjective value: "*man prefers more, rather than fewer goods of the same kind and quality*" is not applicable over time since the valuation of goods can change over time and there need not exist, in value terms, the same goods a few moments later. It is only possible to claim that "*man prefers a higher rather than a lower satisfaction of needs.*" For the theory to be applicable over time, it is necessary to introduce a time-invariant version of it, which is suited to the needs as well as to the goods; a person lives in a time continuum and we need to explain how a person attributes a value over time. Menger (2007) identified that needs with means to satisfy them create a causal relationship. The traditional interpretation of the theory of subjective value usually describes this causal link between a particular need satisfied by a particular economic good (see e.g., Mises 1998, p. 119 who writes generally about the issue "*means of the same quantity and quality are apt always to produce the same quantity of an effect of the same quality*"). However, the mode of the specificity causes several problems for interpretation over time. The specific need satisfied by a particular good that exists today may not exist tomorrow or theoretically speaking, in a few seconds, *in value terms*. The specificity necessarily causes a perception of value heterogeneity; however, the interpretation of subjective valuation overtime must be explained based on some homogenized concept. The problem is not a time or a change per se; a time flow is given; we must deal with it. Change has its endogenous (action-based) as well as exogenous (outer reality-based) character. The problem is to explain how a person assesses goods over time without

evolution, applied to thought per se, must also imply in the context of Lewis (2017) and his description of the emergent properties of the system, that we will constantly exceed the limits of our individual knowledge. This raises two interesting questions: To what extent is this in contrast to the fact that there are clear limits to the knowledge of our individual minds? And to what extent can an intersubjective combination of minds overcome them, i.e., a system of minds and their mutual thinking or thinking about some potential artificial intelligence?

any auxiliaries such as the *ceteris paribus* concept or a concept such as *goods of the same kind and quality* or any other model-static constant presuppositions about an agent's valuation over time. It is also not about leaving this question in the subjective (psychological) domain out of praxeology, as Mises (1998) did; meaning here that everybody does valuations somehow, based on their own psychological background and in an exclusively subjective sense, which is from the empirical point of view correct, but it doesn't describe formal and logical principles of decision-making concerning the valuation. We need to define some concept of the theory of subjective value that is applicable and relevant over time.

2.2.3.1 Proposal of the Modification of the Theory

The modification of the theory was introduced in Pošvanc (2019a) to solve the problem of economic calculation without a common denominator in monetary terms. Although, it is in a different context, it is money we use to evaluate man's action over time. To use the modification of the theory to provide us with some basic concepts usable over time is, therefore, more than appropriate. The modification consists of a slight adjustment and a deeper differentiation of the concept of the theory. It states that man always satisfies some perceived factual and expected (counterfactual) *sum of needs* by some *sum of goods* (portfolio); but it is not the whole picture. There is always a combination of some needs. It is a kind of mental concept which has its own structure (thoughts structure) and which is based on a relational character—ideas of needs are combined together. It is thought by man that the needs (as a sum or a combination of them) are met through the second mind concept—some sum and combination of means. It is also a kind of mental concept with its own relational structure, which we can refer to as a concept of portfolio today. It means that there are two mental concepts—a sum/combination of needs and a sum/combination of means and a Mengerian *value* causality which is not realized on the particular level of the need-good relationship but on the conceptual level of some thought structures of needs and means which have a consequent reflection into reality in the form of a real combination of items of reality which we call economic goods and which constructs our portfolio of real goods. The modification is provided, based on the causal links between sums and not some particular need-good, and the deeper differentiation is provided on the level of goods, where we have to differentiate between the concept of means and real items of reality-real goods. I mean here that there are thought structures (a concept of means and a concept of portfolio) and there are real items of reality which we call goods and combination of goods "a portfolio".[51] The particular level of need–mean relationships is left for empirical judgments. These are claims about the existence of reality, which might be either true or false (a man is able to decide based on the observation whether the claim about the reality is true or false). It means that a person is not only aware of some empirical bond of need–mean e.g., the connection of the *idea* of thirst with the *idea* of water as a means to meet the need which corresponds to real object of reality "water." A person also constructs separately the normative state of affairs as it should be in relation to himself, e.g., I am thirsty, but I wish I were not because I need to live. The *value* causality between the sum of needs and the sum of means is differentiated here on a teleological level, while a person also perceives the empirical bond of a causal relationship between needs and goods.[52] It is suitable to imagine this description as some kind of layered causality. There is an *empirical* level and a *value* compositional and relational level which provides us with a value interpretation of reality; it is created as the normative description of the state of affairs of a person, as something desired or as something it should be. The nature of needs always has some future character, therefore. It is

[51] I think that there is one more general mind concept which leads us to connect the mind concept of means with real items of reality.

[52] Here, we are using the terminology of the post-Kantian Czech social scientist Karel Engliš, which he presented e.g., in Engliš (1930). He states that there are four categories of knowledge: (a) empirical knowledge that is connected with nature, knowledge which describes the world *as it is*, (b) the teleological and (c) normative knowledge which describes the world *as it should be*, and finally (d) formal knowledge which is used as a basis for the formulation of the previous three. Mutatis mutandis to our problem, it follows that a person recognizes the empirical causality among parts of reality, e.g., water—the human body—the elimination of thirst. However, there is another level of *value* causality which is between means and goods, a causality which deals with the nature of value—this is a domain of teleology. It is possible to explain this as another layer of thought, over and above the empirical level of knowledge we use to deal with reality and the human world.

a future structural image (individually human-holistic) that defines the desired state of affairs to be achieved.

The relational character of [the sum of needs—the sum of means] is possible to explain e.g., by Hayek (1952), who shows that an individual grasps their surrounding reality based on the so-called model-map analogy (see interpretation e.g., in Horwitz 2010). The model-map-analogy explains our body-sense-interaction with the surrounding reality. The map is partly biological and partly influenced by society, culture and the religion of an individual[53]; it describes what a person knows about reality, based on learning and past experience. As a model, it is a future-oriented way of thinking, based on the map. It is possible to explain the model as a structure full of abstract principles that can be extracted from the map. The model is, therefore, predictive. The map and model influence each other. The map can be changed if the individual discovers that the prediction of the model does not correspond with reality. If we apply this to our explanation of the sum of needs as satisfied by the sum of means, still on the level of the mind, we can see that the concept of a portfolio is map-based while the complex of needs is model-based.[54] As Pošvanc (2019a) shows, it is not possible for a person to only think about a need per se. In order to satisfy a need, a person necessarily needs to seek a way to satisfy that need, and so, a person seeks a mean—it is a dichotomous relationship. It only seems to us that we are able to define the need per se without the definition of mean (good). It helps to realize the dichotomy by the question e.g.: "*How do we differentiate the needs from any other ideas and how do we differentiate the needs from means*?" It is precisely because needs are satisfied by means; that makes them needs. We are also able to differentiate based on this dichotomy, the real and unreal needs. It is precisely this element of the goods of the dichotomy

[53]I think that the concept of the map is also very intersubjective; it is a mind structure that *tries* to describe reality as it is. Due to (intersubjective) learning, it is not only an individualized part of man's realm, but it also has a subjective and intersubjective character. This brings to my mind question about objective knowledge: Does it exist? Cf. with Popper (1975).

[54]I am very inspired by this explanation by Horwitz (2010), who applies this mutatis mutandis to the concept of the firm. I think that Horwitz is among one of the first Austrians who addresses these stated problems in a similar way, as presented in this text; I mean here that he connects the mental concept of the [map-model] analogy to the reality-based problem of the [balance sheet—business plan] problem of the firm.

which enables us to decide which needs are real and which are unreal or unattainable. A similar conclusion is reached by O'Driscoll and Rizzo (1996), who also points out that valuation cannot only be implied at the level of needs or at the level of goods when they resort to defining the value resulting from the evaluation of the so-called "projected want satisfactions".[55]

2.2.3.2 Scale of Needs, the Concept of Portfolio, and the Overlap into Reality

The value scale is simple; two levels: one, factual (the sphere of a present urgent combination of needs) and, two, counterfactual (the sphere of the possible and the impossible combination of needs). The complexity of counterfactually perceived expected needs can have a real character—these needs are met by a combination of means (the mind concept of the portfolio) acquired by planned actions that can realistically happen and they can also have an unreal character—only imaginary, where the given need may never be satisfied or may not be attainable. There are always some combinations of needs that are impossible to achieve because of insufficient resources and knowledge, while there are combinations of needs that are purely imaginative, with no possibility of having the goods in reality because not everything is possible. Hülsmann (2003) uses the terms factual and contrafactual in terms of "choice" and "any alternative to the choice which may have been the actual choice but this does not happen for some reason".[56] The use of the term "factual" and "counterfactual" is exclusionary. Whatever happened, happened, and everything else was left behind on a counterfactual level. The passing of time, the

---

[55]O'Driscoll and Rizzo (1996, pp. 46–47) write: "*Utility in this framework refers to the rank ordering of projected want satisfactions. An individual may value the prospective satisfaction of his desire for an additional unit of comfortable indoor temperature more than that of his desire for an additional unit of delicious meals. Strictly speaking, he does not rank the wants themselves, because they are mere deprivations and are not valued. Similarly, he does not rank the market commodities themselves, because they are wanted not for their own sake but only for the satisfaction they indirectly produce.*"

[56]It was Chroustal (Chroustal, František. 14.11.2019. Personal interview. Vienna) who pointed out here, that it is necessary to explain the use of the following terms: the factual and counterfactual character of the value scale.

impossibility of repeating a given moment, and thus the impossibility of repeating the choice in question in the classical interpretation of the theory of subjective value and traditionally displaying the multi-level value scale implies the absolute and unrepeatable character of our choice. Strictly speaking, given the particular temporal nature of choice, each choice is utterly unique. A strict position related to the unique character of the choice can be found in Shackle (1992) or Lachmann (2005) as well. However, the relativization of the needs and the relativization of the means (the concept of the portfolio) within the framework of the presented modified subjective theory of value allows us to use the terms "factual" and "counterfactual" in a slightly different and not so absolute form. While "factual," here, is meant to mean "currently selected, elected, manifested in the action," similarly and traditionally, the term "counterfactual" does not have an absolute exclusionary character. It is still very true that choice, its related circumstances, and the perception of needs will never have the same and uniquely identical character, but the relativization of a combination of needs (and the relativization of their satisfaction with means-goods in possession) and therefore makes it possible, later in time, to make a very similar choice or to have, for once, realized the choice persisting character in time (you can use mean-good in many different ways to meet the different combinations of needs). The newly constructed combination of needs implies the possibility of repeating some unrealized needs in a different economic context. At the same time, building a real portfolio allows us to explain the process continuously. The Lego-type relative character of needs and the position of goods within the portfolio enable us to satisfy also counterfactually perceived needs later in time from the point of view of present action and choice. It is not an exclusionary mode.

It has to be stressed that there is no scale of goods (items of reality). It is only the two-leveled complex of factual and contrafactual needs as a mind concept which is thought to be satisfied by a sum of means and transformed into the individual real actions, reflexed by (a) the existing or current portfolio of goods (real items of reality) and/or (b) the expected portfolio concept (as a mind structure of the sum of means) which is either (b1) realistically planned and achievable by some (new) combination of (appropriate, exchanged or produced) means-goods—some potential portfolio, or (b2) which could be only desired and never achieved—a desired portfolio. Until this point, we were mostly on a mental level of the problem and we only slightly emphasized that there was a mind structure of needs, a mind structure of means (the concept of the portfolio) which has its overlap into reality by the composition of the real items of reality—goods, which are acquired by the real actions of people. Essentially, we have described some mind structures as thought structures by which we grasp reality.[57] What is interesting is also that the presented concept has quite a simple overlap into reality. The mental concept of the portfolio (the combination or sum of means) has an overlap into reality in the form of a real accumulation, production, and exchanging of the real items of reality we call goods. The actual, perceived combination of needs is always satisfied by action, such as acquiring real goods that compose the portfolio; man utilizes these goods in order to meet current needs and potential, counterfactual future needs. It follows then, that the combination of needs is purely a mental structure of both the factual and the contrafactual, (real and unreal) needs. Then, we have three kinds of thought concepts of portfolio—some actual or current portfolios, some potential portfolios (thought concepts which are possible and attainable and where we focus our planned actions) and some desired portfolios (thought concepts of what we desire, if …). The current portfolio as thoughts concept has its overlap into reality by what we actually have—a sum of goods. The potential portfolio as thoughts concept has its overlap into reality by what our actions are focused on acquiring when we are dealing with a new combination of goods. The desired portfolio as a thoughts concept hasn't its overlap into reality; we dream about that in the mode of "If I have this or that, I would be in this

[57]It has to be stressed that I don't think these "thought structures" are particular neuronal structures. I follow Hayek (1952), who describes neuronal structures as inevitable for building thought structures. However, there is not one specific kind of precise neuronal structure for these or those thoughts. The neuronal structure and its plasticity only enable us to build some thought structures. If I think about a particular concept, just as anyone else does, it is not so that we can have the same neuronal interconnections which cause the same thought concepts. The neuronal structure only enables to create a thought structure. I don't think that there is some kind of exact equivalence. When I use terms such as mind or thought structures to describe something, as opposed to neuronal structures as well as over them; the emerging phenomena of the self, consciousness, thoughts and ideas.

or that way satisfied." It also holds that the more urgent and complex the combination of needs that can be simultaneously satisfied by the good,[58] the more preferable the economic good is in terms of being included in the real portfolio. The integrity of the view of needs requires that the individual has a holistic idea of life in a time continuum. This can easily exceed its objective length of life and manifest itself e.g., in the context of the inheritance or preservation of real goods for generational descendants. People are aware of their finitude, and at the same time, the continuation of the future generations to which they can adapt their portfolio. The counterfactual structure of needs that we perceive has this character as if stretched in time.

At the same time, the combination of needs allows us to identify, in principle, any extensive and complicated plan. There can be the plan of a few snatched moments, such as eating chocolate so no one can see me; an hour plan (practice); a daily plan (working during the day and going to the cinema in the evening); annual plans (engaging in business) or, a lifelong plan (being a good person). The perceived factual combination of needs is, at the same time, satisfied by the current action. Acting in this sense does not have to be explained in the form of identifying every second of our life, e.g., "*I will take this strawberry, put it in my mouth, I will masticate it five times in order to satisfy 1/20 of my hunger.*" It simply happens as a complex phenomenon. Some actions are more complex and general in nature, while others are very particular. The level of detail depends on the degree to which a particular combination of needs an action requires. This means that sometimes it is sufficient to carry out an activity in the sense of "*I am working all day, which will allow me to support my family*" but sometimes, if I am a biochemist, the activity must be more detailed, as in, "*I have to connect this particular cell very precisely with that one*" The detail of the plan and our actions depend on a subjective assessment of the complex of needs.

---

[58]It is also a combination of features of the economic good as will be shown below. The combination of more features within one good has basically the same effect as the diversification of the portfolio.

2.2.3.3 Consequences of the Proposed Modification

Because we are dealing here with the *sum* of needs satisfied by the *sum* of goods, the concept in the interpretation of economic phenomena is applicable in a time continuum. This is because the sum is a (mathematical) construct of the mind that is formally time-invariant. The concept enables us also to claim that a person will always prefer to achieve a higher (rather than a lower) satisfaction for the combination of their needs through their portfolio over time. They will prefer to achieve satisfaction sooner rather than later; therefore, the creation of their desired portfolio will be subject to their actions. We are also able to solve a classic (Austrian's theory) problem of value imputation. The imputation of value takes place at the level of thoughts or mind concepts, i.e., the *concept* of the *sum* of needs is linked to the *concept* of the *sum* of means. The portfolio is first constructed as the thought concept and only then it is reflected in empirical reality in the form of goods (real items). The imputation of value is the reflection of the causal relationship created on a level between two mind concepts transmitted into reality by the construction of a real portfolio. The importance of the combination of goods in question depends on the extent to which the goods contribute to the overall satisfaction of the sum of perceived existing needs. The portfolio affords us the opportunity to apply the ordinal (Čuhel-Misesian) form of valuation. It also enables us to provide some basic so-called in kind calculation; a calculation without money. This is possible due to the relational character of the portfolio, which is on the one hand constructed by a combination of goods, while on the other, it is the concept per se. A person does not perceive marginal changes in the context of the marginal satisfaction of some particular need by a particular good over time.[59] We apply marginal changes (the law of diminishing marginal utility) on the overall level of the sum of needs satisfied by portfolios. Marginal change thus does not concern something particular, but relative, i.e., the morphological composition of goods within a portfolio. We

[59]The problem with the traditional interpretation of the law of diminishing marginal utility is that it is necessarily applied over time when any additional unit of good may be subject to value perception changes caused by choice, which in turn necessarily precludes the application of the law. See also Chapter 4 of this book to deal with this topic in more detail.

change the relative composition of goods within our portfolio through action; it means that we withdraw some goods from the portfolio as costs of our action in order to achieve a new and more suitable composition of goods. It provides us with a very basic calculation ability. The portfolio is a denominator of the calculation; it provides us with a utility unit, although a very personal and subjective one, but it is our basic accounting standard out of the monetary economy.[60] This is what eventually creates a workable concept of a subjective evaluation in time, where we evaluate *homogeneous concepts*, meaning, the *sum* of needs and the *sum* of goods (portfolio), although the portfolio is formed from different goods at different times and is always different in its composition, whereas the mental concept of the sum from the formal point of view is identical in time. When acquiring goods (by production, exchange, or appropriation), a person strictly prefers the acquisition of goods per se, but marginal change is assessed at the level of the portfolio, which should meet the overall factual and counterfactual perceived needs over time.[61]

---

[60] See an example of the calculation and marginal consideration of state of affairs in Sect. 2.3.5 concerning the intersubjective nature of success/error.

[61] It is possible to solve the problem mentioned by Alfred Marshall in this way as well. To explain the paradox that the more quality music to which a person listens, the stronger their preference for that music can become, Marshall had to deal with the argument that we must assume the invariance of preferences over time in a given law. The problem is solved by Gerry Becker, introducing the concept of social and human capital. I think that the concept briefly presented here, is more abstract and general. Marshall's paradox is very easy to explain from the point of view of the modified theory of subjective value. The point is that we do not see a higher level of preferences associated with a higher consumption of quality music. What we see is a preference for some portfolio (P1) over portfolio (P2), when a marginal change in P2 is realized through the higher consumption of better-quality music. The fact that greater consumption of music implies a higher preference for quality music seems only apparent. The fact is that P2 contains only a higher relative proportion of quality music and is, therefore, preferred. However, the amount of music (good per se) in P2 is irrelevant, given that its position in the portfolio is relative and not absolute. Here, man still prefers a higher to lower satisfaction of needs that P2 provides for some reason in time. The law of diminishing marginal utility is valid over time and we do not have to assume the invariability of preferences. The law does not apply only to music but portfolios generally. The composition of P2 is still dependent on its relative change. The P2 can then theoretically be composed only of quality music because the person responds with a portfolio to the sum of needs. Even in this case, the law of diminishing marginal utility still applies to the portfolio of goods. Thus, if the P2 were composed only of music, the law would be applied in the context of the relative impoverishment of other imaginary goods in the P2, which would be only counter-factual, because they would be discriminated against at the expense of quality music. In my opinion, the concept is also compatible with Becker's

We are treating ourselves in a time continuum as complex beings.[62] It means that the value perception depends on the relational content of needs. The content of needs is always more or less a specific combination of something as it should be. The economic *value causality* between needs and means is, therefore, a more complex phenomenon. This also provides an explanation of some types of actions that most people consider irrational, e.g., suicides, martyrs, or hermits, whose mix of needs—means (portfolio) and related action are different from the mix of people who have more traditional preferences and a so-called more traditional mix of the sum of needs-means (portfolio). Although their combination of needs could be considered strange to others, it is their combination and consequent action that cannot be considered irrational.

We have also reached the point at which we are able to indicate the first part of our solution to given questions about the future which we have to connect with the above-mentioned Hayek–Pavlík theory. The higher and better the diversification of accumulated assets, the better prepared the owner will be in terms of the anticipated and unexpected eventualities of the future, and any changes in the perception of the current number of needs that the diverse portfolio of assets allows. People do not search for some generally valid and specific composition of the portfolio; they search for a subjectively perceived diversification where one person may prefer a higher degree of diversification than another. The portfolio of goods is always composed subjectively and is dependent on the individual preferences of the person and on what they consider to be a suitable composition in accordance with their abilities. It could, therefore, be stated, that we do not estimate the future in its concreteness;

concept, where social and human capital is precisely part of the total sum of human needs. For a description of Becker's concept and problem stated by Marshall, see e.g., Pavlík (2004, pp. 745–751) or in Becker (1997).

[62] I think that to treat an individual as a complex being, and in a time continuum, we ought to turn to the discussion about the imputation of value among early Austrians (see e.g., in Bilo 2004). It is also worth mentioning that Mises (1998) refused to expand on the early Austrian's attempts to describe needs as complexes, which is possible to see in Menger (2007, pp. 129, 145). Mises considers this to be superfluous. Mises (1998, p. 123) writes that Menger and Böhm-Bawerk only "*had to make use of the term 'class of wants' in order to refute the objections raised by those who considered bread as such, more valuable than silk because the class 'want of nourishment' is more important than the class 'want of luxurious clothing'.*" I think that the *class of wants* is a more workable concept which is expanded also in this work.

we relativize by portfolio, albeit subjectively, the specific meaning of the future.[63] By owning various goods and their features and by combining their use, a person responds to the various eventualities of the future, while some do not have to be anticipated. The action is focused on the creation of a portfolio in some concrete form and at the same time, on some future potential—the perceived elimination of uneasiness. I think that the concept presented in this way complements Mises' definition of action. Mises (1998, pp. 14–15) writes:

> *The incentive that impels a man to act is always some uneasiness ... But to make a man act, uneasiness and the image of a more satisfactory state alone are not sufficient. A third condition is required: the expectation that purposeful behavior has the power to remove or at least to alleviate the felt uneasiness.*

Since we do not know the future by definition, we cannot meet the third condition; but we would say that we know the future. However, if we relativize the significance of the future in its concreteness by the sum of needs and portfolios, the outcome of the action, i.e., some kind of goods with which we have enriched and diversified the portfolio, it makes for the possibility of fulfilment in terms of the third condition of the action. The third condition is fulfilled in such a way that the portfolio of goods allows us to relatively satisfy the needs that will arise and will be specifically perceived in the future when it occurs as a combination with other needs. It is also necessary to state that the proposed modification of the theory of subjective value causes a degree of economic subjective relativism. However, it allows an elegant explanation of evaluation over time without having to assume a stable subjective attribution of the

[63]The concept sum of needs met by the sum of means (or portfolio) also allows us to explain logically, the continuity of the action. Shackle and Lachmannn would say that if I implement plan A and I find, over time, given the new economic context, that I have to change it, I am starting from pure logic, from a different plan B because it is different compared to A. This strict discontinuity would mean many problems for men as a result of this very logic. However, this presented concept, a relative one, shows that man is still implementing some plan A, which is only somehow modified—we simply change the relative composition of certain parts of the plan. We only start to implement plan B if the composition of parts of plan B are not possible in order to connect to plan A in any way. This eliminates problems defined by Shackle and Lachmann.

value to goods of the same kind and quality over time. And I think for now this is enough. It is a sufficient achievement. We will have to deal with the conclusion concerning relativism later within the text because it is impossible for individuals to live, based on subjective relativism. I would also note at the end of this presentation that this concept seems to me to be similar to Shackle's concept of *orientations* (see Shackle 1992, pp. 74–80).

2.2.4 How Do We Estimate the Future, and Why We Are Economically Successful

We will begin the interpretation where it is necessary to anchor it—at the level of thoughts and plans. Only then will it be possible to connect the interpretation with reality. As we have shown at the level of ideas and plans, there are combinations or sums of needs that are factual and counterfactual, in nature, and some ideas and plans about how to meet perceived needs are reflected in reality by the building of a portfolio of goods. If an entrepreneur (let's use the term in the sense of an ideal type) can discover what people need in the future, there will be a demand for their goods, which, in return, will allow the fulfilment of the entrepreneur's personal needs and plans. And to fulfill the entrepreneur's personal needs and plans and other consumer's needs and plans requires that other entrepreneurs be able to identify their personal needs; and so on. The entrepreneur must, of course, provide a good that meets the required needs—e.g., offering a horse with a broken leg, or a car without an engine, in order to satisfy the need to move would be business suicide. The goods must satisfy some needs in terms of the mutual interaction of reality, i.e., the interaction of the human body as part of reality with another element of reality or the interaction of elements of reality with each other in the context of a human-defined need, which is reflected in reality by goods, meaning here a healthy horse can be ridden and an engine moves the car while it is drive by a person.

The condition for the success of any entrepreneur is, of course, to discover the needs of potential customers and to adapt the goods they offer to the identified needs. However, it will be argued that this is not a revelation of any particular need. Given the previous claims that needs are always grouped in some complex combinations or sum of needs, the claim should not come as a surprise. I claim that the entrepreneur identifies the complex or combination of needs. One of the conditions for successfulfy delivering in-demand goods to the market is their potential multi-purposeness in the context of the sum of needs. We can imagine this with the example of hunting tools made by our predecessors, e.g., a spear or bow, which are better weapons for hunting wildlife than bare hands and a knife. This is due to the fact that the design of a spear or bow pays attention not only to the effectiveness of killing but also ensures a higher level of protection for the hunter against predators due to its extended reach in comparison with a knife or bare hands. Also, it is possible to use this good in defense against enemies, etc. For this reason, not everything is a loss to the entrepreneur, even in the case of the above-mentioned example of a horse with a broken leg, or a car without an engine, because the goods can still satisfy the need for hunger, the need for spare parts, etc.[64]

Another example could be individual movement from place to place. It is possible to claim that this is some abstract need that humans had 100 thousand years ago as well as today, i.e., some kind of continuing abstract need. While the reason for human movement in the past was probably the search for food, today the transfer is also connected with lifestyle, or logistic chains, or the globalization of production and consumption. From this point of view, this particular need for movement seems to us to be relatively stable throughout history. What we also know is that the need is always satisfied in some specific way—by different kinds of goods. It is empirically obvious that moving on foot, and by horse, car,

[64]In this way, it is possible to explain the paradox of demand for inferior and unsuitable products as well. The demand for them exists precisely due to their certain "multi-purposeness," e.g., to satisfy a demand related to the need to own a rarity that no one else has, or that the a given product is suitable in the context of other compositional needs, e.g., to fix something, etc. From this point of view, it is important to put forward three observations: (a) we either discover this multi-efficiency of the items of reality and make them goods or we intentionally produce them as goods in this way, (b) goods have in this respect their so-called *intrinsic features but not intrinsic value*; it is necessary to differentiate between features and values, of items and goods, (c) the properties of items of reality are the results of the evolutionary process of the combination of some properties created by nature or their intentional construction by man, who combines certain features of reality.

bicycle, motorbike, plane, boat, or train has different characteristics and contexts and has a different form. The specificity of the good in question is related to the specificity of a particular sum of needs related to its specific purpose, but also to the given reality. This means that we move differently and by different means when on water, in the air, or on land. This, on the one hand, is the context which the surrounding reality implies and, on the other, the targeted specific characteristics of the transfer, arising from a combination of other needs, e.g., speed of movement, safety, or comfort, etc. The combination of these factors causes various specific manifestations and combinations of given needs which is then reflected in the form of the goods provided. It is the specific manifestations of a given good that make entrepreneurs compete. The product they offer must satisfy the general and abstract sum of needs as set out above. If the offered good did not meet them at all, it would not be in demand, e.g., a moving car without a motor, or a horse with broken legs. However, this general condition of satisfying the sum of needs must also be specified in some way. It is also true that its concrete form must be conditioned by the fact that not everything is possible. An entrepreneur offering a specific product can only offer it in the context of what is technologically, economically, or practically possible. That is to say, not everything is feasible, and even what is feasible in theory, does not mean that it is economically acceptable. The specific form is always limited by resources in the broad sense of the term. Thus, the specific manifestations of satisfying needs have their economic, technological, and practical limitations on the supply side. A potential consumer may want to travel on a regular rocket flight to the moon, but in terms of resources, it is "almost" impossible today and 100 years ago it was utterly impossible. Of course, this does not mean that this status will not change. Thus, a potential consumer could demand anything from an entrepreneur, but "*anything*" may not be possible. This limitation also means that the entrepreneur is successful at the end of the day, even if they do not satisfy the full range of consumer needs.

As we already know from Knight (1964), by concretization of the product under the given circumstances and restrictions, the entrepreneur tries to formulate or find a target group—a specific market. We also know that the entrepreneur, with his product, is expected to meet some combination of needs. But as already established, not everything is possible. If not everything is possible, the entrepreneur does not have to satisfy any combination of needs. However, he must design a combination for the consumers by which the entrepreneur identifies the market (e.g., the group of people) for whom the entrepreneur produces the good in order to satisfy at least some abstract and general needs that apply to every individual in that group of people. Given the fact that the entrepreneur faces a problem in identifying some *combination* of needs, and the fact that he is dealing with an estimation of that combination, the likelihood increases that some particular needs, not an ideal combination of needs, maybe satisfactory for an individual who is a part of the target group; these needs could be "met," even if not in their entirety, but at least in part through the offered economic good. Production is based on some combinations of features with regard to goods, which correspond to a combination of needs. The specific form of the good and the fact that not everything is possible also implies the adaptation of the consumer. The consumer may want to make his idea of satisfying the combination of their needs with a product an absolute, but in practical terms, this is not possible. The consumer can only choose from what is possible. Therefore, it is skills that make for proper combinations which *allow* the entrepreneur to succeed over time. The entrepreneur is essentially someone who creates combinations and we have these basic options with which to describe an entrepreneur's success, meaning here, to be a successful entrepreneur:

(a) *It is the revealing of a multi-efficiency which is a more successful strategy compared to other ones.* The multi-efficiency in the context of the sum of needs, i.e., a higher rate of potential satisfaction for a combination of several unique needs implies that the entrepreneur who, through offering his goods for the higher variability of satisfaction of needs, will be more successful than another entrepreneur whose goods, in their specific form, do not have these characteristics.
(b) *It is the revealing of a generality-efficiency which is a more successful strategy compared to other ones.* This is due to the fact that it is also a matter of revealing a more abstract and general sum of needs that have a more general and universal character. The more

general/abstract the nature of revealed needs, the more it implies their existence over time; though it may not be the general existence of these needs, in the sense that they are present forever. For entrepreneurs to succeed, it is sufficient that a given combination of needs lasts at least a certain period of time. *The success of an entrepreneur is also subject to the fact that not everything is possible.* This is due to the fact that we will always face some potential combination of knowledge and resource challenges,

(c) *It is the nature of the combination principle which enables an entrepreneur to succeed.* This is due to the fact that the combination of needs and the features of goods produced to meet that combination of needs is relative in nature. It means that both entrepreneurs and consumers face a kind of trade-off in terms of their decisions and the acceptance of possibilities.

However, we cannot stop at a higher degree of generality, a multi-purpose applicability and by the very fact that not everything is possible or in terms of the relative nature of the combinations of needs and features of goods in order to show why entrepreneurs are successful. We have to describe the general principle which consists of also revealing the so far non-existent needs which a person who demands some goods does not have, or, is not aware of their needs, not even in the mode of a counterfactual need. How does an entrepreneur reveal these kinds of needs? How to describe the *core principle*—Smith's invisible hand? Here follows the necessary connection to Hayek–Pavlík's method of evolutionary apriorism.

It is the specific form of the goods which it is possible to produce under some knowledge and resource restrictions which are offered to the market by entrepreneurs in some particular form. It is precisely this particular form where entrepreneurs' trial and error processes take place. It is clearly possible to achieve something through trial and error, while the basic criteria of recognizing success is that a specific form of the good must somehow meet the defined abstract needs. If the good doesn't meet at least the abstract need, it could be described as an error, as there will be no interest in the good (we will describe an exact criteria for the error later). The concrete form is manifested in the fact that the entrepreneur wants to attract consumers. However, to meet the very abstract need solely is insufficient; the entrepreneur must provide some combination of the features of goods that meet a combination of needs. This claim comes from the modification of the theory of subjective value. It is the relational character of a portfolio consisting of goods which is on the radar of a person. Some combination of the suitable features of goods is the same principle which only improves the character of the portfolio per se. This reveals to us that a person is not interested in some economic good per se, a person is interested in some states of affair (a state of the whole portfolio) and a demanded good would cause only a marginal improvement in terms of this state of affairs. However, the principle of revealing proper combinations alone doesn't describe how entrepreneurs do "their job." How do they estimate the proper relational character of the features of supplied goods?

The different specific forms of products (let's imagine now some *product, such* as Smith's *germ cell*) offered by competing entrepreneurs seeking to attract consumers causes a further differentiation of goods. So, we are going to claim that the specific manifestations of the product with which entrepreneurs compete, make it possible to reveal a new sum or combination of needs that did not have to exist until then. Since goods offered in the competitive process are differentiated, i.e., entrepreneurs differentiate goods to satisfy a wider range of combinations of consumer's needs, which is always shown to the consumer in some specific form of the offered goods, consumers are also aware that the goods satisfy some new combination of needs; it could also be some combination of needs not previously perceived by any consumer per se—the product could be a novum per se. This, in turn, allows entrepreneurs to identify a new target group—the market for which they start to produce a new product. This is nothing more than the germ cell principle, and the process of differentiation, as described by Pavlík. This process creates new forms of concreteness, which at a certain stage reach their limits (the demand and competitive process of other entrepreneurs); these are subsequently exceeded through a new differentiation aimed at a new combination of needs, etc. Let us explain this with an illustrative example of a car since a similar example is used by Kirzner (1999).

Entrepreneurs know that a car must move. Therefore, it fulfills some very abstract needs identified in the past, which were previously satisfied, e.g., by horses or carriages. However, the entrepreneurs start offering a new product—a car, for example.[65] The car is successful because it satisfies a combination of needs, while horses and carriages satisfied an older preceding combination of needs. As the car is an entirely new and different type of good compared to the horse and carriage that everyone had, the car entrepreneurs would first be interested in a specific market of people who, for some reason, want to differentiate themselves from others by having a car. It would follow that unlike a horse or a carriage, a car satisfies a complex need differently. *Another combination* means may express a different relative combination of needs and their significance (sitting more comfortably in a car than on a horse, with or without a saddle), or removing a need and replacing it with another (the coordination of the bridle movement is replaced by a steering wheel), or adding some need and features of good to the complex of needs (a car roof which protects the user against rain or prevents a user from getting hurt). Let us focus our illustrative interpretation on the combination of the need for movement and add to this the need for social prestige. Entrepreneurs, of course, realize that the more a given good meets a higher complex of some needs, the more successful they are likely to be. For example, at the beginning of its production, the car could meet only the abstract need for movement in connection with social status. However, the competition between the entrepreneurs means that if they want to be even more successful, the product must be clearly distinguishable from that

[65]However, in this sense, when inventing the car, we cannot imply in the sense of Kirzner (1999), that this is a development that would point to a waste of resources by entrepreneurs, who until then, focused on satisfying needs by allocating resources to the production of wagons or horse breeding. The claim about the waste of resources would be valid only if we knew what creative destruction the automotive industry would bring at a time when entrepreneurs had allocated resources to the production of wagons or horse breeding. The opportunity that entrepreneurs began to spread (i.e., cars) was invented by them; it did not previously exist in any form, even potentially. The invention, which ultimately eliminated almost all entrepreneurs focusing on wagons and horse breeding, consisted of the identification of a new complex set of needs and a suitable combination of resources to produce cars, was a gradual evolutionary process. Cf. with Kirzner (1999).

of their competitors. Since they are still aware[66] that connecting some new features to an older good which enables it to meet a new combination of needs is a successful strategy, they also begin to pay attention to making the car safe. As a result, a better body design was invented. This means that the need for movement, social status, but also a higher level of safety is now being met; it is the safety feature that causes the entrepreneur who came up with the idea to be slightly more successful than others (of course, only if the new feature satisfies some combination of needs over time). Of course, other entrepreneurs do not want to lag behind. If safety has so far been met by a better body design that protects the driver in the event of a collision, entrepreneurs have become competitive in this combination of needs. Based on their success, they see that safer cars are in greater demand than ordinary cars. This motivates them to discover new, specific forms of increasing security, e.g., by inventing the seat belt. The seat belt is then copied by others to increase car safety.

But what is happening in the background of this specific and particular activity? There is a much more abstract need in the form of security, which finds a general segment—the market, i.e., a whole group of clients who *also* want safe cars while traveling by car. But that is not all; of course, entrepreneurs continue to compete. They specify their products, through car equipment or paint, in order to differentiate their goods from their competitors' goods. These more specific goods cause new forms of additional abstract needs to be created, in other words, they target different types of groups of people, where the group shares that additional abstract need. This manifests itself in the design or color of the car (purchasing a green rather than a red car) the equipment of the car, therefore, creates a different kind of need in the form of social status, etc.

Competition between entrepreneurs takes place in a specific concrete mode of specific concrete products. However, success is associated with discovering the right combination of more abstract needs that allow the entrepreneur to shape the market for a group of people who share given

[66]This type of knowledge may not always be explicitly recognized by entrepreneurs. It can easily apply to the so-called tacit knowledge when entrepreneurs only intuitively know that they must have an additional property. Only the reconstruction by social scientists of the events that happen implies that an additional property of good satisfies a new combination of needs.

abstract needs.[67] At the same time, it is important to realize that this is not necessarily a compatible group of identical individuals. As we stated in our modified theory of subjective value, we must realize, that the combination of needs is different for each individual, *but since it is always a combination of needs, their mutual position is always relative.*[68] In other words, it allows the entrepreneur to produce under the constraints of reality and economic resources, a "*safe, moderately equipped, green car*" for a family with two children, as well as for a pensioner or person who thinks green will bring them happiness, or a person with limited budgetary resources who chooses a given offer because of cost. It absolutely does not matter that they are completely different people, with different backgrounds or different views of the world with different personal histories or different social backgrounds. Regularity has only a relative mode, which is sufficient for it to be discovered through entrepreneurial activity and at the same time, to identify its market, i.e., a target group. It is still true that at the individual level of overall needs, the individuals belonging to this target group are absolutely different individuals, who in terms of subjective value may have absolutely nothing in common and may belong to absolutely different cultural and social groups—whether communists or libertarians or working on a farm or in the city.[69]

Therefore, at the level of identifying needs, we see a combination of different types of needs to which the entrepreneur always responds with

---

[67]In certain cases, the target group may be a particular individual in terms of providing a rare and very individual good.

[68]Economic relativism results from the subjective preference of the higher to the lower satisfaction of needs. However, economic relativism creates a problem for comparison. Paradoxically, as the reader will see below, we will solve this through an evolutionary developed and implicitly accepted "agreement" of economic agents.

[69]The explanation at this point is complementary to Hoppe (1997), who explains the creation of Knight's production for the market based on ideal types. The ideal type is replaced here by the relativization of the needs of individuals, which makes it possible to form groups of individuals without claiming that they have the same needs. We have replaced the regularity of the ideal types with a more abstract thought construct. From this point of view, Knight's strategy of diffusion seems as relevant and does not have to be rejected within the framework of subjectivism because the entrepreneur could consider not implementing technology which kills a few workers but to implement technology which only hurts many workers and could weigh what is relatively better.

a specific product. A given product always reaches the limits of its possibilities in order to satisfy a complex of needs that imply a specific target group or market segment. This is because the given concretization of the product causes a new form of differentiation. Differentiation then allows the entrepreneurs to discover other general and abstract needs that people either adopt as new, or that are new combinations of already existing needs. This process is constantly repeated. It is precisely the constant discovery of the given abstract constructions of some complex or sum of needs, which in turn causes the one who reveals them to be more successful and vice versa. This is no other principle than the one described by the invisible hand of the market. It is not a coincidence that entrepreneurs are influenced by some invisible hand while dealing with consumer's needs. However, as it was shown, the logic of the process behind is as it was described by Hayek–Pavlík's method—from concrete to more abstract or from simple to more complex, when higher complexity spontaneously creates new room for new simplicity and we know that it is the result of the Hegelian method of crossing these "limiting" boundaries.

Of course, in the context of an entrepreneur's success, they compete not only by discovering the goods themselves but also by discovering organizational business methods. The process has identical characteristics. Organizational elements or production methods also always have a specific character. This allows entrepreneurs to define certain general principles of their activities. These are manifested in the transition from the workroom to the processes of automated production; the discovery of increasingly common management models re-concretized in the internal rules of the operation of the business unit; the discovery of optimal company sizes; production; specialization, etc.

The proposed solution subsequently implies the possibility of finding regularities in human action in their concrete form. It is not to say that we are all the same and that we behave in a similar manner. It is about revealing a complex of more general and time-invariant needs of individuals who are otherwise completely different.[70] This significantly increases

[70]Given regularities—general complexes of needs or types of behavior in a given area of interest of individuals—are possible not only to identify through the analysis of the so-called big data

the success rate of entrepreneurs in estimating future needs and adapting their business models to these conditions offered by the market environment, both to their consumers and to their employees. As we have shown in the example with the car, the given regularities can even grow into a separate and widespread general need demanded by several people, around which a separate market with separate specialized suppliers will be created.

Discovering general combinations of needs, discovering the specific character by which a combination of features of goods will respond to the identified complex of needs, and choosing a combination of suitable resources to construct the good is not accidental. It has a rational character, i.e., it has been come up with as a result of intellectual activity based on the differentiation of current knowledge used toward the future. Success or failure is associated on the one hand with the correct or incorrect estimation of abstract complexes of needs, but can also be connected to the right or wrong combination of resources focused on the production of the good, or formulation of the target group—the market, etc. It is possible to state that we, as entrepreneurs within the meaning of ideal types, are combinators of knowledge with regard to how to meet other people's needs, by some combination of means (goods).

The combination of these circumstances also implies the possibility of learning from economic success or error. This is not a lesson learned from a particular event that Shackle will never repeat again and is always unique; this is a lesson learned from the application of the above-mentioned principles within the relative importance of the revelation of the sum of needs. This means learning from experience, e.g., in the past, an entrepreneur may have incorrectly combined the specific properties of the good. These errors can be avoided in the next business attempt so that the combination of the given properties in its specific form is more accurate (we will describe the creation of the criteria of success and error

today but also based on these analytics, it is possible to identify behavioral patterns that are usable for further identification of new products and services which have the character to satisfy a complex of newly discovered more general and time-invariant needs. It is necessary to emphasize that these time-invariant needs need not exist indefinitely. It is satisfactory for the entrepreneur that they exist for some unspecified time which, however, is sufficient for building his/her business model.

a little bit later). However, as previously pointed out, the economic error can also be used advantageously, or at least in the context of the elimination of absolute losses (the example of a horse with a broken leg or a car without an engine).

What did we illustrate? We illustrated the possibility of explaining operational principles of the invisible hand by linking the process to the modified theory of subjective value with Hayek–Pavlík's method of (intersubjective) evolutionary apriorism, using the example of how entrepreneurs discover people's needs and why they are successful in meeting those needs. We also described how the not very clearly described term *Verstehen* works. We showed, too, how it is possible to produce, in terms of Knight's solution "for the market." Similarly, we have shown how entrepreneurs find and discover novelty (Shackle's context). Entrepreneurs must relativize the *concrete* significance of the future which cannot be estimated in its concrete form. On the contrary, it is necessary to adapt the *desiredness* and *proximity to the truth* to the general and time-invariant complex of needs. The complex formed by different combinations of needs relativizes the significance of a specific need or its exact reflection in reality and in time. It is also possible to identify, against the background of our interpretation, how entrepreneurs create Shackle's concept of the *scheme* and enable the satisfaction of needs due to *limitations*. It is impossible not to see how the specificity of business production implies a divergence of expectations. It is also possible to identify regularities based on this interpretation—in the form of general and abstract combinations of needs, which enable the entrepreneurs to focus on a successful satisfaction of a consumer's combination of needs. It remains for us to connect our theory to Hayek and explain the problem he has been dealing with almost all his life. The problem of coordination, i.e., the existence of social order.

2.3 Economic Coordination and Ordering: Process Description

At this point, it is necessary, to start with the same question that Hayek (1937) chose at the beginning of his program: Let's paraphrase: "*Why does the subjectively captured data on which we make decisions correspond with objective facts of economic reality*?" Before we begin to answer this question, it is necessary to make two remarks on the question itself. We must first fill the gap between the subjectively grasped economic data and the objective economic facts of reality. We must realize that all objective facts of economic reality are either created, based on the very subjective actions of individuals (e.g., simple production process) or the intersubjective actions of individuals (e.g., complicated production processes or exchange). We have to realize that the reality is "as it is." It is a human intention realized by human action which creates some kinds of economic reality facts. First, it has to be an intentional plan; this plan has to be transformed into the subjective or into the intersubjective action which produces some objective *historical fact* of economic reality. The objective fact of economic reality could only be the *outcome* of subjective or intersubjective actions. Subjective intentions followed by subjective actions tend to be very personal for those who want the state of affairs solely for themselves and are solely subjectively focused; this produces some subjective consideration of the objective (historical) economic state of affairs. There are also intersubjective actions. Here lies the main problem of Hayek's question: how it is possible that more and more human subjects economically understand each other based on the fact that they can interpret the intentions and plans of others only from their very subjective point of view? This is the gap we have to explain. However, the sequence of argumentation must be as follows: (1) The subjective perception of data (signaled by others); (2) The intersubjective assessment of data, which leads to (3), The interpersonal coordination, in the form of continuation in the established direction of action or possible action adjustments, and (4), The objective facts of economic reality (result). Then the sequence restarts.

Objective data, such as the price of a good is always the *result of the exchange* of goods and money (or in the barter economy, the exchange of goods for goods). *Whenever* people *agree* on some form of coordination and *implement it*, the price becomes an objective fact of reality. If they do not agree, the price as an objective fact of reality has no reason to arise. It will remain in an unrealized subjective form (the asking price), or displayed in some intersubjective tool—e.g., an order book, or expressed in the form of an oral offer, or is displayed in the offer of the shop or the price list of the entrepreneur. Historically, an objectively created price can only be compared on an objective level with another historical price. The historical and once realized price which results in the exchange only gives us information about the subjective views on the exchange that took place in the past. In other words, what two or more individuals perceived in terms of past value based on then-existing exogenous and endogenous influences. This is interesting information for humans—comparing history and present events. However, the historical price is not linked to our plans in any other way except as a historical aspect of the realization of some part of the plan, which already happened. Plans lead and take into account the future *only*, and the future itself can still be influenced. The context of our plan is reflected in the assessment of the change in the portfolio of goods. Within the context of the whole portfolio, this means, what a person must give up in exchange, and what they get in a return within the context of the newly created portfolio. At the value level, this is related to the value a person must give up in the context of the overall perception of their needs being met, compared to what they will get in the context of the overall perception of their needs being satisfied.

Therefore, the *bid* and *ask* price are present on the market only if intentions to exchange some part of the portfolio exists[71]; the existence of bid and ask is determined by the fact that human subjects consider enhancing their impoverished portfolio. What creates exchange is spread between goods which are intended to be exchanged between two or more humans; it does not matter if they are considering the monetary or barter economy. The *bid* and *ask* process has an explicit subjective character, unless it is mutually accepted. By stating bid or ask we *only*

---

[71]Apart from many past prices which arose when one party of the exchange accepted the subjectively perceived *bid* and the other party the *ask*.

assume or expect that the ask or bid price will be accepted by others. The bid and ask process, therefore, only assumes an intersubjective character. In the case of a nonmonetary economy, this character (the subjective and expected intersubjective) is determined as the ratio of one good to another; in the monetary economy, the given character is determined as the ratio of good to money. The question is, on what basis does the subjective preferences expressed in terms of bid and ask price, change into information that has an objective meaning for these individuals, so that they can grasp and interpret identically? Objective information about the past price is neither inspiring nor important. It is always the will that determines what is inspiring or not. An objectively generated historical fact (the price) *cannot be* what conveys information to acting individuals about their mutual plans. It is too late for that.

However, we see something else in the market that we should focus on: *Spread*. It has *no subjective character but* has an explicit *intersubjective character*. An objectively incurred price (i.e., if someone agrees to make an exchange—becomes a bid or ask (depending on which angle the trade is viewed) is the result of an intersubjective assessment of the input data present at a given point in time. At a subsequent point in time, after an objective price is agreed upon, the assessment is made again; however, it is now based on other data that expresses itself within the spread. The past is already lost for us and its intersubjectively perceived circumstances from time $t - 1$ are irrelevant to our further decision-making in terms of their specific objective representation of the past price. The past can only be useful to us in an abstract time-invariant form. Only such a form could be used at any time and in any temporal context. It manifests itself only in the form of *revealing a change* in the intersubjective perception of data compared to the subjectively perceived past.[72] Actions aimed at the future always have a certain form of uniqueness in their *concrete form.*

[72]It is possible to see the distinction of some past prices with intentions of individuals expressed within the price spread; meaning that e.g., if the price of one apple was 1 USD a month ago and now the seller asks for 1.5 USD, we can also see if there is anyone who is able to take this ask; it could be that there is no one for some reason. This shows us the distinction between the time a month ago and the present. It is useful information for us; however, it is not decisive because there is no bid on apples today or a poor bid. The past price has no connection to the present evaluation of a situation by agents on the apple market. It is something else that forces the bidder not to bid.

Even if the action seems to us to be completely identical to an action performed before, due to the relative character of the sum of needs-sum of goods relationship, it still has a different concrete economic context, which in principle, is unrepeatable. Here we must agree with Shackle, since the past price, as an objective fact of reality in its concrete form, is not based on what we decide for the future; it could be psychologically inspirational but it cannot be the logical principle for decision-making within the scope of praxeology. The principle has to be something else. The past price only has an informative character; it has already happened. What has happened, cannot influence; only what is yet to happen can be influenced. Coordination must take place within the future plans and intentions. The past is interesting to us, but as Shackle (1992) notes, the past does not suggest that coordination will take place in the future.

This leads us to the second related remark, which is the need to modify Hayek's question itself; we need to expand it slightly. It should be phrased as follows: "*Why does the subjectively given data (respectively, the subjectively captured data based on which we make decisions) correspond with the objective facts of economic reality that result from coordination? What intersubjective tools do we use to coordinate our actions towards the future?*" In principle, the answer is quite simple, though more difficult to explain. The answer we will defend is as follows: "*This is because, as humans, we seem to (as if) spontaneously agree on certain intersubjectively perceived standards which ultimately appear to us as objective standards for assessing economic reality; It is because we perceive some economic intersubjective facts that allow us to cooperate with each other.*" If we used a combination of F.A. Hayek and K. Engliš terminology, we would have to describe the spontaneously created and spontaneously agreed standards of human cooperation, i.e., a normatively determined system of standards applied in the teleological world. This kind of simple answer can cause doubts and, therefore, we must explain it in a relevant way. However, first, we have to describe some basic economic intersubjective phenomena, which provide information to market participants and the interpretations which "forced" our predecessor to come up with some standardization around these phenomena, in order to understand each other more precisely. The sources of information about intersubjective phenomena can be considered as:

(a) An exchange spread
(b) An exchange spread over time—interest
(c) The process of entrepreneurship or what others want.

These sources are, however, only one side of the coin. The second side of the coin is the process of standardization of provided information which leads to intersubjective standards of:

(d) success/error (and economic calculation as intersubjective accounting standard)
(e) profit/loss
(f) costs.

These intersubjective standards can be considered as essential, given that they relate to exchange, exchange over time, and the economic activity—entrepreneurship—that allows exchange. This essay does not claim an intent to describe all existing intersubjective economic phenomena that are used in coordinating our economic activities as humanity. The essay merely focuses on these basic ones from which it is possible to derive, in more detail, other particular and already specific intersubjective economic phenomena that are related to these basic phenomena.[73]

2.3.1 Price Spread and Subjectively Perceived Prices

As stated above, the objective price—the historical fact of exchange once realized, is not a key factor for the mutual coordination of people. It is a historical fact that implies that some coordination has taken place in the past—two persons agreed on the exchange ratio of the two goods and in the given circumstances, they both considered the exchange to be a beneficial act. Since this is only the result of some action by some humans,

[73]These can be many things—a person's credit score based on which he/she gets better interest from the creditor, better capital equipment, increasing the trust of the entrepreneur, the company's history, the specific know-how of the individual/company, or the fact that it is a stable customer. In principle, these are different types of information that arise in the intersubjective interaction of people with each other, some of which have a purely historical character while others are focused on the future and contribute to the basic coordinates of our behavior.

this result was preceded by some coordination. One cannot coordinate with another without a coordination process. The existence of an a priori procedure leading to an exchange agreement implies three things. First, something to be exchanged must exist. In the broadest sense of the term, not only can you trade real items of reality, but also promises and ideas, as various types of financial instruments show us today.[74] When something exists, it can be exchanged in the present time—here and now, traded for something else here and now. Finally, it implies something that is offered and demanded. The fact that something is offered (an impoverishment of portfolio) and demanded (an enrichment of portfolio) implies the existence of two currently perceived prices. Menger has written about the fact that there are always two prices on the market and briefly summed it up in Weiner (2012, p. 13):

> *…for every good in every market, there is not one price but two different prices. If one comes to the market to buy, one must pay the offer (also called the ask). If one comes to sell, one must take the bid. The offer is always higher than the bid.*
>
> *… In the very act of buying at the offer, one fact is implicit. The seller has traded away his goods and received his money. Satisfied, he leaves the market. The next offer in the stack tends to be higher. This phenomenon, of buying at the offer with the result that the next offer is higher, is called "lifting the offer." Analogously, selling at the bid with the result that the next bid is lower is called "pressing the bid".*

While the objective final price—in the form of an agreement at the ask level or an agreement at the bid level—is in the past for us, it is something we cannot change, the *order book* itself shows the intentions and the plans of traders. Mises (1920, 1990), Hayek (1945), and Hülsmann (1997) do not ignore this fact, but they do not operate with it at all when explaining the economic calculation or the problem of coordination.[75] I

[74]These are not only existing products but also existing commitments or combinations of given commitments.

[75]Rather, there are the founders of the Austrian school, such as Menger, Böhm-Bawerk, who explain market coordination in the context of the bid-ask spread through their examples of horse markets.

believe the reason could be that they are inspired by Mises (1920, 1990), who, through an objective fact (the price), solves the transition from the subjective perception of economic circumstances to something tangible to all people—the price, i.e., an objective fact. Mises (1920, 1990) omits or overlooks this, that even the relative intersubjective quality in the form of a *spread* of the bid/ask price, which is shown by the order book is a tangible fact. Nonetheless, it has not an objective, but an intersubjective character. Still, the intersubjective nature is quite sufficient. I think that the closest to this finding is Hülsmann (1997), who tries to explain the economic calculation based on the current prices, not explicitly historical ones. Hülsmann's explanation is, however, similar to Mises's interpretation; he did not address the spread problem.[76]

The spread is shown in an order book. It shows us how closely the individual market players coordinate mutually diverse and currently perceived intentions and plans. Of course, today, the order book has a much more sophisticated form compared to what existed in the past and today it is expressed in money/currencies. Whether in the monetary economy or the nonmonetary economy, the degree of coordination of individuals in the given market is expressed by the extent of the price spread. It is the uninteresting level of the range of the spread that informs us with regard to what extent the plans of market players are or are not coordinated. The wider the bid/ask spread, the lower the coordination and vice versa (the process is described in more detail in Chapter 3; here we are providing only a brief introduction). The spread concept is easily applicable to our modified theory of subjective value, based on the satisfaction of the sum of needs by the portfolio of goods. The existence of an exchange spread between two people, e.g., Alice and Bob, is related to the two assessed states of their portfolios. Let us first describe what happens before two people decide to set the expected bid-ask subjective prices for exchanging goods. Let's create an example. Both Alice and Bob face the narrowing and widening of their *individual spreads* between the current, potentially achievable and desired portfolio; while the motivation for the desired portfolio (Pd) stems from a dissatisfaction with

[76]The inspiration for spreads comes from the works of prof. Fekete and his followers, such as Keith Weiner, whose works are primarily focused on the problem of spreads.

the current portfolio (Pc), it could only be some potential achievable portfolio (Pp) which will be chosen; however, everything depends on the range of the individual spreads which are formed on the level of the individual comparison of the existent state of affairs (Pc) to some potential and desired state of affairs (Pp or Pd). It has to be stressed that it is possible for Alice or Bob to realize the spread because they are able to compare the composition of goods within Pc, Pp and Pd and realize which state of affairs is better, compared to other states of affairs, defined by the portfolios in question. It is also important to emphasize that all this description is future-oriented (we are describing intentions, expectations, or plans) without any intention to look at the specifics of past prices and past exchanges between Alice and Bob, which could or could not have taken place.

From an individual perspective, the exchange should narrow the spread between the current and the desired portfolio. A satisfactory state, without any intention to exchange, would imply that Alice's portfolio P-current-Alice (P-current-Bob), satisfies the desired sum of needs over a subjectively perceived time frame. If so, Alice (or Bob) is not motivated to change the current situation in the form of PcA (PcB). However, perceptions of needs may change as well as the fact that the Pc can change. This means that PcA (PcB) is no longer a suitable portfolio and Alice (or Bob) is motivated to strive for some desired P-desired-Alice (P-desired-Bob). This is caused by the perceived widening spread between the PdA (due to a new combination of needs) and the existing PcA, while PdA can be achieved either by the individual production activity of Alice or by an exchange with Bob; mutatis mutandis for Bob. Both options (the individual production activity or the exchange) are considered in a context that is more satisfactory for Alice or Bob. In case they decide to exchange, the following will happen:

Suppose that apples are part of Alice's portfolio and pears are part of Bob's portfolio. Assuming that both Alice and Bob are interested in a new composition of the portfolio PdA, PdB, which would be achieved by an exchange of pears for apples. The PdA enriched with pears and impoverished with apples is thus Alice's desired portfolio, where Alice assumes that the new composition of PdA will satisfy her combination of needs more than PcA; if Alice did not assume this, she would not set a price for apples in the form of a bid price for pears. For Bob, the opposite is true.

However, the exchange may not be completed depending on the range of bid-ask spread. This is created by assessing the extent to which the desired PdA—which is composed so that Alice gives up part of the apples and obtains part of the pears—corresponds to what can be achieved by the exchange. The exchange will only take place if, for example, Alice gives up 3 apples and gets 5 pears, but it no longer takes place if Alice requires 6 pears, and Bob, in turn, would require 4 apples. This would mean that the potentially possible composition of P-potential-Alice and P-potential-Bob is not suitable for either of them. Both would then have to give up a larger number of goods; perceiving that the obtained composition of the PpA and PpB portfolio would jeopardize the satisfaction of their needs (that is why they do not prefer PpA and PpB) the exchange would not take place; their individual spreads would be widened by the exchange, not narrowed. It has to be stressed that it is not a question of apples or pears, but a question of the portfolio composition which is considered which, in turn, has an impact on the range of the individual spread of either Alice or Bob. If the exchange is not realized, it means that e.g., Alice's spread between PcA and PdA is narrower compared to PcA and PpA and Alice prefers a more current portfolio compared to any other potential; mutatis mutandis for Bob. The decisive factor is not the "apples - pears" spread per se; the decisive factor is the individual spread with regard to Alice or Bob. The "apples - pears" spread is only *inter-subjective information* for market participants with regard to Alice's and Bob's intentions and expectations.

The spread exchange can be wide or narrow for several reasons. Alice's PcA could contain e.g., an insufficient number of goods required by Bob in exchange or, conversely, Bob's PcB contains an insufficient number of goods requested by Alice in exchange. Both Alice and Bob judge what to give up compared to what to gain. But at the same time, they assess the given activity in the context of their desired PdA, respectively, PdB. Alice can easily demand more pears from Bob. However, if Bob loses too many pears, it would jeopardize the overall satisfaction of his needs. Therefore, Bob is willing to sacrifice only the number of pears he has chosen, and if he does not exchange pears, it is clear that the composition of PcB is better than the PpB. Later, of course, Bob may be willing to get rid of even more pears than before, perhaps because he has obtained oranges. The composition of the portfolio, which contains oranges in addition to pears, makes it possible to get rid of many more pears than before by gaining the number of apples offered by Alice. The result could be that although Bob's portfolio now contains nominally fewer pears than expected before, it would satisfy his needs more than the previously composed portfolio because of the composition of goods (pears, apples, and oranges) in question. The degree of economic coordination between Alice and Bob when exchanging apples for pears therefore increases.

The range of exchange spread as intersubjective information gives market participants necessary information for possible coordination. It is not the past prices which coordinate us. Neither is it the subjective prices as bid or ask per se; it is the spread which bid-ask together forms, and it is its range which provides a sufficient information for market participants to know what to do and what not to do in order to increase their satisfaction. It has to be stressed that the "apple-pear" spread is only information; it is not the process of the coordination. It is information about the intentions of market participants. If the spread widens, it means that either Alice or Bob experiences some change concerning their desired, potential, and current portfolios, which are composed, additionally by other goods and that the combination of apples and pears with other goods creates a state of affairs which changes their satisfaction of needs. Subsequently, this leads to the change of the conditions on the "apple-pear" market. If the exchange spread narrows, and from Alice's point of view the ask from Bob is accepted as a bid from Alice, the degree of coordination increases. Given that we can imply that either the desired composition of PdA and PdB coincides with what can be achieved in the exchange or the individual spread of current and potential portfolios is narrower compared to any other situation which Alice or Bob considers. In the case of a non-existent bid or ask price, the discoordination on the "apple-pear" market is absolute. The reason for the non-existence of a bid price for the offered goods of the entrepreneur may be the existence of a more affordable alternative to some other goods, which the buyer could purchase from another manufacturer. The absence of an asking price may be the existence of some restriction that prevents him from selling his product, and so on. It must be stressed that it is this activity that we receive intersubjective information from each other. This is possible because the information format has the same formal-time-invariant principle which is based on the subjective assessment of the deprivation and enrichment of the portfolio, which is the very same in both Alice and Bob's case.

2.3.2 Interest: An Intersubjective Tool for Decision-Making Over Time

The concept of interest must be considered as an important intersubjective tool for decision-making and coordination. It is related to debt exchange. Debt exchange is not necessarily a more sophisticated way of exchanging. On the contrary, surely a direct (barter) exchange is, from a *logical point of view,* a special kind of exchange in time. Barter is based on a very short intersubjectively perceived maturity of obligation or zero maturity when neither party to the exchange considers time between the acts of receiving and giving to be significant. In principle, every exchange takes place over time. We sometimes perceive only a given moment in time to describe the given exchange as a debt. However, debt only seems to be a more complicated construct. Graeber (2011), who follows many works of social anthropologists, shows that if we imagine our predecessors with a lower level of awareness then logically, they may have had, then they would have taken advantage of the debt.[77] Debt can also take place in a mode of lower awareness.

[77]Graeber (2011) argues that debt inevitably precedes a direct barter exchange, i.e., that debt was the original concept for the creation of money. The so-called problem of *coincidence of wants* defined by Jevons is possible to solve by debt exchange when time is inserted between the discrepancy between the exchange of one good and another good, which the other party of the exchange does not want at a given time. Time allows for the harmony of mutual needs to occur later, and we need not presuppose them immediately at the time of exchange. The second aspect is that debt in quasi-family ties in a clan or primitive group should not be overlooked due to the possibility of its effective recovery and the low level of information costs of keeping debt records due to the size of the group. The third aspect, defined by Graeber, is that the barter exchange took place with someone our predecessors didn't know, rather than someone they did. Making an exchange with strangers forced our predecessors to close the deal once and for all at a given moment of time, because they may not have met the other party of the exchange ever again. This does not apply to a clan member. In this respect, the potential information cost associated with recording a debt in the community had to be absolutely negligible compared to the costs that would result from the potential recovery of a debt from a foreigner. It is therefore likely that barter was more often used with foreigners. Of course, barter does not need to be excluded in the community either. From the point of view of our essay, however, it is not essential to decide definitively whether the debt or the barter was the

The exchange has two basic components—normative and economic. The normative component implies a rule (if/so) and at the same time implies reciprocity related to the rule (I will give you something—you will also give me something). The economic component of this exchange implies the manifestation of subjective preferences. The presupposition that our predecessors had a lower level of awareness is quite reasonable. Isn't it, therefore, a contradiction to presuppose the existence of debt exchange within these prehistoric communities? Given the fact that any group of people must follow some kind of rules, the prehistoric group of people had to follow rules as well, albeit unspoken ones and only spontaneously created. If we apply this assumption in the context of our predecessors, whose self-awareness may not have been as strong as ours is today considering that they lived in groups, it is logical that the norm precedes a *full awareness* of their individual needs. The point is that a quasi-need, as an economic component of a given exchange, can also exist in a mode of the absence of full awareness and can only have an instinctive character. However, this does not apply to the norm. A norm cannot be a quasi-norm. The norm itself, in the mode of the lower awareness of our predecessors, *must have* the real character of a norm that is connected with life in the community. It is an implicit part of the community and it manifests itself in the norms of distributive justice because the community is ontologically other than the sum of its individuals. As Lewis (2017) shows, the interconnectedness of the elements of the system causes the spontaneous emergence of emergent phenomena. In our case, prehistoric (unspoken) norms have spontaneously formed the background of the quasi-conscious activities of members of a given community. They *did not follow* those norms in the mode of self-awareness. This implies that the debt exchange could also have been an integral part of prehistoric community life.[78]

---

primary phenomenon of some prehistoric clan. However, as Pošvanc (2019a, 2020b, 2021) shows, the debt exchange is a key phenomenon for the discovery of the economic standard of calculation and money because it provides structure (of mind) which is future oriented and usable in the economic interactions of individuals within a particular economic community.

[78]The statement is in accordance with Hayek–Pavlík's theory of the origin of catallactic rules when Pavlík (1999) applies Hayek's theory of cultural evolution to the norms of distributive justice, which were probably followed by groups of our predecessors. Empirical (supporting) evidence is also provided by social anthropology (e.g., Graeber 2011). However, to connect the

Debt exchange is also a particularly important economic intersubjective phenomenon. It allows the expansion of time-consuming capital structures (so-called roundabout methods of production) which is an interesting empirical fact or consequence of a debt exchange. What is more important, is the perception of the time between the provision of one good (or principal good) at time t and the repayment of the debt by another good. This includes the phenomenon of interest (principal and interest) at time $t1$. A barter exchange is extremely limited in this sense. This kind of exchange motivated our predecessors to an abstract perception of economic phenomena (plans, ideas about the future) and also motivated them to strive for a concrete expression of plans and ideas in the form of future results. Based on the fact that one good was provided at time t and the elimination of a lasting obligation by another good at time $t1$, it was possible to perceive the following stimuli:

(a) the existence of the obligation in time, not only by the direct participants involved in the exchange but also by others in the community

---

empirical findings of social anthropology to an economic interpretation related to the emergence of economic ties of exchange is only possible when we divide the problem into the normative and economic context. Once we focus on the problem from two perspectives, normative and economic, it is possible for an economist to understand normative concepts such as reciprocity, altruism or the concept of gift, as an integral part of a prehistoric exchange, without being in contradiction with economic findings that any exchange has a solely subjective value inverse character, meaning that one part of the exchange prefers something they receive to something they had to give up, which is certainly not any kind of economic *value* reciprocity, altruism or act or gift.

However, economists should accept the fact that primitive exchanges took place within the context of meeting the quasi-needs. This presupposition is necessary to follow because we should presuppose a lower level of awareness on the part of our predecessors. Economic concepts related to the expression of individual subjective preferences arise only subsequently, with the birth of a higher degree of self-awareness. The economic component of exchange (as explained by economists) and its subjectivist interpretation of a value inverse and mutually beneficial act is possible only after our predecessors' minds had undergone sufficient differentiation and a fully conscious human subject emerged. Until then, it is necessary to interpret the economic component of the exchange based on the quasi-need or instinct. However, once the differentiation of the mind ended, and a conscious person emerged, the economic component of exchange must be interpreted individually and based on a subjective value.

To focus more on the nature of debt exchange and to divide the problem of exchange into economic and normative parts, creates quite a vital possibility for the connection of findings between the social anthropology, as well as and the economic camp of scientists.

(b) the possibility of implementing some economic activity between time t and $t1$, which leads to the elimination of the obligation
(c) the actual elimination of the obligation for some good, which could also become the standard for consistent further exchanges.

The debt exchange realized by our predecessors was thus gradually created in the concept of sedimentary history. This is what we now call economic planning. Today we see the phenomenon of interest as a part of debt exchange; initially, this perception was not present (it was implicit). Böhm-Bawerk (1930, p. xi) implies that interest is/was part of the "price" of a previously provided economic good from one individual (now called a creditor), for the elimination of liability later in time, from another individual (now called a debtor). For interest to be a coordinating phenomenon, it must be in the nature of a spread. Pošvanc (2020a) defines interest as a spread between a direct and an indirect way of satisfying needs over a period of time, as considered by at least two people, i.e., between the assessment of one's own action against the activity of another, aimed at satisfying their needs over time. Interest, as a concept, must have gradually developed against the backdrop of the primitive and very simple debt exchanges implemented within prehistoric communities. These simple debt exchanges provided the first sedimentary history for the possibility of differentiating this concept as a separate phenomenon. Only the subsequent standardization of these exchanges, together *with the creation of money*, made it possible to fully conceptualize that phenomenon. The awareness of interest could only arise based on the differentiation of principal and interest, which became possible through money. Until then, the interest was only an implicit and intuitively used part of the spread of debt exchange.

The concept of interest as a spread is again easily applicable to our modified theory of subjective value, based on the satisfaction of a sum of needs by a portfolio of goods. The concept also allows us to better identify the so-called natural interest (Wicksell 1936) or what Mises (1998) called originary interest. The interest spread is produced in a more dimensional way. Participants of the exchange assess the same spread between their actual possible (desired) portfolios. However, they assess in advance, the manner in which these needs will be met in the future; whether it is more suitable to meet needs directly (their own production activity) or indirectly, (by exchange over time) and, what may happen to the above-mentioned spreads between actual and possible and desired portfolios, through this assessment. Due to the decision to make the exchange over time three new phenomena, needs to be considered, namely:

(a) time preference
(b) interest
(c) the normative character of the deal.

All three phenomena have an impact on the realization of the exchange over time. To describe the concept of natural interest, imagine that Alice is a creditor and Bob a debtor. Alice must first consider whether Bob's request for apples could deplete her PcA at time t. If this does not jeopardize meeting her needs, she can enter the exchange. However, she is also considering the time $t1$ when Bob had to eliminate his debt by offering pears. Alice considers whether the enriched portfolio PpA with the addition of the pears (which includes the phenomenon of interest) at time $t1$ is more or less suitable for her. The time period from t to $t1$ could also create circumstances that would cause her portfolio PcA to be without apples and her expected PpA would be without promised pears. So, she considers some kind of securing acts (law, collateral, etc.). Bob considers the situation from the opposite point of view. He could have a potential portfolio PpB with apples from Alice at time t which would enable him to meet his immediate needs compared to the state of affairs provided by his actual PcB. However, he will need to eliminate his obligation at time $t1$. He therefore considers some PpB($t1$) which must include pears at the time when he must meet his promise to Alice. He also considers whether the securitization requested by Alice is suitable for him within the context of the immediate meeting of his needs and of providing pears to Alice in $t1$.

The assessment of the situation is quite different compared to an immediate exchange. While the above example of exchanging apples for pears implies that apples and pears were acquired by the participants as a result of previous economic activity which involved the cost of producing exchanged and existing goods and assessing whether the exchange would pay off in terms of possible (desired) portfolios, the exchange over time is different. Alice and Bob also assessed the method of achieving the desired composition of their portfolios, while they both still had a choice of their own activities associated with some costs. Alice, due to her savings, can assess Bob's activity and Bob can offer his preferred action to Alice. It means that both Alice and Bob can access some alternative economic activity. This activity is possible to access because Alice is able to provide the required good to Bob at the time of the exchange, which will allow Bob to build a new capital structure that provides pears. We can see that the situation creates a clear image of Alice's postponement of time preferences concerning the meeting her needs over time by her PcA. It creates Alice's claim and Bob's obligation, a natural interest spread, and normative circumstances with regard to the securing of the exchange.

The postponement of time preferences are not related to any particular economic good but are related to the fact that in the case of an exchange over time, the creditor's portfolio is impoverished (for the duration of the exchange) by the good which is allocated to the debtor at time *t*. The time preference is connected to the fact that the perceived sum of needs may not be met by a portfolio impoverished by apples. Over time, Alice is able to compare only the state of her portfolios; she does not know if she would need the apples sometime in the future. She assesses her savings (the portfolio) and asks herself whether she can give up the apples. Perhaps Bob would ask for too much from her portfolio; she may feel that meeting her needs is jeopardized and would therefore not enter the exchange. Bob, on the other hand, is in a position to meet his needs immediately, due to the exchange. He could be involved in an alternative activity that may not be possible without Alice. He can act immediately using his portfolio PpB. Alice provides him with "zero-maturity" goods which enables him to alternate his actions. However, he provides her with e.g., a one-month maturity obligation expressed as "the pear." We see that Alice does not need to be motivated in order to express her time preference if her PpA is not compensated properly by the pear or if Bob is not able to accept some "if/so" terms of the exchange.

Pošvanc (2020a) explains that interest is an intersubjective phenomenon of debt exchange as such and as a spread resulting from the assessment of the possibility of the direct and indirect satisfaction of needs over time by two economic actors. We can describe the natural interest spread which can arise only if Alice shows her time preference and Bob is able to accept normative terms of exchange; otherwise, the natural interest spread would stand in the counterfactual area of action. The natural interest manifests itself as the spread between the potential portfolio achieved through direct economic activity and the potential portfolio achieved through an exchange over time. Alice, with some savings in the form of P-current-Alice, assesses the following situation: She must incur costs (C-Alice) to achieve the economic project E-Alice, which will bring some R-Alice-good into her portfolio; she tries to achieve Portfolio-potential-Alice by (PcA − Ca + Ra). However, at the same time, she can assess the composition of PpA1 while she still thinks that she will spend the costs Ca to achieve the economic project Ea. This will bring the good (Ra) to the portfolio; however, at the same time, she has the opportunity to acquire I-from-Bob-good (a pear in our example) if she *can* sacrifice good D-Alice (an apple in our example) from PcA to Bob today, without jeopardizing the satisfaction of her needs. So, she considers PcA1 (without Da but with a claim to Bob) today and PpA1, which will be composed as PpA1 = (PcA − Ca + Ra + Ib). From Bob's point of view, this is the opposite situation when he assesses whether the requested good (Da) will ensure the satisfaction of his set of needs so that he will be able to provide the good Ib in time *t1* to Alice. Bob assesses two possibilities concerning his future economic activity; either he will try to achieve some PpB or some alternative PpB1. Assuming that the PpB will be achieved as (PcB – Cb + Xb), meaning that he is producing product Xb at cost Cb. The second alternative is PpB1 (PcB +Da – Cb1 + Yb – Ib) which can be realized based on what is provided by Alice and what causes alternative costs Cb1, connected with alternative production and the alternative outcome of Yb. This also enables the provision of good Ib to Alice at time *t*1. It should be noted that PcB consists not only of what Bob had before in the form of PcB and good Da from Alice; it also consists of an obligation to Alice.

The natural interest as a spread is then generated from Alice's point of view as well as from Bob's point of view. Alice considers the spread of (PcA versus PpA) to the spread of (PcA1 versus PpA1) which defines her reflection of the natural interest and Bob considers the spread of (PcB versus PpB) to the spread of (PcB1 versus PpB1) which defines his reflection of the natural interest. However, natural, or originary interest emerges or is manifested in the reality only if they agree on the exchange as the spread between (PcA1 versus PpA1) and (PcB1 versus PpB1). Both of them define the intersubjective phenomenon of natural interest. It is a spread of the given considerations within realized exchange. We cannot define it as the rate because we don't have money incorporated in this basic description to differentiate between principal and interest. However, money only expresses the process of its emergence in a more precise way.[79]

The extent of a given spread then implies a degree of coordination between Alice and Bob over time. If the desired terms of the debt exchange—consisting of time preference, interest, legal conditions are accepted, it means that Alice and Bob consider the exchange to be economically and legally possible. The debt exchange is therefore agreed upon and can be implemented. Based on the given exchange, a new capital structure that incurs the cost of Cb' and the outcome of Yb

[79]It must be stressed that natural interest arises only if Alice is able to demonstrate time preference and if Bob agrees to the legal conditions of the exchange. All three phenomena influence each other. If the natural interest spread offered by Bob is not attractive to Alice, she will not demonstrate a time preference. If the legal conditions of exchange are too strict for Bob, he will not be able to enter the exchange. If Alice would endanger meeting her needs to give the economic good D to Bob, she will not enter the exchange. These spreads are discovered today at the level of society by the banking or financial sector.

Before money was invented, we were not able to express the spread in some good because we did not have a *common* denominator. Once money was invented, Bob was able to consider his spread between PcB1versus PpB which could be e.g., 10 M, so he was supposed to eliminate the debt by 110 M (100 + 10% of interest). The second advantage is that they express both spreads, in the same way, using the same denominator M. This is possible because we are able to express the portfolio in the form of money and so we are able to define spread more precisely. In practice today, it is realized as follows: if Alice considers lending 100 oz of gold, it depends on whether she is not jeopardized by this decision, in terms of her whole satisfaction of needs. Bob asks for 100 oz and offers 10 oz as interest, which is a decision tool for Alice. They both also consider some legal aspects of the exchange.

When using the terminology used by Lewis (2017), natural interest is actually an emergent phenomenon. It cannot be described as shown in Pošvanc (2020a) at the level of the individual. It can only be realistically described at the level of interacting individuals or community. It is thus a new characteristic of the economic system of cooperation. Interest rate, expressed in money, thus literally arises spontaneously—it is that emergent phenomenon of systematic economic activity which is related to the allocation of resources over time.

is created, the creation of which was enabled by the provision of Da. If Alice is unable to or is not motivated to provide Da, the capital structure does not arise. The range of the spread is affected by several circumstances. On the one hand, it is the time preference associated with Alice's portfolio, the risk associated with the Cb'/ Yb capital structure, the attractiveness of the Ib-good (pear) requested by Alice, and also various legal aspects of the exchange in the form of collateral from Bob or legal guarantees associated with the provision of Da and the return of Ib, etc.

In this respect, interest is an emerging phenomenon that does not exist without the intention of two or more people to carry out an exchange over time. Interest has been and is still used by people to make decisions related to the shape of the capital structure toward the future. As Hülsmann (2002, p. 101) shows, interest is an economic phenomenon by which we decide where our capital resources will be placed. The premise is that Alice will not provide the capital goods until Bob has offered something attractive that arouses Alice's interest. If Bob offers something different, Alice directs her resources where she considers them to be more appropriate and thus eliminates the project Bob offered where the capital structure does not arise.[80] Interest is generated as an *offer* by the debtor, which is accepted by the creditor for the provision of capital goods. The mutual interaction of debtors and creditors thus determines the nature of the capital structure based on the time preferences of members of

[80]Two remarks need to be made here. The first is that within the monetary economy the whole process takes place only through money when Alice provides money as principal and Bob buys for the provided principal capital goods (created in the past in a very similar way). The combination of these capital goods activates a new economic process, which produces a new product. Bob must also sell this new product later in time for money and returns the principal and interest from which it is possible to differentiate, due to the money. The second remark relates to the fact that this explanation does not necessarily refer to higher or lower nominal interest rates preferred by Alice. She may also opt for a lower proposed nominal interest due to two facts: (a) the debt exchange is a complex phenomenon; Alice may prefer a lower nominal interest rate due to higher collateral or a better reputation on the part of Bob, while there may still be a higher interest rate offered in the market by other potential debtors. However, related terms of the exchange with Bob are not as attractive to Alice as with others, (b) Bob creates an obligation to Alice (or Alice creates a claim to Bob) which becomes part of her portfolio and it could be that Alice is seeking something similar to what is offered by Bob (lower interest, but with lower risk and better conditions) because she has other exposures to others members of the community and the deal with Bob is, therefore, more preferred within the context of her portfolio PpA1; in other words, the spread between any desired PdA1 and potential PpA1 is depressed by the deal with Bob but not with others who could offer higher interest rates.

the community and what legal conditions follow. At the same time, the capital structure reflects the estimate of the future, i.e., it is formed with respect to the future potential income of the debtor to eliminate the debt previously incurred in time. This means that in order for the borrower to provide a product that others would want in the future he must, on the one hand, estimate the right combination of people's needs and, on the other choose, under some existing constraints, a coherent combination of resources to meet those needs.

The principle of resource allocation is based on the combination of the interest rate for the planned project with the combination of other factors (collateral, legal conditions, business plans, etc.) offered to creditors from borrowers. A more appropriate *combination* of interest rates and other debt exchange factors then determines the nature of the capital structure. Interest, as an economic phenomenon of debt exchange, determines the importance and prioritization of plans, as well as a realistic assessment of the plans by owners of existing capital resources in the context of offers of plans by borrowers. In other words, the interaction of potential creditors and potential borrowers determines what will and will not be done in the future.

2.3.3 The Entrepreneurship Discovery Process, Competition, and Pricing

According to Foss and Klein (2009), within the Austrian School of Economics, there are three basic approaches to the subject of entrepreneurship that complement and differ in emphasis with regard to what it means to be an entrepreneur. The first is the Knight–Mises approach to the entrepreneur as a resource allocator, where the emphasis is on property rights, which is a rational estimate of consumer needs that the entrepreneur makes through *Verstehen*. The second is Hayek–Kirzner's approach to entrepreneurship as a function of a higher degree of coordination or a higher degree of equilibration of economic phenomena. Like Lewis and Lewin (2015), we could say that the entrepreneur is actually the initiator of a higher degree of order, which is based on the price system specifically in the case of Kirzner (e.g., Kirzner

1973) through arbitration. The third approach is based on Schumpeter's (1983) opinion. He identifies the entrepreneur as an innovator, one who permanently initiates the market disequilibrium.

The attentive reader may have noticed that the context of the second description of the intersubjective economic phenomenon of interest, as well as the context of the first intersubjective phenomenon bid/ask spread, is related to two approaches to entrepreneurship: an entrepreneur as a resource allocator (Knight, Mises) and an entrepreneur as the initiator of higher coordination (Hayek–Kirzner) vs. Schumpeter's, an entrepreneur as an innovator, in the sense of disrupting the existing degree of coordination (here presented entrepreneur as rational/evolutionary spontaneous combinator). The above intersubjective economic concepts (interest and price bid/ask spread) are the foundation of the business discovery process if we use Kirzner's terminology. Entrepreneurial discovery, whether as resource allocation, respectively, in terms of a higher degree of coordination, or the disruption of coordination, must necessarily take place in the sense of what Shackle writes, at the level of ideas and plans, which are subsequently implemented in reality. Mutual coordination of economic activities can only take place within the future. It is not possible to change anything that has already happened or that is happening right now. However, coordination is possible at any point in time into the future, regardless of pre-implemented plans and ideas, which can always be modified and changed. Our proposal to call the entrepreneur a combinator reflects the use of this term.

Coordination also takes place in a competitive environment, which is made up of subjectively different individuals, with subjectively different plans and a subjectively different view of reality. We have described the evolutionary description of the basics of how business discovery takes place above. The process has an evolutionary character, i.e., there is a certain "germ cell" of the proto-needs combination that the entrepreneur is focusing on. This causes the product to differentiate. Differentiation then creates variability in the specific form of satisfying needs. However, multiple and competing for specific forms of satisfaction of needs inevitably leads to a kind of "encounter" of limits of the satisfaction of a particular combination of needs. These guidelines motivate entrepreneurs to cross those boundaries with new combinations of property characteristics aimed at different, i.e., more widespread or a better satisfactory combination of some needs. In principle, it is an endless repetition of this process.

We have pointed out the rational nature of the activity which is not driven by "blind" evolution but is created by specific people, while the process of selection through consumers determines the evolutionary direction of where the next process of business discovery will go. Thus, the competition is not a presumed phenomenon of this process, which is often assumed in order to explain a business activity, but a consequence of this process. It is an emerging phenomenon associated with people's lives within the community. Robinson Crusoe does not compete with anyone on the island. Competition as a consequence of business activity can be simply explained through the above-mentioned spreads which arise between the existing and desired portfolios of entrepreneurs (mutatis mutandis companies).

Let's assume that we have entrepreneur Alice who specializes in the production of good U-Alice, which satisfies the combination of needs (A, B, C). In order to create Ua, she must incur costs Ca from her portfolio. Suppose entrepreneur Bob specializes equally in the production of U-Bob, which satisfies the same combination of needs (A, B, C) while spending from his portfolio cost Cb. Alice and Bob also want to satisfy some of their subjective needs through their individual portfolios PcA and PcB; that is why both Alice and Bob decided to produce Ua and Ub. Their subjective goal is to achieve the desired portfolio of PdA and PdB and therefore they produce Ua and Ub. The desired PdA or PdB generates a spread against the current PcA and PcB. They can narrow the spread by a higher sales rate for Ua or Ub. Narrowing the individual spread motivates them to provide such Ua, Ub, which are desired by consumers. Therefore, they are motivated to either produce Ua or Ub for more advantageous costs or to produce such Ua or Ub that satisfies the best and the most desired combination of needs (A, B, C and potentially D, E ...). Let's suppose the success of Alice against Bob which implies that the spread between the current and the desired portfolio of Bob is changing, forcing him to either repeat what Alice is doing or be better in meeting the sum of needs of his product compared to Alice. The competition is then the result of these efforts—not the premise of any entrepreneurial activity. It is the personal spread of Bob which "forces" him to be more successful, otherwise it would not be possible to achieve his desired PdB.

In the context of competition and business discovery, prices also arise. The resulting market prices are not a coordinating element of the process; they are a depiction of some historical event, a historical economic context. Prices that emerge on the market are interesting. They provide us with interesting information to understand how the change of some conditions and processes of evaluation of an individual *has spread* over the markets. However, past prices have no decisive role in setting new prices on the market. They are the results of some activity of the entrepreneur and his client, whether it is a price in the nonmonetary economy or a price in the monetary economy. The price is the result of the evaluation process, dependent on what the entrepreneur wants to achieve and what can be achieved in terms of competition or the budgetary constraints of the client. The mantra of past prices and their influence on future decisions must be abandoned. For the purposes of this essay, it is sufficient to show an alternative view of the formation of price in the market process.

To illustrate a simplified description of the origin of the price, let us infer that the demand for an economic good U, exists from a client, Charlie. Let us assume also that there are producers, Alice and Bob. How is the price calculated? It will be the result of assessing the spreads between the desired and potential portfolios of the three human subjects. Both Alice and Bob are, of course, interested in selling their U to Charlie. Let's say that they have their actual portfolios PcA and PcB, which contain the U. They come to market with their ask price of the U on the market. The price reflects how much U they want to get rid of for the good M from Charlie (the M need not be money; however, it could be). Suppose Alice is willing to sell U for 10 M and Bob for 11 M, and Charlie comes to the market willing to buy U for a bid price of 5 M. The 5 M is part of his actual-current PcC portfolio. It is clear that in these circumstances the sale of U for M will not take place. Absolutely subjective requirements that are different stand against each other.

What must happen for a sale to take place and a decision of the price ratio of U/M to be made? The price from the previous day, which was, let's say, U/12 M or the price from the previous month, which was U/6 M is of no help to Alice, Bob, or Charlie. Today, there is a new situation on the market that corresponds to some evaluation by Alice, Bob, and Charlie. Today's assessment takes into account the idea of Alice, Bob, and Charlie's desired portfolios, to which they want to be able to respond in the future in order to satisfy their individual needs, as much as possible, with the newly composed portfolios PpA, PpB and PpC. So how can today's price of U against M be set? This is again a question of the individual spreads between some Pc and Pp of Alice, Bob, and Charlie. The price U to M at the U/8 M level can only occur if Alice and Charlie are willing to widen their individual spreads between actual Pc and potential Pp and thus narrow the price market spread of the U/M; i.e., if Charlie is willing to get rid of more portions of M and Alice is willing to accept less M, if, for some reason, they are willing to accept that the desired portfolios will not be achieved. At the same time, the resulting price implies that for some reason, they are willing to widen their individual spread between their current Pa and their potential Pp. This, therefore, affects the price of U/M, which we finally see on the market. Whether Alice and Charlie are willing to close a given trade for U/8 M still also depends on Bob, who also assesses his individual spread, which, like Alice, he is willing to expand or not. If he is willing to widen his individual spread, i.e., accept a different composition than originally desired for the portfolio of PpB, thus causing the market price spread to narrow, at U/7 M. Charlie, therefore, concludes a trade with Bob and not with Alice. However, if Bob is willing to widen his spread between desired and some achievable portfolios only so that the exchange would take the form of U/9 M, then Charlie will close the trade with Alice and not with Bob.

What forces Alice, Bob, and Charlie to change their view of their desired portfolios? There are many circumstances that influence the spread between their individual portfolios. It could be factors that create limitations related to possibilities of the technological process of U's production or, it could be factors related to the evaluation of what Alice and Bob are willing to give up and/or gain within the context of the composition of their portfolios. Indeed, what Alice or Bob are willing to give up cannot ultimately jeopardize their perceived satisfaction of needs; what they gain must be evaluated as a relevant contribution to their Pp that will satisfy their needs. Bob may not have the proper combination of resources to produce a better U than Alice. However, it could also be that Alice has debt and needs to decrease her individual spread due to these circumstances which force her to sell the U to Charlie at a price more beneficial to Charlie, irrespective of the production process Alice uses.

This description is valid in either the monetary or non-monetary economy. It does not matter if the good M is money or an apple. Entrepreneurial discovery is, of course, aimed at making entrepreneur Alice and Bob narrow their individual spreads between their existing portfolios and some desired portfolios as much as possible. Of course, they have options for achieving this, such as: innovating the U so that the U can satisfy a better combination of needs; to increase/decrease the ask price; to change the number of Us produced; to change the organization of U's production; get better debt conditions from creditors, etc. These are traditionally described different types of business strategies, the only goal of which is to narrow the individual spread between their existing individual portfolios and some asked portfolios of these entrepreneurs.

2.3.4 The Meta-Standards and Standardization as a Basis of Evolutionary as Well as Rational Ordering

Up until this point we have been dealing more or less with some sources of intersubjective information for potential cooperation and coordination and we have shown some potential examples for how the coordination could happen based on this information. However, it should not be sufficient to end the interpretation at this point. We have to answer the question set out in Hayek (1937); or a modified version of it as presented above. To show the source of the information is namely one side of the coin. The second side of the coin is the standardization of this information. We have to, therefore, consider the normative intersubjective emerged economic standards that allow people to coordinate their behavior in the economic system, which we reconnect to Hayek–Pavlík's theory of evolutionary apriorism. The identified standards will also allow us to remove economic relativism which stems from the modified theory of subjective value because we will introduce a common standard as if it is a common language, so that everyone can interpret the sources of intersubjective information in the same manner. The reader should not be surprised that this "rational economic language" emerges spontaneously.

The intersubjective economic phenomena described in the previous section, bid/ask spread and interest, are created in the context of business discovery and competition and do not yet answer exactly how people can coordinate, based on this intersubjective information toward the future. This is the subject of the following sections. The above-mentioned intersubjective economic phenomena could not work without spontaneously agreed intersubjective economic meta-standards. These standards are generally necessary for better, proper, faster, and more precise transference of economic intersubjective information. However, again, it is a result of the outcome of human activity, not a presupposition of cooperation. To focus on intersubjective meta-standards, it is important to emphasize that the above-mentioned phenomena—spreads and entrepreneurship—are areas around which various types of specialized market activities are created and economic institutions emerge. We can consider this as an empirical supporting fact for our search, which is observable through the banking and financial sectors in the area of debt and the phenomenon of interest, or specialized exchanges and markets in the case of sale and the purchase of goods and services, or specialized business units and forms in the area of entrepreneurship.

These "areas of interconnections" had a rather simple character in the past; they took place at the level of "individual vs. individual" with quite simple supporting economic institutions. However, as evidenced today, they have gradually become the subject of institutionalized and specialized business; provision of these types of institutions and standards is demanded by humans. The interest rate today is a factor of banking entrepreneurship activity; coordination of exchange is provided by specialized stock exchanges and many business units have investors and form many specialized business institutions—different types of companies. However, if we look in detail at these activities, these are always activities that emerge out of the coordination of plans, ideas, or expectations. The discovery of interest rates and conditions of debt exchange is related to long-term plans and is provided by specialized institutions—banks or the financial sector. The bid/ask price spreads or order books that show these spreads are provided by exchanges that standardize conditions of exchange and definitions of traded products. Entrepreneurship activity is provided by specialized business units with their rules, such as shared ownership, with professional management. All of this is created around spreads which are developed as a result of plans, ideas, or expectations.

Given that these phenomena relate in principle to people's thoughts and abstract processes, it is not at all surprising that humans have created internal and mutually recognized rules in these areas related to debt recovery: collateralization, trade rules, codes of business ethics, product standardizations and so on. These are all rules and standards that, in principle, connect the plans in question with reality in the "if – so" mode; i.e., if something is planned but does not happen, it may happen, whether in the form of a penalty or in the form of some kind of economic fine. From this empirical context alone, it should, therefore, be clear that the area in which we are looking for coordinates of the economic interactions of individuals is the correct one. Within the given activities, whether it is the price spread of existing products, the allocation of resources over time, or the business discovery itself, information is created that must be mutually interpreted and used by individuals. It is necessary to realize the fact that some information can be interpreted by one person as positive information and by another as negative information or, even as no information (people can ignore it). The interpretation depends on the needs of the individual. The activities that generate this information are, on the one hand subjective, but they create intersubjective connections given that they are based on a mutual economic interaction between people. However, in order to understand each other and be able to interpret the *interactions* in an identical way (it is not necessary to use information in an identical way), the *economic intersubjective meta-standard* is necessary.

Therefore, we have to focus primarily on laying down the very foundations for the concepts of *economic success/ error* and the related concept of *profit/loss* and *costs*. These meta-standards led our predecessors to the present time standardization in the form of market institutions, which is realized at the higher level of economic relations.

The term "standard" generally implies an agreement between two or more people, while the agreement implies rational—intellectual behavior. The problem, as we have shown in the context of evolutionary apriorism, is that we should not assume that everyone has been fully aware of the "standard" at all times. We, therefore, face the problem of conscious "agreement" or "acceptance" on a given meta-standard at the same time; this implies that an agreement on a given meta-standard could not be conscious. The origin of the agreement on the given meta-standards, as well as following the meta-standard, must be explained in the context of prehistoric man, who would not have been aware of the "standard." As the theory of Hayek–Pavlík's evolutionary apriorism shows, it is the identification of certain values and beliefs that sediment and they seem to "settle" as the basis of spontaneously realized economic activities in the mode of incomplete-consciousness. When the Ego comes to a higher degree of consciousness, that knowledge is already automatically used, and it arises, emerges, as a spontaneous independent feature of the economic relations in question.

It should be noted also that the approach we have chosen differs from the institutional interpretation of the problem of coordination which is based *primarily* on the institutional framework of our action; i.e., it is the institutions that provide the coordinates for our actions in an uncertain world. Regardless of the fact that described concepts here are normative standards, it is possible to consider them as economic (teleological) meta-coordinates of our *economic decision-making*. The institutional normative framework described in the works of Hayek after 1937 or in the Lachmann's system, or through the works of Lewis, and others, is the outcome of this process of meta-standardization. From the argument presented here, we try to connect in principle the institutional evolutionary explanation (Hayek and post-evolutionary Hayek followers) with Misesian rationalism (intentionality resulting from human action) to preserve the valid elements of both approaches; it is about the incorporation of rationalism into the cultural-evolutionary institutional interpretation of the coordination of individuals. To achieve this task, we need to define some very basic, non-consciously emerged phenomena which humans used to solve their economic interrelations. It is possible to call them meta-standards.

As part of solving the problem of coordination, we will focus on the description of several standards. We will show that the given standards have both a subjective and an intersubjective character and that it is their intersubjective character that enables the coordination of subjective economic activities. We will show the origin of the intersubjective characteristics of the given standards in the context of the above-mentioned sedimentary history of knowledge in a spontaneous way as the basis for specific activities of individuals in the past. We will also point out that there are other economic-normative types of standardization.

2.3.5 The Concept of Economic Success/Error: Its Technical (objective), Subjective and Intersubjective Nature

We made quite a lot of preparatory arguments in order to finally approach our aim in describing the problem of success/error directly through specific criteria. We have demonstrated some existing arguments, we proposed a methodological evolutionary path given by Hayek–Pavlík's method, we have introduced the modification of the theory of subjective value, elaborated upon the role of the entrepreneur and we have identified sources of information for potential coordination and elaboration success/error. All this was needed in order to describe the concept of success/error. The problem of economic error, i.e., what exactly does it mean to make an error from an economic point of view, is not a new problem. However, there is no extensive discussion about the concept of economic error in fundamental terms regarding this concept, i.e., how to actually define an economic error. Surely, you must have said to yourself many times: "*it's a pity that I didn't do this or that then … I just made a mistake.*" We detect the error ex post when we compare the current state of affairs against some past assumptions. The assumption made caused us to make a decision; subsequently, we perceive the result of that decision as an error or a success. Even today, when planning, we imply that we can make an error, or succeed. The problem of the concept of error is not as clear-cut as it seems; we need to precisely explain the concept of error. As we will discover, it is not entirely easy. The problems will develop the consequence of future planning; it is important that we compare the same concepts and not compare pears with apples. Here are a few examples to illustrate the problem in the context of error identification.

Let us assume that the probability of some phenomenon occurring, in reality, is very high, and we act accordingly. We are almost certain (as Hoppe 1997 says, practically certain) that phenomenon A will cause phenomenon B. Let us assume we act on that premise. However, in the future, phenomenon B does not occur, regardless of the fact that A was produced. Can we then explicitly say that we made an error at the time we carried out the activity A? At the time, we explicitly assumed that, based on our knowledge, B would occur; our knowledge implied the phenomenon of B and not another result. However, B did not occur. So, did we make a mistake or not?

Let's take another example. Let us assume we opt for some economic activity A, which we expect to increase our satisfaction of needs later in time. However, our satisfaction of needs did not occur. Did we or did we not make a mistake earlier? The problem we face is that we assumed one thing in time *t* and the future by changing circumstances, we assume something else. Does that mean we made a mistake earlier? We did not have the knowledge at time *t*, which we have later on. Should we consider this in the context that every moment of our lives is so unique that in this respect, there is no real concept of a mistake at all? And if it is true that everything is so unique how could we even learn from an error? So, is the concept of error a subjective delusion?

Another example. If I said that it is a pity I did not do activity A instead of activity B, which, in the future, I am convinced that if I did B earlier in time, it would have been much more advantageous to me. How do I know that if I had carried out activity B earlier in time that economic circumstances would have remained the same and that activity

B would not have affected other circumstances and that the same circumstances would have occurred that lead me today to say that B would be a better activity than A? After all, I do not know of any alternative history. So, can we even compare any economic phenomena over time? At the same time, how could I be so sure that my alternative action B today would mean exactly how I perceive B today? From an objective point of view, I could only talk about an error if I knew the future. If I knew the future, I would have known that B would be better for me; however, with full knowledge of the future, I did A instead. Only then it is true that I have objectively made a mistake. However, as each of us knows, we do not know the future; if we do not know the future, how can we say that we made a mistake in the past? The fact is, that we do it and can learn from errors. Or does it only seem to us that we are capable of learning from errors?

So, what is the essence of the concept of error? What exactly is an error? How do we recognize and identify it, so that we can learn to avoid similar errors in the future and thus improve the state of affairs and satisfy our needs? As the reader sees, again, we solve in principle the only problem we stated at the beginning of our work, i.e., how we grasp the future. This will be the basis of our perception of error.

2.3.5.1 Mises, Kirzner, Hülsmann and Shackle–Lachmann on Error

Before approaching the solution proposed here, which again does not claim to be complete, let us examine what other authors such as Mises, Kirzner, Shackle–Lachmann, and Hülsmann have to say about error. They were/are interested in the concept of error from various points of view. Mises (1998) says that man realizes mistakes and economics "*deals with real man, weak and subject to error as he is, not with ideal beings, omniscient and perfect as only gods could be*" (Mises 1998, p. 97). However, this does not mean that a person's actions are irrational. On the contrary, according to Mises, his actions are always rational; he always acts in the best way in order to meet his needs. The fact that he later evaluates that the given action did not ultimately lead to the desired result is not a consequence of irrationality, but a consequence related to the degree of our knowledge. For example, in the case of a farmer from the past who calls on the gods for a better harvest compared to a farmer from the present who uses new methods of increasing fertility, where the present farmer knows more about cultivation than the former. However, from the point of view of Mises's action, both act rationally, with only a different degree of knowledge. A farmer from the past did not act irrationally and did not make an economic error. On the contrary, he behaved rationally in his context; he did not have the knowledge that the farmer has today nor does he have the knowledge that the farmer will have at some point in the future. In Mises's view, the same is true of any entrepreneur; the successful entrepreneur is not distinguished from the unsuccessful one by the concept of error, but by their skill in estimating the needs of others. It must be stated that for Mises (as if) there is no possibility of the realization of a real mistake, there is only the ignorance of knowledge and the ignorance of a better estimate of the future needs of others, including oneself. Ignorance can, of course, be constantly corrected and removed to a higher degree and replaced by a lower one. However, according to Mises, this is not a mistake. The inability to detect an error retrospectively is related to the concept of purposeful action.

This means, as Kirzner (1978) points out, that the very axiom of action which is based on a purposeful change in the state of the satisfaction of man, it is impossible, from a retrospective point of view, to declare that man has acted wrongly. One can only seek to be better informed, have better skills, or to better combine resources than he has done. However, this does not mean that he made a mistake. What Kirzner does not suggest is that Mises's mistake is only possible in the context of the other-one person. Although Mises does not explicitly mention the phenomenon of error intersubjectively, he points to it. This can be seen in statements such as: "*Entrepreneurial errors result in losses for the inefficient entrepreneurs which are counterbalanced by the profits of the efficient entrepreneurs*" (Mises 1998, p. 298). Without the context of the other person Mises could not speak of a successful and unsuccessful businessman; action must be rational, i.e. it is the difference between a successful and an unsuccessful entrepreneur—meaning here, an entrepreneur who is more skilled to better anticipate future needs as opposed to one who is not so gifted; this allows Mises (or any observer) to declare that an entrepreneur has made a mistake and that we are beings who make economic errors. Otherwise, he would contradict his presuppositions about rational action. The error, from this point of view, is a relative feature of entrepreneurial comparison.

While Mises states that the existence of error is a natural part of being human, Kirzner (1978) searches deeper for the origin of an economic error. This shows that this problem is slightly neglected in economic theory. As an example of the attempt to relevantly define the concept of error in terms of scientific knowledge, he gives the example of the discussion between Benedetto Croce and Vilfredo Pareto. Croce distinguishes between the so-called *technical nature of the error* and the *economic nature of the error*. Technical error is related to the knowledge of the surrounding reality. In the words of Mises, it is a comparison of knowledge, e.g., two farmers, one invoking the gods and the other guided by the actual knowledge of what is best to produce the finest crops. The difference in knowledge is related to the subjective error of one and the correct decision of the other.[81] Croce tries to identify the economic nature of the error in a similar way. He claims that an economic error occurs when a person acts against himself, that is, against his beliefs or the goals he has set. Croce talks about a mistake of will; that occurs when a man indicates a need, but in fact, wants something else. This concept has been criticized by Giorgio Tagliacozzo, who shows that there is no such thing as a mistake of will. It is not scientifically possible to distinguish between right and wrong goals.

As Kirzner writes, once we accept the assumption that one has the opportunity to change one's goals tomorrow, which were different

[81] Of course, this does not mean that the first farmer must be, by definition, unsuccessful. On the contrary. If the first is more successful, then in addition to invoking the gods, he unknowingly did something that ensured that his harvest was more abundant (if the goal is to grow as many crops as possible). And our knowledge has yet to reveal the unconsciously realized causal connection which is still attributed to God by the farmer. As can be seen, the technical error is rather related to the degree of knowledge of the surrounding reality. It is related to the *class probability* of how a group of phenomena behaves, when, as Shackle states, the probability rate shows the degree of our non-knowledge of the one hundred percent knowledge, i.e., to an absolutely certain extent in terms of the determination of phenomena.

yesterday, then it is not possible to speak of any wrong goal. Kirzner (1978, pp. 169–172) explains that from the point of view of acting purposefully, it is not really possible to state retrospectively that we have made a mistake in the past because even then we acted purposefully. However, Kirzner realizes that the existence of an error is indeed something that also exists from a scientific point of view. It's not about lamenting what we want in a different way which would have been more beneficial. We can learn. Kirzner, therefore, comes up with the concept of the so-called *genuine error*. He illustrates it with an example of a man who walks down the street and observes the offer of apples for 1 USD, but he enters the second store a little farther from the first one and buys the same apples for 2 USD. According to Kirzner, this is a clear economic error; however, this creates a suitable condition for entrepreneurship. Some people who are more attentive than a regular street pedestrian would take advantage of the difference and reduce or eliminate the price spread that exists in the market. However, Kirzner does not say explicitly that this is an intersubjective phenomenon when discussing the error.

Kirzner (1992) also criticizes ultra-subjectivists, Shackle, and Lachmann, for their interpretation of the problem of error based on the impossibility of estimating the future. From the interpretation of the Shackle–Lachmann system offered so far, it can be easily implied that there is no such thing as a mistake, since every event in our life is very unique and the mind responds to it in a unique and unrepeatable way. Although many of Mises's interpreters would probably disagree with me, the position of Mises (without the above-mentioned remark about an error in the context of the other one) is, in principle, similar to that of the ultra-subjectivists. The only difference is the context of the explanation and the higher degree of consistency in the argument of the ultra-subjectivists that, based on action arguments, its future orientation, and novelty, it is necessary to say that our perception of error is a chimera. Rather, it is the lower level of consistency of Mises argumentation that seems to protect him from identical, however incorrect, statements. In fact, Mises does not have room in his system for a priori intersubjective phenomena which, he implicitly and unconsciously identified in the description of the error. Before we present our approach to the concept of error, let's look at the discussion of error presented in Hülsmann (2000), who has some very interesting insights into the subject.

Hülsmann (2000) states that the concept of error/success is directly dichotomous when incorporated in choice. We all know that sometimes when we make decisions our actions can lead to success or failure. An error has several psychological forms that are very difficult to define in precise terms; we refer to mainly, "*whims, fancies, follies, greed, jealousy, illusion*" (p. 5). Hülsmann (2000, p. 5) considers the following to be an error: "*error is the failure of the choosing person to select the project most important for him.*" Like Kirzner, he points out that the concept of error cannot be described in the context of the psychological evaluation of our actions in the context of imaginary preferences. It is a choice that causes action and consequently, we are satisfied with the action or not in terms of our needs. Hülsmann perceives error and action in the context of objectively existing reality. The subjective evaluation is directed, based on objective features of reality. Hülsmann (2000, p. 13) states:

> *Something does not have high utility* ***because*** *we value it highly. Our valuing must be reasonable; it must assess the object's utility correctly. In other words, something is not (objectively) important* ***because*** *we think it is or want it to be. Our thoughts must be fitting and our wants rightly understood to gauge its real importance.* (In bold are the original italics)

The value, regardless of the fact that it is subjectively determined, has, according to Hülsmann, an objective component. According to him, that objective component is implied by several authors such as Condillac, and Jevons, when they differentiate between a value that has a subjective character and one that has objective importance, which they call the *utility* of economic good. Hülsmann literally says that it is not possible to make a choice and an associated assessment without avoiding the assumption that there is an objective component of the assessment of that option. Hülsmann is skating on very thin ice here; this is not about the objective existence of reality per se (yes, goods have their objective features), but he implies some kind of *objective evaluation of reality* (based on these features), while at the same time claiming that sometimes the objective component of the evaluation is objective only for the evaluator and for no one else. This is a special approach to what the objective value of the economic good or project means, but understandable from the point of view of the concept of error. This is due to the fact that, especially when evaluating over time, we need to compare comparable concepts, which is what Hülsmann is probably trying to do by implying the existence of an objective component of evaluation.[82]

Another important Hülsmann view of the concept of error is related to the fact that he uses it in the mode of counterfactuality; this relates to the consideration of several competing projects that appear to us to be essential and between which we decide (at a given time) based on what we consider to be correct, while the implementation of other projects is considered a potentially wrong decision. This is important in terms of the dichotomy of success/error action. Action and error thus do not depend on knowing the future. Action can be both successful and unsuccessful, even in the context of the uncertainty in which we act: "*the notion of success is only a comparative element of our understanding of the world*" (Hülsmann 2000, p. 14). In this way, Hülsmann tries to respond to the skepticism of the ultra-subjectivists. Success/error is only implied in the action, not dependent on it. He argues that we can never prove that our actions either *cannot be* wrong or *must be* wrong under certain conditions. Once we choose an action, its success/failure depends on empirically determined individual conditions. We will make a mistake if we compare the implications of our actions with other actions for which we imply more appropriate results at the time of decision-making. Hülsmann (2000, p. 20) writes:

> *One has to identify other concrete actions that would have been possible and determine whether they would have been more important. In short, one cannot apply equilibrium analysis by reference to any* a priori *standards. The standard of comparison must be a concrete action that also could have been performed in the same concrete historical situation.*

[82]As we will see below, this problem can be circumvented by our proposed modification of the theory of subjective value, where we apply the time-invariant nature of evaluation to the concept of thought and not to the surrounding reality per se.

Within the choice, therefore, we compare the action with the alternative action here and now and not the action with another action that we could potentially perform in the future. Here again, however, Hülsmann has a problem with the concept, meaning here, that we do not know the alternative history. If we do not know it, we can't actually determine the standard of comparison. If this is to be only a counterfactual standard of comparison, we remain only at the psychological level of "*what if/maybe*," which Hülsmann himself rejects. Again, we will have to make a modification to otherwise logical statements indicating that we are comparing at least two alternatives when making a decision; however, we must ensure the concept is applicable and generally valid over time, otherwise, we are not able to connect it with action. In principle, we are seeking criteria to assess two intended projects and explain why we think that one is correct and the other is not. It is wrong to move to the counterfactual area and at the same time compare the decision over time as well. While it is true that we cannot detect an *ex ante* error, meaning here, that we consider only alternative projects in the ex ante mode in the context of error avoidance. We need criteria that are not just psychological. On the contrary, we must show and prove that our actions either cannot be or, conversely, must be wrong under certain conditions and circumstances. Otherwise, it cannot be the case that we detect the error ex post, given that we do not know of an alternative history that would show us that we made the error ex post. In other words, we must identify some a priori conditions of error which in the context presented by us will, of course, have the character of evolutionary (intersubjective) a priori criteria. If the argument in Hülsmann (2000, p. 20) were true, that "*the standard of comparison must be a concrete action that also could have been performed in the same concrete historical situation*," he must admit that ultra-subjectivists are right. Because from a specific point of view, nothing like "*the same concrete historical situation*" exists; as we have already said, we do not know of an alternative history against which it is necessary to assess individually perceived factual and counterfactual projects.

Hülsmann further shows how difficult it is to analyze errors in an individual—e.g., Robinson Crusoe, where we simply know nothing about his value scale and intentions. Hülsmann claims that we can only evaluate him as a mother evaluates her child, whether he is really doing the best from the point of view of the mother and whether he is making mistakes according to her view. And if we want to embark on the evaluation of Robinson Crusoe's action at all, then we must at least assume some stability of his value preferences for the given evaluation; but it would be just an attempt, not an objective evaluation. An objective evaluation could only be attempted if Robinson Crusoe was able to identify his mistakes in the context of the deviation of plans and reality. What is interesting and at the same time strange to me is that, in the end, Hülsmann rejects an obvious intersubjective view of the concept of error. He claims (2000, p. 22):

> *The first thing to emphasize is that we are still interested exclusively in the success or failure of individual actions. It would be groundless to argue that the choices of other market participants determine which of our actions are right or wrong, for this does not affect whether our actions actually are right or wrong. General equilibrium is reached when all individuals choose what is for each the most important course of action. We do not have to bother with the question of whether the general equilibrium is ever reached, however, as long as we are sure that it can be reached.*

It is interesting and strange in terms of how his argument progresses. He argues that the market compares not only the activities of an entrepreneur in terms of the action he chooses but also in the context of other entrepreneurs, which explicitly implies an intersubjective comparison. He also gives the example of two ice-cream vendors. Their products are considered by the market to be identical products, but they sell them at different prices. One sells ice cream in front of a school and the other in front of a retirement home. It gives various examples as to why different prices of a given product are possible under different or individual conditions (one seller does not tolerate children) or objective conditions (the other seller has to deal with a gang of schoolchildren) and so on. He states that Stephen Shmanske would say about this situation that the market is not in disequilibrium, given the lack of a perfect information benchmark that market participants do not have, and do not care that the identically perceived product is sold at different prices. However, the argument can be set against Kirzner's argument that the opposite is true and that it is an objective error. Hülsmann concludes this contrast only by asking, "*Who is right?*" He replies that comparing two ice-cream vendors is a relevant comparison, although we do not know whether all eventualities were assessed by both vendors as well as the alternatives that ultimately led to different prices. However, Hülsmann ultimately asks himself to what extent the discovery of such an error is relevant. He replies that everyone has to judge for themselves. Finally, he concludes that the standards of what is and is not successful are constantly changing, because only ex post can we compare what is, with what would be, in the context of assessing some other alternative and thus revealing our mistakes. However, if it were true that our standards are constantly changing, how would the principle of comparison work at all? Do we have any explicit answer to the concept of the error once an error can be assessed from one point of view, and on other occasions from another point of view, even for one person? Based on this kind of interpretation, we would not be able to say anything at all about how people can coordinate with each other and learn from each other's errors.

It is a pity that Hülsmann (2000) did not focus much more on the intersubjectively mentioned nature of the error and is satisfied with the statement that it is up to one's individual assessment, whether we accept such a nature of the error or not. The possibility of an individual decision to assess the intersubjectively detected error, e.g., in the case of the ice-cream makers, implies that in this way it is possible to actually identify the error. And given our research, the reader may notice that concerning intersubjectively perceived economic contexts, individuals can set standards for their perception and comparison. At the same time, it must be stated that Hülsmann's argument about the constant change in the standards of what is and what is not success leads to a significant degree of relativism, where one would not be able to assess anything over time, which is very similar to the position of ultra-subjectivists.

Paradoxically, it is precisely the intersubjective comparison that, in my opinion, allows the concept of error to be explained; as I have tried to show above, it was this intersubjective possibility that the authors had examined very intensively. Ironically, at the individual level, the ability to identify an error is much more problematic. Before embarking on an overall explanation, I will only try to entice the reader into believing that intersubjective comparison is very instructive in the context of the error. If we imagine either the above-mentioned Kirzner's or Hülsmann's example—about the apple shop or ice-cream sellers—then we see several features. First, we compare two human actions at the same time, i.e., in the same economic context. Second, we imply in the examples that two identical situations are related to a product that is treated in the same way by the market. Third, we imply that information about given differences is transferable and discoverable. It is clear that in the context of both cases, we can think of diverse reasons why the prices are different and why this is not a mistake; whether it is a case of the consumer's pleasure in buying apples in this store and not in another store; perhaps because there is a pleasant seller, or because the ice-cream seller does not sell in front of the school because he does not like teenagers. In the context of the error, however, these are surrogate problems that can be solved by standardizing the rules for trading.

In contrast to the examples of Kirzner and Hülsmann, who describe a very underdeveloped market, we see standardization in developed markets today. In developed markets, a standardized product is traded in a standardized way in terms of the form and content of that product, which ultimately allows not only for the identification of the action-error, or in order to eliminate it (e.g., by arbitration), but also implies the existence of an intersubjectively identified error. Despite the possible subjective (Lachmann's) nature of the perception of the situation (i.e., Lachman's subjective interpretation of prices), we are able to understand in an identical and standardized way, all participants of the market in the very same way, even if one or other market participant decides to use this information individually one way or another. The same can be implied in the specific examples given by Kirzner and Hülsmann; errors in given markets can be effectively identified *if* there is standardization; ice-cream vendors can sell a standardized product (e.g., standardized ice cream product from the chamber of commerce), or there exist standardized ethical rules for marketing products or enforcement of ownership rules where the enforcement protects not only the consumer but also entrepreneurs. Once standards exist, we know what comparisons should be made. In other words, even in the examples of Kirzner and Hülsmann, it is possible to imply that the intersubjective nature of the error is a relevant concept. But we also have to deal with the individual recognition of success/error decision. So, the questions we face are, what is an economic error, and what is its nature? Can it be identified only at the individual or even at the intersubjective level? How do we recognize that we have made an error and how can we learn from it and not repeat it, if it is true that the circumstances under which it occurred may never be repeated?

2.3.5.2 Technical Nature of Success/Error

Based on the above-mentioned dispute about the concept of error, it is obvious that the problem has several levels. We perceive the concept of economic error in the context of the surrounding reality. The surrounding reality is the object of our interest in terms of satisfying our needs. The technical nature of error as identified by Croce is related to the degree of our knowledge of the reality we use to satisfy our needs. The identification of the error is also related to the assessment of the plan and the attendant result. If (from a technical point of view) the result does not match the assumptions, we look for reasons why this did not happen. We first decide either to eliminate the causes and improve our knowledge, e.g., we find better methods of crop production and abandon the invoking of gods, which is less successful. The second possibility is that, if the elimination of the given error does not make economic sense, we incorporate the identified error into our plans, e.g., we include it in the overhead costs (e.g., an accidentally broken bottle). In other words, eliminating the error associated with accidentally breaking one bottle per billion makes no economic sense. It is better to become accustomed to it then to solve this problem. The third possibility related to our limited knowledge of reality is in the various types of insurance relating to the frequency of occurrence of certain phenomena (*class probability*). This type of error has an objective character that is as tangible to everyone in principle as it is.

Subjectively, in this case, only the economic nature of the technical error is perceived, i.e., whether or not it pays to deal with it in the context of our plans and whether we know how to deal with the given error economically and meaningfully. At the same time, this does not mean that the assessment of an error does not change based on an intersubjective perception of these errors. It can easily be that the state of economic acceptance of some technical error (economic ignorance of technical error) within one entrepreneur's plan, causes a higher success rate in another entrepreneur's plan. The second entrepreneur can economically and meaningfully eliminate the technical error, e.g., by another combination of capital resources which causes the elimination of the technical error and, consequently, achieve economic success, as a result of ignoring the technical error of the former. The technical error is part of the concept of economic error. The formation of technical error is based on the knowledge of humans concerning reality and the causal explanation of its principles. This knowledge is incorporated step by step into economic decision-making. However, our task is to describe the emergence of a meta-standard of economic error that the technical part of the error uses.

2.3.5.3 Subjective Nature of Economic Success/Error: Portfolios Structures and Spreads

The second level of grasping the concept of error stems from a subjective view of reality. It is always a specific person who perceives the surrounding reality and the actions of others in the community. Given the fact that the dichotomy of error/success is necessarily related to the action, Hülsmann (2000) rightly focuses on the assessment of the error in the context of a counterfactual project. The problem faced at the subjective level is Hülsmann's request for evaluation, which has both a subjective and an objective part. The interpretation of the problem in Hülsmann (2000) is problematic because as part of reality (the project takes place in reality), Hülsmann applies certain objective evaluation elements to the project. However, it is the kind of person who grasps and interprets reality in the context of our subjective evaluation. In subjective evaluation, there is no objective element of evaluation, derived from objective reality. There is only the attribution of value to elements of reality, based on their objective properties. However, this does not imply an objective component of the evaluation. Evaluation can only be subjective. The fact remains, however, that in order to evaluate over time, it is necessary to compare something that is comparable.

I claim that we can also solve the problem by using the above-mentioned modification of the subjective value theory when it comes to satisfying the sum of needs through the sum (portfolio) of goods. The concept of the sum of goods used to satisfy the sum of needs is reflected, through a portfolio of goods/projects. This is not an assessment of successful/unsuccessful goods/projects per se, but an assessment of successful/unsuccessful changes to the composition of the portfolio, i.e., someone is assessing how a marginal change of the portfolio meets the perceived sum of factually and counterfactually perceived needs in the time continuum. The time-invariant component, which is evaluated and comparable over time, is a portfolio concept that is the same in the past, present, and future. The single goods/projects that make up a given portfolio are relativized by the given concept and have only a relative position within the portfolio. The success/error is then evaluated identically, as Hülsmann claims, but as we see in a different and comparable context. The action is focused on the change of a portfolio. The implemented projects aim to create such a portfolio construction that will ensure a higher degree of satisfaction of needs in time. Successful actions versus some erroneous actions (not all but only possible) are ex ante evaluated factually and counterfactually in terms of portfolio composition. Ex ante, any action which doesn't bring the preferred state of the portfolio is eliminated into the counterfactual sphere of action and only one action is chosen that a person expects is likely to bring about the desired change. This means that a successful action could be considered to be the one that causes the resulting portfolio of goods to meet the needs as expected and vice versa, while the fact remains that people always prefer a higher to a lower satisfaction of needs. The success/error is also evaluated in the relative and not the absolute mode. However, this is precisely the point. Ex post, we can decide that the action focused on the composition of the portfolio was successful/unsuccessful because of the preference for a higher to lower satisfaction of needs. If the action doesn't result in an exact image of the satisfaction to be compared to some particular projection, it doesn't mean that the action was *entirely* unsuccessful. A man can perceive a better set of circumstances in relative, not just in absolute terms, in order to compare the state of affairs to the plan. However, is this enough to recognize the subjective error?

Unlike Hülsmann, the standard of comparison (portfolio) in its formal abstract form is identical over time and only its specific form changes. The ex ante criterion for comparing success/error is always the *expected state of the portfolio* in the context of expected (factual and counterfactual) overall needs. The criterion of success/error is, therefore, related to the future, not to the present. However, when we state that the criterion for the success/error is always the *expected state of the portfolio*, the attentive reader may remind us that as a matter of fact, we are unable to define an *expected state of the portfolio due to ever-changing needs*. So, based on this, we wouldn't have any criteria at all. It is very true that the sum of our needs is ever-changing; basically, it is still some kind of flow or process. It is impossible to define its state per se unless we still or stop our mind, which causes stops to the perception of time flow. Does it mean that the ex post evaluation is not possible? It is. Basically, we cannot focus on a particular state of anything. We are facing the problem of flow. Therefore, we can only evaluate an approach to some kind of expected satisfactory state of affairs. So, what exactly do we assess ex post, i.e., what do we compare in terms of the present with the past? We compare the spread; the spread between expected (ideal) and the ever-changing portfolio used to meet our changeable needs and the portfolio which we actually acquire again and again. If this spread is depressing, we are more successful than unsuccessful. This way we are able to define fluxional criteria for the evaluation of the change of the portfolio over time which constantly changes its composition to meet an ever-changing combination of needs. This flowing criterion is necessary due to the fact that the will is the constant flow that is heading toward the future. This means that the ex post assessment of success/error always takes place in the context of how the acquired portfolio can eliminate or mitigate the state of *potentially perceived* future uneasiness.

How is that possible? It comes from the modification of the theory of subjective value. As we already know, the theory implies that the preference scale is two-dimensional: factual needs (here and now) and contrafactual needs (some combination of future needs); while the contrafactual has a real (possible and realizable) and unreal character. For this reason, we build a suitable portfolio to meet the widest possible combination of needs. The real nature of a combination of needs is one that implies that we can satisfy a certain combination of needs with a portfolio of economic goods. The second part of the counterfactual area of needs, however, is various intended needs, which, for some reason, cannot be satisfied with a portfolio of goods, regardless of the fact that a person would, of course, want some ideal and desired composition of the portfolio. As an example, it may be a magic wand but it can also be something "more realistic," that for some people remains unattainable, e.g., social prestige gained, whether by driving an expensive car or sailing on their own yacht when limited by other factors in achieving the given needs. The theory implies a casual *value link* between factual and counterfactual perceived needs and a portfolio of goods. It is clear that a person wants an ideal portfolio, however, a person can only have a possible portfolio, which comes from the fact that not everything is possible. A person has, therefore, an actual portfolio (Pc) and wants, an ideal one (Pd) and always acquires one that is possible (Pp). The spread among portfolios emerges. As we know, creating a spread among portfolios is possible because the concept of a portfolio is relational in nature. The portfolio consists of several goods and, thus, it is possible to identify changes in the form of a ratio of the relative representation of goods within the portfolio. This creates the spread between Pc and the Pd and the Pp and the Pd. Each Pp becomes some Pc. However, the change of Pc to the Pp is motivated by the effort to achieve some Pd. The target state of the portfolio is to satisfy factual and counterfactual perceived needs. As the combination of needs changes in time, so must the view of Pc – Pp – Pd.

The concept of error is then evaluated, depending on how the spread among Pc – Pp – Pd narrow/widen. The success/error is that it is evaluated, based on the range of the spreads in question. The narrower perceived spread between the Pp and the Pd implies that the economic activity in question, that caused the change of the Pc to the Pp, is successful and vice versa. The narrower the spread between Pp and Pd, the greater the success rate. The attentive reader should note that the description of this dynamic does not depend in any way on the specific goods and the representation of the goods in the portfolio of an individual. The specific economic activity is evaluated within this context or we could say benchmark. It is an improved knowledge of reality and the needs of others that enables an individual to achieve a narrower spread of their personal Pp and Pd. However, this is possible to achieve not only by better knowledge of the reality and needs of others, but also by improved knowledge of ourselves and the better composition of our Pd. It could happen that, for example, an older person with acquired knowledge adjusts the required scope of the spread between the Pd and the Pp. The reason may be because the person knows that not everything is possible, abandoning meaningless expectations of satisfying needs (e.g., in the form of making magic), recognizing the limits of economic possibilities, or requiring less effort in terms of changing things at the end of someone's life, or changing demands to meet needs, etc. It is also true that the wider the spread between the Pc – Pp and the Pp – Pd, the greater the economic activity of the individual aimed at eliminating the uneasiness that stems from the extent of the spreads and vice versa; in other words, the greater the efforts to eliminate former mistakes.

In this way, we can say that an error is made within a different economic context connected with the past, in the present as well as the future without any logical inconsistency. As for the elimination of errors in the context of the future, we do not know the future in its concrete form. However, we can grasp it because we relativize its concrete form by portfolio. This means that we are preparing for as many potential events as possible that the future may bring regarding the portfolio. And the more eventualities we can eliminate, the more we are able to satisfy some complex of our needs that we perceive in a factual and counterfactual mode or even those about which we do not know anything yet, which will only arise as a product of our mind later on. What individual or interpersonal strategy is chosen is already a different question in this context. Whether it's building a highly diverse portfolio of goods, or trying to exchange part of a portfolio with another person, or inventing money as the most liquid commodity in order to eliminate the need for vast diversification and to ensure that we buy what we need, no matter what our future needs are (under given budgetary constraints). The concept of subjective economic success/error is based on the differentiation between what is suitable as a part of the portfolio and what is not. The concept of a portfolio gives us some kind of ex ante and also ex post criteria for the evaluation of decisions at the time at which we arrive at a decision (the factual and contrafactual sphere of the action) and also later on, when we compare the present with the past.

The very basic idea of a portfolio is based on the idea of diversification or being prepared for more eventualities which the future brings. This feature of human activity comes from the normative notion of our thinking. Our thinking is based on the idea "of things as they should be." The possibility of formulating this normative state causes us to be able to visualize some eventualities and compare them with the state of affairs "as they are." Due to this, we are motivated to diversify. It is the very notion of our action. We are not squirrels, "making" their "portfolio" in the sense of ever repeating the same activity due to the fact that it is instinctive behavior. We want to satisfy our needs intentionally, essentially in terms of their combination. And the possible combination of needs is, in principle, infinite. This infinity of the combination of needs, the ever-changing reality, forces our thinking, forces us into making certain combinations of goods—a portfolio. It is possible to claim that the notion of the diversification by portfolio has an evolutionary aprioristic character, since the degree of diversification need not have been very vast at the dawn of mankind. It has also some kind of individual character; hermits need less diversity than others. However, as the conscious man emerged and higher and higher economic interactions of men emerged, it became an unstoppable characteristic of human actions.[83] The key factor of the individual degree of portfolio diversification is, therefore, an important characteristic of a person living within the economic system. Therefore, it has to be stated that from a subjective point of view it is, therefore, apriori a preferred situation to possess

[83]I think that the best empirical evidence of this is money. The invention of money, basically, enabled our predecessors to eliminate the problem of diversification of any portfolio.

a portfolio that has better diversity over the others, while this range of diversity is already very individual.

There are two basic problems with the description: it is provided on the conscious level of man and it states that the diversification of the portfolio has an apriori character and a provided criteria for the recognition of the individual success/error. To eliminate both problems, we need to provide a conjectural history, which shows the operation of the concept on the vague level of our prehistoric predecessors, as well as showing how this meta-individual-standard for recognition of success/error emerged and how the criteria of the success/error happens to be apriori a valid mind structure of man. We have to explain, basically, how it is with the concept of a portfolio in terms of a connection to some idea of prehistoric human beings. Is it possible to presuppose that they used the concept in some semi-conscious way? Could it be that the concept of a portfolio is some kind of meta-standard or "germ cell" of the concept of error? From the empirical point of view, we found many examples that our predecessors hoarded things and parts of reality to protect themselves against an uncertain future. Even though we are unable to identify when the start of this hoarding (as a portfolio composition) began, it is obvious that this kind of activity is very natural and was an inseparable part of the lives of our predecessors from the very dawn of humanity.[84] However, we are not too interested in empirical facts that could be interpreted in many ways. We are trying to logically deduce why our predecessors chose the concept of the portfolio as a concept. The defining reason behind it might be that it offered the possibility of describing the process of differentiation. As was described above, Pavlik (2004) shows that the basic principle of conjectural history is the description from the abstract (simple) to the concrete (more complex). It cannot be the case vice versa. And the concept of the portfolio permits this description from simple to more complex or the differentiation of

[84]What is interesting, from this point of view, is that according to Smail (2014, p. 118) the particular activity of over-hoarding among some people is a form of unnatural behavior. It is possible to trace it with some kind of certainty as far back as only a few centuries. However, Smail already mentions that in Footnote 24, that "*The International OCD Foundation suggests that a reference in Dante's Inferno constitutes evidence for hoarding behavior in the past.*" However, he considers this not compulsive hoarding but avarice.

the whole and the parts. It enables us to describe the process from the unconscious (the quasi-economic) to a conscious economic activity.

The interaction between prehistoric man and reality had to start as the acknowledgment of the vague human mind which differentiated itself from reality. If we are able to imagine anything about those prehistoric times, we have to start thinking with the claim that our predecessors were part of that reality, armed with certain evolutionary abilities (we can only speculate about this) which later led to the emergence of free will. If we accept such presuppositions about the existence of groups of these beings, who had instinctively usurped certain parts of reality, we can then claim that we are dealing here with some group instinctive behavior which resulted in the creation of some group shared portfolio. This concept could help them to differentiate between outside reality (everything else) and the group (prehistoric men and parts of reality) as one common entity. The concept of the whole, i.e., everything, meaning here the reality and prehistoric men as the unconscious part of the reality, was differentiated as "we" and "our" parts of reality from "everything else." This kind of differentiation took place automatically, as prehistoric men took and instinctively integrated with reality, and started instinctively to use parts of reality for food and survival. The dawn of consciousness started the process of the differentiation between the "we" and the "reality." The portfolio of economic goods first had an intuitive character and had to be considered as joint or common, as the group of prehistoric men was considered as united. At this stage of development, it is possible to speak only about the group behavior due to the lack of higher levels of self-consciousness of the members of these groups. However, as Pavlík (1999) shows, it is possible to speculate that these prehistoric groups were already governed at that time by the norms of distributive justice, which lay down the basic guidelines (sedimentary history) for the catallactic rules; general rules which enabled the existence of bigger societies. However, the opportunity for some kind of differentiation within the prehistoric group between some concept of "group portfolio" and the concept of "economic goods" as parts of the group portfolio is already observable within the different options required to compose the group portfolio. Our predecessors could see that one component of a portfolio (e.g., with antelope meat) was preferable to another composition of the portfolio (e.g., only with some fruits) to meet their needs more satisfactorily. This difference shows that some parts of reality (an antelope) were also desirable and that the economic activity had to be focused on hunting antelopes. Based on this activity, groups of prehistoric men could start to realize the concept of the portfolio, as something they were commonly trying to achieve and the concept of goods, as parts of the portfolio. The activity could also lead to the differentiation of value. Different portfolios (consisting of different goods) enabled them to recognize that some parts of the portfolio were preferable to other parts, meaning that they could start to differentiate between the attribution of different use-values to different goods.[85] It has to be stressed that the concept of group portfolio as something given or as something which is a part of the group compared to the surrounding reality to which our predecessors belonged with their vague minds is a simpler idea compared to a personal portfolio, composed of particular goods. The sequence from simplicity to complexity is as follows: nature as a whole—pre-human vague minded beings with a group portfolio—a rising individual mind and its individual portfolio—particular goods. It means that recognizing the concept of goods per se is a more complex mind structure that presupposes consciousness, other human beings and a full differentiation of the will from nature and the group.

We can move a step further. It could well have happened that one group met another group. This occasion enabled further differentiation between other wholes and parts of reality, meaning that prehistoric men realized that there were "some others like us" and "they have their parts of reality," meaning here some other groups of prehistoric men and their instinctively acquired possessions, and "everything else" (there is still the reality out there). These economic interactions led to further differentiation between the concept of portfolio and the concept of economic goods. It was possible to realize (still vaguely) that the group possessed certain parts of reality that were similar to that which the other group had, and that it was possible to exchange certain parts of the portfolios of one group for other parts of the portfolio of other groups. It must

[85]The term attribution of "use value" is used in the Menger (2007, pp. 226–236) sense.

be stressed that within the group there is very little room for the differentiation of the concept of economic goods exchange. As Pavlik (1999) shows the norms of distributive justice *only* laid down a basis for catallactic rules. It follows that the barter exchange of one good for another good within the group had to be very limited due to the distributive character of the rules of the group.[86] It has to be stressed that due to the presupposition of vague consciousness on the part of our ancestors and the concept of group behavior, it was meeting other groups that allowed us to explain the concept of the barter group exchange and the connected concept of so-called *exchange value* attributed to economic goods. We can move another step further. Due to their growing self-awareness, it was possible for prehistoric men to realize that there were parts of reality that consisted of "me as human, conscious, subject" and "what is my possession - my parts of reality (portfolio of goods)" and the "group," as well as the "reality." This was possible due to the growing self-awareness of man and the intensity of economic relations among our ancestors that consisted of the growing intensity of the specialization of labor, exchanges among members of communities and foreigners, or debt exchanges within communities. This kind of differentiation process leads us finally to the definition of the portfolio of conscious man and the concept of economic goods. The differentiation basically continues until today as we recognize many aspects of reality as new goods; we are dealing with many portfolio strategies; we are dealing with portfolio strategies on the level of financial instruments, and there is no reason to suppose that this differentiation will end. It will continue further and it will provide us with many new concrete criteria in order to recognize individual success/error, based on the spreads between our ideas of the portfolios in question.

At the end of this description, we face an empirical question of individual strategy in order to achieve his or her suitable states of affairs which provides the content for the individual success/error evaluation. In principle, this could be any personal strategy. To describe strategies from the point of view of the individual is not possible. There are as many

[86]The argument about the distributive justice within the group also supports the Graeber (2011) statement that debt exchange was a more common feature of the prehistoric group than the barter exchange, since the barter exchange was more or less an exchange between strangers.

strategies as there are individuals; as there are many individuals, there are many strategies. If we could suggest some kind of abstract level in order to describe this empirical context, I would choose the following principle. We can divide strategies into (a) cooperative, (b) semi-cooperative and semi-non-cooperative, (c) individually non-cooperative, (d) principally non-cooperative. Voluntary cooperative strategies are the main focus of this work. They come from individual economic action and voluntarily economic interaction with others, we called this the concept of a free market. The semi-(non)cooperative strategies are those that are prone to claim that we, as a society, consisting of individuals, need some kind of political action in the field of individual interactions. These are strategies that accept a great opportunity in order to meet individual needs solely using the free market, however, they accept some roles for enlightened leaders or politicians in order to make available certain kinds of basic skeleton frameworks for otherwise free actions. The individually non-cooperative strategies to achieve a suitable state of the portfolio, are those of hermits or persons who commit suicide. They are trying to escape from the societal world or from the world. The principally non-cooperative strategies are those of thieves, murderers, warriors, tyrants, basically people who are trying to achieve their satisfaction with activities that are dangerous for others. Most of the information connected with precise criteria used to identify some success/errors that have an impact on individuals and their personal satisfaction of needs is given between semi-cooperative strategies and in principle, non-cooperative strategies. We face many kinds of political systems. It is unrealistic to claim that all of them provide nothing for society or that everything is exploitation or theft. It is a grey zone with some clearly given and recognized extremes. Why? Because there could be some enlightened rulers or politicians who would want to set up some free and voluntary society. However, there are also some tyrants and dictators, who are clearly the negative extreme example. It is also possible to see that the strategies which politicians provide are often voluntarily accepted. It is not only the power that persuades others to accept their operation within society. However, there are many parts of our societal life enforced by political power, which clearly hurts free individual interactions. There are some social problems that seem equally suitable for resolution, based on political decisions. We will not address all these problems within this essay. We have been solely focused on the *economic criteria and character* of the question of individual error/success evaluation. Having a short digression from our task was important because the reader needs to be aware that the problem we are faced with us is not an easy one—it is basically due to the empirical multi-character of a strategy chosen by someone while interacting with others, which explains why the interaction of individuals is sometimes very problematic.

2.3.5.4 The Intersubjective Nature of Economic Success/Error: The Concept of Economic Calculation as Accounting Standard for the Comparison of Activities Within a Community

The third level of the concept of success/error stems from economic coordination. As mentioned several times above, it is mainly this (intersubjective) nature of the error that the above-mentioned authors "circled" around but did not name or explain it explicitly. The intersubjective error, as the term "intersubjective" suggests, is a success/error that is subjectively perceived by at least two people and possibly observed by a third person. This implies some kind of agreement, the time-invariant-logical-formal character of the success/error; if there is an agreement between two people, there should be no problem extending the agreement to other participants within the community. The only problem would then be the promotion of that particular standard through the community. However, as the reader will see below, this is, of course, only a model description in the sense of "*perceived by at least two people and possibly observed by a third person.*" The concept of intersubjective error and its expression is not so easily defined—the description, based on three people, is only illustrative. In fact, it is quite the contrary. It is a new level of assessment of the economic situation, which necessarily arises in the *wider* economic community, when it is not possible to explicitly define the term "wider," e.g., by the minimum number of people. The essence of the matter is that it is an emergent phenomenon, which arises in terms of the connection to the higher complexity of the problem of evaluation, when some common evaluation standard of success/error in the community is subsequently spontaneously formed. Below we will address the issue in more detail.

Intersubjectivity implies that it is a mutually shared evaluation standard of success/error, which can be used to compare the economic activities of all individuals.[87] An error or success is perceived by the same human subjects in the same manner. For this condition to apply, there must be some criterion according to which both (and all involved) individuals will identify a success and an error. The standard must be durable and applicable over a period of time, it must be understood equally by everyone involved, and eventually by newcomers. The standard must also bring identical information to everyone, regardless of the related claim that the interpretation of the information of a given standard can *also have an individual* and unique "Lachmannian" character.[88] The subjective error standard for comparison at the individual level is a portfolio of economic goods and considered spreads among current, potential and desired portfolios. As mentioned above, a portfolio allows an individual to compare his success/error over time in terms of the possibility of higher/lower satisfaction of personal needs. But that's not all. Yes, the portfolio allows the individual to identify a very individual calculation and his own accounting standard. The individual is thus able to assess whether spending a unit of good from the portfolio and acquiring another unit of good into the portfolio is a meaningful economic activity for him. In other words, a person can calculate, even without money, and the denominator for assessing the situation is the overall state of the portfolio. As we have already indicated in the description of the modification of the theory of subjective value, the concept allows a person to assess their situation at the value level in the sense of the ordinal assessment of

[87] As it is possible to see e.g., in Kirzner (1978), the concept of error even appears to be a genuine one. It even seems to Kirzner that not to recognize some arbitrage opportunity is an objectively valid error which implies that the meta-standard we are dealing with is quite deeply incorporated in the minds of people and they commonly use it.

[88] As the reader will see later, this concept is even the basis of our current distinction between efficient and inefficient economic action, or profit/loss. The standard based on the concept of intersubjective economic error is thus one of the main coordinates of economic social coexistence.

the state of affairs, meaning "more—less" (Čuhel-Mises's diction). At the same time, it allows for a very subjective and fundamental cardinal calculation—comparing the expenditure of a marginal unit of goods from the portfolio and obtaining a marginal unit of goods into the portfolio because a person sees a marginal change of the portfolio. A person is, therefore, able to identify a cardinally expressed marginal change in the composition of the portfolios in question related to a change in the composition of goods, where a person spends one good and acquires another one. Let's provide an example here, because it is crucial.

Let's say that a man has in his possession (portfolio Pc): fire, some hunting and cultivating tools, 1 kg of meat, 10 kg of wheat, 100 L of water, and 30 days of life (let's say that meat, wheat, and water enable him to live for 30 days). He stands before the following decision; either he has to spend 2 days of his life hunting in order to gain 5 kg of meat or he has to spend 15 days of his life cultivating the soil in order to gain 100 kg of wheat. We do not have a universal comparable denominator for the consideration of which of his possible actions is more effective for him. However, he makes a decision. Based on what? Based on the marginal utility, of course. The only difference is that he did not consider the dollar value of his actions, he considered two possible overall situations compared to his present state of affairs, meaning here that Pc and two possible portfolios Pp1 and Pp2 while Pp1 is composed as (Pc—2 days of his life—some consumption of other goods + 5 kg of meat) and Pp2 is composed as (Pc—15 days of his life—some consumption of other goods + 100 kg of wheat). He makes a decision, based on the marginal change of the portfolio; we are not able to provide some comparative analysis, based on a general denominator (the dollar value), however, the decision based on the principle of the comparison of portfolios is possible. He, subjectively, is able to recognize what suits him more or less and he, subjectively, is able to recognize the (cardinal) changes which are considered. We have to be very careful here with this statement. It is not in the cardinal sense as we know it in money terms today, since money is the common denominator of our actions and our portfolios. It is only a sediment of the cardinal expression—out of the monetary economy. A person is able to recognize relational morphological differences of given current and imaginary potential portfolios; these relational morphological differences basically enable us to claim that the decision, whatever it was, was made within the mode of marginal utility that was greater than zero while the expression "greater than zero" has today an explicit cardinal character in monetary terms. It is the morphological differences that enable a person to recognize a more and less suitable state of affairs while these changes are based on cardinal changes of a morphological character of relations of goods within the considered current and potential portfolios. A person realizes an individual and very fundamental calculation based on the differences in the relational morphology of portfolios in question. The accounting, denominational unit, which is very individual, is the portfolio of goods; it provides us with what we call satisfaction or utility but it has to be stressed that it provides us with utility only at the level of the whole portfolio, which the whole provides us with, in order to meet our needs. The individual calculation is a consideration of the range of morphological changes of the structure of goods within Pc compared to Pp1 a Pp2. The structures are created through a consideration of meeting some combination of perceived and expected needs. The basic cardinality concept is given here by the comparison of the relation of goods within portfolios, as whole structures; a cardinality shows us as a change of the structure of the portfolio caused by some replacement of goods, e.g., such as the change from Pc to Pp1 when the utility of the Pc is changed into the Pp1 and a person recognizes the change of the range of the utility, albeit very subjectively. This is true either in the context of an exchange or in the context of an individual (entrepreneurship or production) activity, or within the basic activity of the appropriation of items, meaning here all possible kinds of actions which are focused on the change of the relational character of goods within someone's portfolio. The only difference in comparison to today's state of affairs is that we calculate today, based on a common denominator which basically expresses the range of this morphological change in terms of a common intersubjective tool—money. In the past, this was an individual level situation.

Based on this, we can derive a situation in an economic community that spontaneously creates a mutual accounting standard for the comparison of activities of community members. This means that we need to identify a shared accounting and "benchmarking" standard based on principles that are valid on the individual level. As we will see, in my opinion, this is not a transition that is some kind of average, in terms of the individual standards. It is a more complicated construction of the mind/thought structure—the standard of accounting, which, once created, is used by each member of an economic community for mutual comparisons. This is, of course, a very well-known problem of economic calculation and the problem of money; at least it is a well-known problem within the Austrian school. However, we must first show the characteristics of the standard outside its monetary expression and then describe the origin of its monetary nature.

Given that we live in a community and due to the abstract nature of the concept of the portfolio at the individual level of two non-cooperative individuals, the portfolio already allows for some basic mutual comparisons and implications of error against each other's actions. This means that the composition of my portfolio is different from that of my neighbor's, thus I may imagine that if I had his portfolio, I would be either better or worse off presently or in the future. This can be applied mutatis mutandis to the group behavior of prehistoric men. However, this still does not lead to any general normative-economic principle—the standard. In the case of two non-cooperating neighbors, it is actually a comparison of conceptually the same thing, but with fully individual, standards. Even at this level, however, if e.g., Alice envies Bob or admires or repeats what Bob does, this does not mean that Bob must perceive the situation in the same way, meaning here that Bob is satisfied. It is only Alice who could speculate with regard to what she would do in Bob's position.

However, to describe the intersubjective standard, we need the economic interaction of more people. Given that the standard is an emergent phenomenon, the condition "more people" is a necessary condition for its emergence; it has to be stated that we are not able to define what exactly "more people" means (e.g., How much is it?). Although it may seem at first glance that this is an ambiguous and empirical question, it is not. The question has its aprioristic character as well. Emergent phenomena are formed against the background of some specific activities and against certain parts of the system (within this context—society). It is the complexity of the many activities done within the system that will eventually cause them to arise. It means that less complexity only causes different emergent phenomenon to emerge, or there will be no emergent phenomenon at all. It is the complexity of relations among parts per se, which determines what kind of emergent phenomenon emerges or if it emerges at all. The different levels of complexity cause a different morphological structure of relations. Therefore, the question of "how much does it take to cause this or that emergent phenomenon?" is connected to the type of emergent phenomenon in question. It means that if there are only two members of a community who deal with certain kinds of standardization, the standard will be different than the kind we see today, when the complexity of human interrelations is far more different or there might be no standard at all because the complexity between two men is quite low. Consequently, the origin of emergent phenomena is caused by the fact that the individual parts begin to form some complex of interconnections and their own morphological structure causes a de novo phenomenon to arise; a phenomenon per se, which is composed of certain parts, but its decomposition into the parts is not possible anymore (see e.g., Lawson 2019) because of the strength and vitality of interconnections and because a new phenomenon proves the validity of its existence, when it responds better to problems that parts of the system have faced less successfully.[89] It is possible to say that a new layer of the composition of parts of reality is being created, when the necessary and sufficient condition for the existence of a given phenomenon changes. A necessary condition for a given phenomenon is no longer its parts, but it is the morphology of relationships that causes it to be a new kind of phenomenon. The phenomenon has its lower layer composed of parts, but the necessary condition of the given phenomenon is based on the morphology of the given relations, not the parts of the given system; this is the necessary context of Hayek–Pavlík's interpretation of evolutionary apriorism.[90] So, what criteria (common to all of us)

[89] I think that this description is, for the sake of the argument, sufficient. However, I see that it has to be detailed more in my following essays on the subject.

[90] I think that this is also the reason why we saw many different kinds of money and calculation standards during the history of man; and we will see many more. It is a matter of complexity that we are trying to eliminate with these emergent phenomena, while still dealing with the very same concept of debt as the Smithsonian "germ cell."

allows us to reveal the mutually subjective side of the problem in order to turn it into an intersubjective one?

It is the exchange that qualitatively changes any situation that is perceived purely on a subjective level. Exchange is a state where Alice prefers portfolio P-desired-Alice, which will be enriched with goods X—which she will receive from Bob—and impoverished by goods Y, which Alice gives to Bob over some existing portfolio P-current-Alice which will contain X in addition to other goods (and vice versa in terms of Bob and his portfolio). Alice assesses whether the PdA is more advantageous than the PcA. On this basis, she can subjectively evaluate her profit/loss if she makes an exchange. She considers whether obtaining PdA will satisfy her needs more than the original PcA. The exchange of goods X and Y also reveals part of Bob's preferences and part of Alice's preferences, against a marginal change in their portfolios. The exchange implies that Alice is offering Y which Bob wants and vice versa. In having what she wants (X), Alice depends on her offer. The offer depends on the unveiling of Bob's combination of needs and on the combination of features of offered goods (Y), which Bob evaluates as satisfactory to meet his combination of needs. The subjective evaluation and Alice's higher satisfaction depend on her knowing how to meet Bob's needs (and vice versa in terms of Bob). This knowledge provides what Bob wants and partially what Alice wants. As we see, this knowledge has an intersubjective character. The success/error of Alice is dependent on the knowledge of what Bob wants and vice versa. Basically, this is the area where the intersubjective success/error stands. It is Alice's knowledge that must be evaluated to ascertain if she is able to provide something that Bob wants and it is Bob's knowledge that must be evaluated to assess whether can provide something that Alice wants. What is interesting is that, given their combined information, if they agree on the exchange, they will both be (ex-ante) successful. Erroneous knowledge would result in an offer from Alice that Bob does not want and vice versa. Non-exchange informs us that Alice or Bob has incorrect knowledge or they ignore each other. The second interesting point is that this knowledge is accessible to a third one. It is because the act of exchange has a formal-logical character. However, this type of exchange will take place once and will end. The economic plans of Alice and Bob are revealed to them only at this clearly defined time of the exchange of X and Y. However, once the exchange has taken place, the plans of Alice or Bob will be shrouded again in a "subjective veil of secrecy." The coordination of their further actions is "controlled" only by the institutional framework of the community (i.e., by the rule that Bob does not steal something from Alice after the exchange).

But we need to explain a shared, lasting, and mutual standard, or some criteria, which I and anyone else express in the same way. A standard that allows mutual comparison, even when it is still true that, from a subjective point of Lachmann's view, we can interpret the information which will be understood, regardless of the way it is presented. We will not stop someone from interpreting this or that as he/she wants. In terms of the coordination of individuals, we just want to explain that if a person wishes to compare with another, then this kind of standard will allow him to proceed with the comparison. The exchange, which is realized and at the same time finished here and now, cannot be applied to the explanation of the intersubjective economic concept of success/error. In the *economic* coordination of plans, i.e., within the coordination of economic intentions and ideas toward the future, based on the exchange here and now, the structure of the duration of the interaction in time would be absent, which would cause the non-existence of standard and criteria. The exchange here and now does not allow much room for the detection of the criteria of an intersubjective error. To imply the exchange here and now, we would be able to assess the error only from the subjective level of two people and the implication that if two people enter the exchange, it is advantageous for them both, which further implies that ex ante, they both assumed that the resulting state of their portfolios would much better meet their expectations than if they had not entered the exchange.

But how to derive a comparable criteria of intersubjective success/error from our intersubjective activities? Basically, we need some kind of apparatus for the comparison of knowledge concerning what the other one wants. We already know that it is the knowledge of Alice and Bob within the exchange here and now which provides information about their success/error activity. We know that it is not possible to derive any standardized economic criteria from this. Yet, we also have another type of exchange—the exchange over time. It provides us with the needed time structure. The exchange over time unveils plans of two or more individuals for longer periods of time and provides us with the duration of that plan. There are plans concerning the coordination of individual activities which are of main interest to us. It is, therefore, appropriate to search for criteria. But where exactly? I think the best possible area is a differentiation between knowledge which brings us a better or worse state of affairs; meaning that based on some specific criteria, humans have to recognize which knowledge brings them a higher to lower satisfaction of needs and a better diversification of their portfolio. Although an exchange here and now causes a higher relative rate of portfolio diversification than an individual human activity, it still causes a lower relative rate of portfolio diversification than debt exchange. I see three basic reasons. First, in the case of a debt exchange, the parallel activity of the creditor can also take place, i.e., the creditor continues to carry out his activities as before. Second, the debtor can implement his project which would not have arisen without the creditor's contribution, i.e., the debtor would only have to deal with his original activity, which he considers to be less productive. Otherwise, he would not have been interested in resources from the creditor to alternate his action. Third, debt exchange enables more flexibility; With debt exchange, any plan can be changed or adjusted to new conditions later in time. For these reasons, the potential diversification of the portfolio is highest in debt exchange; lower in the exchange here and now, and lowest in individual human activity. In principle, the spread between a potential portfolio and a desired one will narrow through exchange, but more through the exchange over time. Here lies the reason for the expansion of exchange activities in general.

In other words, the debt exchange not only provides us with a time structure for the creation of lasting and intersubjective criteria with higher possibilities to meet a higher combination of needs, but it also makes it possible to differentiate between knowledge connected with higher compared to lower spreads of portfolios in order to meet someone's needs. We are faced with three important coordinates connected with the debt exchange. It is a phenomenon of interest and time preference connected with the portfolios of savers (expressed in the maturity of the debt) and the normative conditions of the debt exchange, such as the question of the collateral, "if – so" principle (meaning if the promise is not fulfilled later in time, the debtor must do this or that instead of the promise) and any other legal conditions connected with the relationship between creditor and debtor. All agreements to do with these problems of debt exchange have an impact on the definition of the intersubjective standard. Basically, these are ex ante and ex post criteria we use to assess successful or erroneous knowledge that is transformed into the actions of individuals.

In current practice, the standard is expressed in money or currencies. Money or currencies are our intersubjective tools that we use to decide which intersubjective economic activity is more productive than any other. More precisely, it is a communication tool for assessing the knowledge of someone who produces a product for someone else. However, we have gone too far with the description of the characteristics of the standard. We have to realize a more general description, which will be valid both outside the monetary economy, and subsequently, also inside the monetary economy. The description of the origin of this standard (in general terms, not necessarily in monetary terms) is based on the principle of the creditor's agreement with the debtor, i.e., based on the principle of the debt exchange. As we will show below, a debt agreement can also have an implicit character; it need not be a conscious act of the agreement. At the same time, the agreement is not a standard per se; it is only an activity on the backroad of it, from which a standard can be created. The debt that arose at time t must be eliminated later by the debtor at the time $(t + 1)$ in the repayment required by the creditor at time t. To eliminate his obligation, the debtor must carry out an economic activity until time $t + 1$, which will ensure the creditor's request, e.g., in the form of the good M (it is not necessarily money, however, I call it "M" because it is an act of spontaneity that has caused these "Ms"—whatever they are,—to become money at the end of the process). The agreement creates an abstract, intersubjectively transferable, tangible and in a time-applicable concept of the commitment/obligation expressed in commodity M. Thus, man creates a time-lasting preconception in the mind in the form of a commitment from time t to time $t + 1$; this mutually expresses two subjective expectations about some future state of the portfolios of at least two people.[91] The non-fulfillment of the obligation can be considered an intersubjective error and, conversely, its fulfillment can be considered an intersubjectively perceived success. From the point of view of the current perception of the situation with money, the above-mentioned is the meta-principle of the intersubjective success/error.

The reader should not get the impression that we have defined the intersubjective economic success/error in a normative way in terms of the legal fulfillment/non-fulfillment of the debt exchange. The normative nature of the fulfillment of an obligation implicitly includes the economic nature of the fulfillment of the obligation. The economic nature of intersubjective success/error is, of course, expressed by the repayment of what the creditor asked (today principal and interest).[92] But what does the outcome of the exchange tell us from an economic point of view? A debt agreement involves the interconnection of two ongoing plans of two individuals. The commitment agreement establishes a binary standard on the basis of which both the debtor and the creditor can determine the success/failure of their activities over time. This depends on the fulfillment/non-fulfillment of the obligation later

[91] Based on the obligation expressed in M, it is possible to derive the prices of other goods, which will be expressed in M over time (from time t to time $t + 1$), when the debtor will demand good M for the results of his activity X, which must, of course, be demanded by other members of an economic community. The debtor must either find, produce or exchange for the results of his activity what the creditor requires at time $t + 1$ between time t and $t + 1$. All three activities economically initiate the use of M, i.e., generate an exchange demand for the good M, albeit to varying degrees. The first two options initiate the exchange demand M only on the site of the debtor—he has to return M so he must either find it or directly produce it. In this mutual intersubjective context (creditor–debtor), the good M acquires an exchange calculation status only in terms of the internal part of the portfolio that the debtor has to sacrifice (the internal costs) to find or produce some unit M, which he has to return later in time. However, the real motivation comes when exchanging the results of the debtor's activities for M, when the exchange demand for M is also perceived by other members of the community. The debtor then produces some goods, which he exchanges with other community members for the good M, which he has to return to the creditor later. In this way, the price of the M expressed in other goods is created, which leads to a price level in M, as well as a price spread—the demand and supply price of the M against other goods over time.

[92] In the initial stages of the development of the standard, interest was composed of debt exchange only implicitly in the form of a natural interest spread. Our predecessors were able to discover interest rate only after they were able to differentiate (identify) the monetary principal and the monetary interest rate, for which they first needed to identify the concept of money. See Pošvanc (2021) for more details.

in time and the evaluation of whether the result of the fulfillment/non-fulfillment of the obligation is perceived as a state of the portfolio that satisfies more or less the needs of the creditor/debtor. Based on this agreement, two people calculate—and assess economic activity over time. The calculation process takes place within the evaluation of the portfolio concerning the good, M; the creditor evaluates the enrichment of the future portfolio by M for the fulfillment of his debt to the debtor in the present, and the debtor evaluates the possibility of providing M in the future and the enrichment of his current portfolio by the repayment provided by the creditor.

The standard is "proposed" in this respect by the creditor; this is because it is the creditor who owns already what a debtor seeks. The fulfillment of the obligation means delivering the good M by the debtor. A creditor should be satisfied if his portfolio at time $t + 1$ is enriched by M (the obligation is fulfilled) and the enriched portfolio satisfies his needs, as expected, in terms of greater portfolio diversification, compared to the previous state before he entered into an exchange at time t. It should be noted that the creditor continues to carry out their own economic activity, which he expects to bring him a portfolio composition that will satisfy his needs more than any other economic activity. However, he simultaneously decided to activate some of his savings, which would be not used. He was able to demonstrate the postponement of satisfaction with regard to some of his needs since his portfolio was depleted by the goods which were provided to the debtor at time t. The fact that the creditor gave up some savings in favor of the debtor at time t implies that the impoverishment of his portfolio at time t did not jeopardize the satisfaction of his needs over time. If some of his needs were not satisfied, he would be unable to provide part of his savings to the debtor. We can also say that his time preference in terms of meeting his needs through his portfolio, allows him to provide resources to the debtor for the possibility of enriching his portfolio by M later at time $t + 1$. This implies that the delivery of good M at time $t + 1$ meets the expectation of a higher portfolio diversification.

It is possible to see that the intersubjective character of success/error is influenced by the ability/inability of the entrepreneur (the debtor) to build/not build such capital structures which enable/do not enable the production of products whose combination of features enable/do not enable the optimal combination of needs on the part of customers. The information on subjective plans, expectations, and a combination of needs is transformed into intersubjective information about the success/error of debt exchange. The information has a time-invariant-formal character that is accessible by any third party interested in the particular debt exchange and who has the ability to include the concrete character of the information into his/her own plan. This means that if any third party wants to buy the claim or wants to clear his claim/obligation to this exchange, this intersubjective information can be grasped in time and dealt with. The time-invariant-formal character of the information is based on the consideration of spreads between actual, potential, and desired portfolios. It follows that the provided criteria of debt exchange enable interpersonal coordination based on the subjective consideration of spreads among the portfolios of the individuals concerned. It is the formal structure of the information which is the same, meaning here that the information is created via the interaction of individuals, it lasts in time, it is concerned by depressing spreads of individuals who are interested in the information among their actual, potential and desired portfolios, it has its reflection in reality in the form of some goods, it is governed by some rules of a community; it acquires its character empirically as a result of these last two conditions. Therefore, it enables coordination even though the specific content of the information is different over time; meaning here, any production process from simple pencils to complicated rockets.

The intersubjective error/success standard actually provides us with mutually tangible criteria. At the same time, the standard does not guarantee coordination itself. It is a prerequisite for some coordination, and coordination is only possible if the information needed to coordinate individuals changes from subjectively perceived information to intersubjectively comprehensible information. The structure of given intersubjective information actually deals with the success/error of knowledge in terms of how to satisfy the needs of other people. It is a matter of knowing how to use certain existing resources (owned by the creditor) in order for it to be used in a capital structure or plan created by a debtor, which has a period of existence, and which results in a product that satisfies/does not satisfy the needs of others. The morphology of these relations, their interconnection across economic communities, i.e., their connection with other structures, is different in their content, while they may follow each other up or be unrelated, forms the basis of an intersubjective robust thought structure suitable for the subsequent differentiation of what kind of knowledge is (relatively) successful and what kind of knowledge is (relatively) unsuccessful.[93]

The question may arise whether, from a subjective point of view, the creditor will be satisfied with the new composition of a given portfolio; meaning here, an ex post evaluation and what kind of information does this bring? From a subjective point of view, after the time $t + 1$, once the exchange is closed, any creditor or debtor may ultimately evaluate the exchange as his subjective error or success. The subjective aspects of the success/error don't disappear, nor does the Lachman ultra-subjective possibility of any assessment of a given interaction. This

[93]How to imagine such a thought structure—is it intersubjective in nature? The story of our son can serve as an example. When he was born, he was gifted with a plush dog named "Avor" from a friend. When he was 1.5 years old, we were on a hiking trip and we lost "Avor." My girlfriend was crying because "Avor" had been with us for a year and a half. As a result, we bought the same new "Avor" so that my son would not be sad and we bought two of them; so as not to have identical problems in the future. My son did not notice that he had a new "Avor," but he noticed that they were two of them. A big surprise—how was this possible? They were similar, (the same toy), but they were still sewn a little differently. The result was that "Avor" has a brother. Without a new name; after all, the toys were similar. We have been with "Avor" and "his brother" for three years. My son takes care of them as he "feeds" them, puts them in pajamas, communicates with them and we live this story with him. What are we looking at? At the family intersubjectively created thought structure. We also transferred the structure to the grandparents; our close friends know the story. The thought structure exists, is the subject of conversations, is based on the differentiation of empirical reality (at least with regard to different toys), the given structure lasts—my son is still interested in the toys, and even if he stops as he gets older, the story will probably remain in our memories.

This is, of course, a different shared thought structure compared to the intersubjective economic success/error standard. The standard has a society-wide character, perceived by foreign people between each other. However, the important point in the example is that it is the morphology of relationships of the different parts of reality, the time sequence of their connection and duration, our motivations and the motivations of our son, the transfer of information (even outside the family), which stands behind the existence of the thought structure. Of course, no one other than us is interested in its further transmission and use. However, in principle, I think that the creation of our family structure and society based intersubjective structures is identical. The difference in the case of society-wide standard structures is, of course, the above-mentioned degree of complexity, the morphology of mutual relations, the duration of structures, and the various layers of which it consists, in so far as economic, legal, and as well as social circumstances are concerned.

is already the domain of the subjective perception of the given situation and thus the domain of the subjective success/error evaluation. The subjective perspective of the outcome of debt exchange, whether considered a success or error, does not have any impact on the character of the intersubjective consideration of success/error. The realization of the process of the debt exchange itself creates criteria for the intersubjective economic consideration of the activity. Due to the fact that the debt exchange has a time-invariant-formal character, it is possible, essentially, for anyone to evaluate its outcome—whether the debtor was successful with regard to his obligation or not. Both intersubjective outcomes, either success or error, create information that can be considered by others. All outcomes considered from subjective and intersubjective perspective transform important information about the success/error of created capital structures that would not be created without the debt exchange, or we can say without a decision by both creditor and debtor. It follows that the outcome of this activity can be considered ex post from the subjective and intersubjective perspective. The outcome could have these possibilities from the point of view of the creditor as well as the debtor:

(a) subjective success and intersubjective success,
(b) subjective error, and intersubjective error,
(c) subjective error and intersubjective success,
(d) subjective success and intersubjective error.

If we look at the outcome from the point of view of the creditor, the subjective success and the intersubjective success means that the creditor evaluates the diversification of his portfolio as successful because the debtor fulfilled the agreement—he has delivered promised goods and he is better off. The subjective error and intersubjective error mean that the creditor is not satisfied with the diversification of the portfolio because the debtor did not fulfill the agreement. However, we have two other options. The subjective error and the intersubjective success mean that the debtor fulfilled his agreement, but the creditor is not subjectively satisfied with the range of diversification ex post. The last possibility is that subjective success and intersubjective error means that the debtor was not able to deliver the promised goods; however, for some subjective reason, the creditor is satisfied with the portfolio composition ex post.[94] The same is true vice versa, from the point of view of the debtor.

It should be obvious that due to the subjective part of the ex post evaluation of the activity, the intersubjective character of the evaluation of the outcome could relatively affect the subjective character of the rate of success/error. The creditor could speculate ex post about a different allocation of resources which would provide a better diversification of his portfolio. The debtor could consider the outcome as very successful if the rate of his profit (after the repayment of obligation) is more than expected, or it could be only satisfactory, as expected; however, the success could also be anything in excess of the repayment of the obligation to the creditor, even though the expected outcome was different. Due to the time element, it should also be clear that the intersubjective concept of error has a very flexible character. It could be that the debt conditions are renegotiated during the duration of the debt exchange. The voluntary acceptance of some degree of error by the creditor toward the debtor could lead to the renegotiation of the debt conditions; after renegotiation, the project can be considered successful. Another possibility is writing off the debt in order to use collateral from the debtor, which eliminates the losses of the creditor, or the possible sale of assets that were the subject of the project financed by the debt. In this way, it is also possible to eliminate a certain degree of intersubjectively generated economic errors. The division of the problem of success/error with reference to its subjective and intersubjective character enables us to see the criteria which influence the coordination of economic agents more clearly.

What is important to remember about the intersubjective nature of economic success/error information is that it is created and spread only

---

[94]Although this last option seems unlikely, it can occur. It may happen that later in time e.g. the creditor evaluates that even if he got rid of a goods in the past and the debtor eventually gave him nothing (the debt exchange went bankrupt), it is still better than if he kept the good and the debtor returned to him what he had promised; in this case, from the creditor's point of view, these may be goods which, at both times t and $t + 1$, would have to be disposed of in certain circumstances in order to satisfy more of his needs—e.g. if he found out that at time t the good he gave to the debtor did not benefit his health and also at time $t + 1$ the good that should have been obtained from the debtor would also not benefit his health.

by those who directly participate. They, by their mutual actions, create a given benchmark. Others, such as hermits or those who are not interested in participating in the activities of an economic community, can either voluntarily adopt the standard or ignore it. If they come into contact with the standard (they observe what others are doing) but avoid explicit participation in the activities of the economic community, they should at least understand it. This means that they should know what it means to use a given standard over time. It follows, given the intersubjective nature of a given standard, that Hülsmann's individual assessment of whether or not one decides to use and participate in a given intersubjective standard of success/error, still applies to some extent. However, the differing view from Hülsmann's (2000) is that this standard is recognized as intersubjective in nature and thus provides criteria for the economic assessment of interpersonal activity. The intersubjective and subjective concept of error implies that there is a subjective and an intersubjective concept of profit/loss and costs which must also be described. We will get to this subject as soon as we briefly outline how this model binary standard of success/error could become the n –nary standard of the economic community, i.e., the standard of monetary calculation.

2.3.5.5 The Intersubjective Nature of Economic Success/Error: The Development, an Extension of the Economic Calculation Standard and Its Unification into the Money Format

The above description of the characteristics of the accounting calculation standard is a model one. We have described the characteristics of the structure of a given standard between at least two individuals. The model description implies an agreement between two (and more) people. However, this description is not suitable for describing the origin of the standard. The standard was not created in the mode of one conscious individual versus another conscious individual, meaning here it is not an agreement per se, a conscious thought structure of the standard. The standard was created spontaneously in the mode: a community of prehistoric individuals with a vague ego—the intuitive activities of these group members—the spontaneous creation of the standard—the differentiation of the standard and the higher degree of Ego differentiation—the discovery of the use of the standard by individuals as it was given to them. We can also imagine this process as if we had N-times binary debt exchanges (which create a structural base for the standard) among many members of some economic community which step by step, coincide into the realisation of the debt exchange in one common standard of one good M (meaning here money) which is subsequently used to compare binary intersubjective economic plans (or representations of successful or erroneous economic knowledge) of members of this economic community. The reason for this spontaneous coincidence, based on Hayek–Pavlik's description of evolutionary theory, should be given as a higher complexity of the problem our predecessors faced, meaning here e.g., the higher the number of exchanges in the community, the higher the pressure to clear the debt, stretching the time of exchanges, their higher level of complexity, or their expression in a higher number of goods, creating pressure to solve the problems through a higher degree of abstraction. The implementation of the exchanges creates a situation that the community solves as a problem. This creates pressure to express the debt exchange in some unified medium of exchange M (money) or by several parallel goods M. This implies that the expansion of the standard is proportional to the importance of debt exchanges in a given economic community. Their expansion and repetition create a mutually assessed economic-legal concept of success/error of two or more men—an economic calculation in money terms.[95]

Before describing the given conjunctural history, it is useful to add a note here. For the last hundred (plus) years, the description of economic calculation (meaning here our standard) has been considered in the tradition of the Austrian School of Economics, based on the work of Mises (1920, 1953), where Mises presents his concept of regression theorem and his theory of economic calculation. The problem with Mises' interpretation of these phenomena is, in short, that Mises derives

[95]The mass participation of human subjects that creates the defined intersubjective concept of success/error takes place at the institutional level today when specialized entrepreneurs—banks—mediate the demand/supply for savings and mediate the discovery process of the nominal money interest rate.

future-oriented action from a particular state in the past; in my opinion, this is a methodological error. And although he himself avoids determinism[96] (see e.g., Mises 1957, pp. 73–94) the influence of the past in its concrete form on the emergence of phenomena such as economic calculation or money, is indisputable and we can say the influence has an important place in his system (see more details in Pošvanc 2019b). In Mises's work, therefore, we see that the standard of economic calculation can be imagined primarily in monetary units, and the explanation of the calculation in the nonmonetary world is circumvented by the statement that it is a simple *in kind* calculation; likewise, the derivation of the calculation from the past price (not only the monetary price) also leads to an infinite regression, which on the one hand does not allow for an explanation of the beginning of any calculation and on the other hand is in direct conflict with the fact that the action is focused on the future and the future economic context, while the past as well as the present, depicted in objectively incurred prices is forever, in the Shakleian sense, lost (for a detailed critique, see Pošvanc 2019a). The regression theorem has identical problems, where Mises also derives the purchasing power of money from the past industrial price of a commodity (e.g., gold), which sometime in the past began to function as money. It means that the last industrial price of a commodity (e.g., gold) was supposed to serve the function of deriving the purchasing power of money. However, the regression theorem does not explain how the subjective attribution of the so-called exchange value of an industrial commodity, from which its marketability is derived, becomes the general societal state of money's objective exchange value, on which the phenomenon of moneyness of the commodity depends; it is a state of affairs in which the subjective and objective attributions of the exchange value of a commodity inevitably coincides and the de novo-money-phenomenon arises (see detailed critique in Pošvanc 2020c). Although

[96]It is the chapter of *Determinism and Materialism,* in which Mises explains the problems of determinism and the free will doctrine; he referred to his position as *activistic determinism* (Mises 1957, pp 177–183). Mises is not a pure determinist; however, his suggested solutions are based on the influence of a particular past on our decisions. I consider this a methodological mistake.

Hayek (1937, 1945) begins to direct the problem of economic calculation to the problem of knowledge, it must be stated that his solutions or considerations still remain in the context of Mises's work and his conclusions about the monetary nature of calculation and the emergence of money. This is regardless of the fact that Hayek begins to describe the problem of social ordering after 1937 and created his system of the cultural-evolutionary origin of normative rules that allow successive generations of people to use such evolutionary knowledge for the improved possibilities of their economic coordination. On the one hand, we have a Misesian a priori approach within the theory with its own problems and which does not solve the description of these phenomena evolutionarily. On the other hand, we have Hayek's approach, in which we already know that, according to Pavlík (2004, pp. 21–22, see also the quotation on page 50), Hayek places too much emphasis on the unconscious nature of norms (in the broadest sense of the term) which allows for interpersonal coordination. It seems to me, therefore, that the Hayek–Pavlík's evolutionary apriorism (which is some kind of combination of apriorism and evolutionism) in combination with the presented modification of the theory of subjective value makes it possible to eliminate these problems in order to explain the dawn of moneyness and the money-calculation phenomenon.

The principle of individual calculation outside the monetary economy can be explained through the concept of portfolio, where so-called *in kind* calculation takes place in two modes: (a) a comparison of two portfolios before and after an economic activity in terms of a higher compared to a lower satisfaction of needs by the portfolios in question, and (b) a representation of the cardinal calculation that appears as the background to this assessment in terms of the marginal impoverishment of the portfolio by some unit of goods and the marginal enrichment of the portfolio by some acquired unit of goods. It is a time-invariant universal principle, a mental structure that is used both in the *in kind* calculation and in the monetary calculation. In terms of the terminology of Hayek–Pavlík's description of evolutionary apriorism, the structure is the above-mentioned "germ cell". And what we need to explain, in principle, is how this individual, albeit universal, structure for everyone evolves into a mutually shared unit of account or an accounting standard for everything. As we have shown above, this is also related to the problem of detecting economic success and error. The structure brings information to a person, when this person makes a mistake in time and when and on the basis of which he can learn; in principle, a person tries to compose the most suitable composition of his portfolio from his subjective point of view, which aims to satisfy a complex range of subjective needs. At the inter-individual level, however, we need to assess one's knowledge of how one can meet the needs of others. Therefore, the universal principle of economic calculation and its superstructure in the form of monetary calculation is related to the universal principle of the individual detection of success/error and the inter-individual assessment of success/error of people who satisfy each other's needs by virtue of their own activities. These two areas need to be linked, and at the same time, it is necessary to show how we gradually move from the individual level of calculation to the inter-individual social level of the general standard and thus create a standard for assessing inter-individual knowledge with regard to meeting the needs of others. And that is exactly why we need to use Hayek–Pavlík's description of evolutionary apriorism, which we will apply to this problem.

We have described above a suitable concept in the form of debt exchange, the nature of which makes it possible to provide a suitable solution to the presented problem here. It is apparent that intersubjective information about the satisfaction of the needs of the other one in the exchange here and now will arise and disappear at the time the exchange took place. It is a characteristic of debt exchange that lasts in time that is a more suitable candidate for describing the emergence of an interpersonal standard for assessing entrepreneurship success and error. The structure of the agreement between the creditor and the debtor has both normative and economic characteristics. In principle, Hayek's program after 1937 focuses on the development of broader normative characteristics of the functioning of the social order. However, it is clear that there is a second (teleological) side of the coordination problem. Economically, we look at decisions about the allocation of existing economic resources in a broad sense (land, labor, and capital) within some production structures (economic plans), which should result in a product that satisfies the needs of either the borrower or other people. Against the background of debt exchange, two new phenomena are gradually emerging—time preferences and interest rate. Time preferences associated with the impoverishment of a portfolio by a good devoted to the debtor for some time and delaying the satisfaction of the current needs of the creditor and a natural interest phenomenon that takes into account the decision of the creditor and the debtor (as we already know, an interest is an intersubjective phenomenon) on the economic conditions of debt repayment.[97]

The mutual interconnections and compositions of debt exchanges within an economic community gradually create a new morphological structure of economic interconnections in a given community and thus increases the complexity of the problem facing the members of the community. The new structure of ties creates, among other things, new stimuli and phenomena. Individuals within the community see the possibilities of clearing debt, the time characteristics of debt, the normative conditions of debt, the time preferences, but also results in higher satisfaction of their needs. This additionally increases the complexity of the problem, which, if it begins to go beyond some border which, given the vaguely conscious Ego of our predecessors, may not be even particularly significant, puts pressure on the problem to be simplified. This comes in the form of a spontaneous inclination to one or even a few commodity/ties in which the morphology of the relationships is clearer, simpler, and more understandable to our predecessors. The inclination toward one commodity, which has certainly already been used in the given relations and which just leads to the given simplification, is not caused consciously. On the contrary, it is a spontaneous discovery that a durable, divisible and well-usable commodity that had already been used only in particular exchanges has the appropriate characteristics to express the morphology of the relationship, first in a small way and, if it is a suitable commodity, then in the wider community context. The following standardization of the given exchanges (e.g., by

[97] See section "2.3.2 Interest – an intersubjective tool for decision-making towards the future" for the description of the natural interest phenomenon.

the rules of the community), their successive re-expression in the particular commodity, subsequently makes it possible to explicitly distinguish between principal and interest, whereby interest becomes a visible monetary phenomenon of the debt exchange. The debt exchange became a more standardized tool for decisions over time and people discovered a very important and explicit ex ante/ex post criterion for debt exchange–monetary interest. The repetition and even expansion of the number of debt exchanges, expressed in one or more money commodities, made it possible to compare economic activities that represent knowledge about the intensity and efficiency of meeting others' needs for money. It is as if a new *monetary-level* of interactions was created per se over the layer of nonmonetary-goods interactions. It was not possible to decompose this new phenomenon (a new layer) into its parts anymore, it simply started its own "life." However, in order for this to be an evolutionary concept, we have to describe the gradual emergence of the standard (monetary calculation); the concept must also be explainable in a mode of unconsciousness. We should describe the process from the simple to the more complicated or from the abstract to the concrete, i.e., we have to use the concept of the debt exchange as the formula of a "germ cell". As Graeber (2011) shows, the use of debt is quite rational since members of the group know each other, the group follows specific rules, and there is no extensive information asymmetry which results in the problem of obligations.

Explaining the origin of the given standard requires, in our case, the presumption of the existence of a prehistoric community. This is a rational assumption. The community implies the following rules; we already know that rules or norms do not necessarily have to be followed in the conscious mode, i.e., consciously formulated. The norm is part of any societal behavior otherwise it is not possible to describe a society, i.e., some small clan or group of prehistoric men. This norm is part of the instinctive behavior of any prehistoric group or, as Lewis (2017) explains, it is a new spontaneously aroused feature of the new ontological entity, for example, a small community or group of prehistoric men. The norms we deal with are so-called norms of distributive justice. We have to show how it is possible to connect the concept of the debt exchange within the concept of the norms of distributive justice which prehistoric groups followed. Pavlík (1999) writes about the norms of distributive justice as follows:

> *The best definition of distributive justice can be found in Aristotle's work Nicomachean Ethics: in which justice is defined as a state of affairs when the proportion between the unequal merits of various persons is in correspondence with the proportion between unequal quantities of things (goods, money, honours, military distinctions or even social status) which those persons gain as rewards for their meritorious activities in favour of the society as a whole; similarly the proportion between punishments of various persons must correspond to the proportion between their crimes concerning the degree of their detrimental influence on the society as a whole. Distributive justice in this meaning, however, is originally applied to small social group performing collective or conjoint actions and publicly distributing the (commonly owned) goods resulting from a joint effort. The principle of distributive justice presupposes that the contribution of each individual to the common benefit (his merit) can be immediately seen and compared with the contribution of other individuals; the immediate visibility here means that in principle each individual can see and compare the merits of his neighbours. This in turn presupposes that all acting individuals share the same aim because the comparison of various individuals' contributions is possible only in relation to that common aim: these contributions are evaluated as more or less effective means for fulfilling the aim. On the other hand, the inequality of individual contributions presupposes a kind of division of labour, but this division concerns only the inevitably various character of various individuals' activities as oriented to the same aim; division of labour exists here only in the frame of conjoint action. The visible basis for the comparison of various contributions of individual persons is here the various degree of physical effort as applied by various persons.*

We need not imagine the debt within the prehistoric community in any sophisticated way. That is not the point. What is important to imagine are very primitive and very elementary activities which have some temporal character, and which are vaguely "considered" by members of that community. If the "*principle of distributive justice presupposes that the contribution of each individual to the common benefit (his merit) can be immediately seen and compared with the contribution of other individuals,*" it is not very difficult to visualize the principle in some extended time continuum. If so, it is not very difficult to claim that the contribution of each individual of the group was compared over time or in different time segments connected with different activities of the group, e.g., hunting, the collection of fruits, or fight and so on. This helps explain the creation of basic sedimentary thinking and primitive language structures[98] with regard to the concept of debt exchange; meaning the distributive justice among members of a group in time, which emerged circumstantially with these activities. We can clearly see the concept of obligation, the postponement of time preferences, e.g., in hunters who were able to use collected fruits and later on, provide meat to collectors. It is possible to speculate that we can see a very primitive character of natural interest spreading. It is also possible to speculate that if members of the community did not submit to the norms of the group they were probably persecuted. The further development of the concept is the question of the higher consciousness of men, with opportunities to make more complicated exchanges based on the debt principle within the group; this could have been combined with some barter exchanges within the groups but also with other groups of similar humanoids. The concept of normative justice over time *facilitated* many concrete forms of debt exchanges within the primitive groups which reached certain limits of implementation. This occurred because of the increasing complexity of these activities, such as the additional use of time, utilizing too many goods as the objects of social justice, and the potential to clear debts within the community, and so on. These circumstances forced the mind to make things simpler and led from n-numerous binary standards (debt exchanges with more goods[99]) to the more abstract standards. The process of standardization could have had many empirical forms from

[98]These language structures which enable thinking needn't have first been spoken, in a similar way to that which as we do today. It is possible to speculate about some combination of sound and sign with regard to primitive language gestures and expressions.

[99]As Szabo (2002) points out, it is already 500 goods which cause that member of the community to face the possibility of 25,000 prices (500^2) if they are the object of the exchange. It follows in the context of our speculations that it is not necessarily a question of too many goods, the potential problems of chaos are already caused by a few goods used as the object of the debt exchange. However, these only highlight the tension of only using a few commodities within debt exchanges, while the empirical decision for the use of certain particular commodities could also be motivated by other empirical, religious, societal, or cultural contexts.

political (designated centrally by some chiefs) to religious or cultural characteristics.[100] The limits of concreteness of too many debt exchanges produced some chaos or problems with the orientation of prehistoric men. The limits were "crossed" by certain simpler but more abstract methods of doing these activities. The new standards were implemented and created by the first commodity—money. These standards, which of course compete with each other, provided new economic information to our predecessors. This meant the provision of a more precise expression of intersubjective success/error criteria which ensured that they would be more interested in narrow spreads for their portfolios. The best possible money commodities were able to reflect the natural interest and ensure the mediation of debt exchange, not only within communities, but also with other communities "won" as commodity money.

From an empirical point of view, the process could be explained as follows. First primitive groups used only the norms of distributive justice over time. We are not able to provide any empirical evidence for this statement. However, rising consciousness forced our predecessors to face more complicated economic activities within the group. They were pushed to record debt. The probable tool used within the context of certain primitive legal systems or in a certain group or groups within a few extensive areas were, so-called, tally sticks. The tally sticks represented some commodities—these were very primitive money standards. The intensification of economic relations created new problems connected especially to the limitations of primitive legal systems used for debt recovery, in particular, the use and limitation of tally sticks, the fact of their limiting durability, the necessity of their legal recognition beyond particular groups, the possible existence of asymmetric information among groups. There were also needs that were connected with the more precise verbalization of given phenomena with regard to debt exchange such as time preferences, interest and we cannot forget the legal conditions of the debt, influenced by cultural, societal, and religious circumstances. All these circumstances led our predecessors to solve these problems with full commodity money standards. It has to be stressed that

[100]An interesting description of some empirical examples to do with what kinds of goods were used as money commodity goods, is given in Einzig (2014).

this process did not stop here as we know professional banking activities started to emerge and replaced the commodity standards with fiduciary media and currency standards.

The transition from the expression of debt in a small community governed by its rules, to the general expression of debt in commodity money, and at the same time the emergence of a price system in a given commodity had already been influenced by the development of the division of labor and trade. Borrowers inquiring about a money-commodity for a creditor who exchanged their products for a given commodity caused higher and higher monetary demand for the commodity; this gradually expanded into the development of inter-communal trade. Only the higher degree of economic cooperation and interconnectedness of individual communities allowed more intensive use of debt exchange, which had already been standardized against the background of legal systems and spread through specialized entrepreneurs—bankers. This type of institutionalized business banking activity focusing on discovering the level of interest rates, the standardization of debt exchange conditions and the professional creation of the economic standard of calculation, enabled the rise of the modern currency monetary standard. It is an intersubjective standard in which we today express the success and error of our intersubjectively assessed economic activity, in the products of banks—in currencies.

While commodity money was used for individual debt intermediation, currencies are a product of banking activity—institutional entrepreneurs in the field of debt intermediation. Banks issue currency = immediately payable liability = zero-maturity debt which is the expression of what banks have on their assets. In this respect, banking activity is an extension, a new layer of relations over commodity money in the form of debt clearing, debt expressed in currencies over time, and the clearing activities between debtors and creditors. Banking activity is, in principle, the business activity of debt relationship management on a societal scale, a great coordination mechanism of our economic plans, expectations, and intentions. Banking activity subsequently creates a monetary (intersubjective) standard in which users of the currency (either voluntarily or involuntarily, due to possible political influence of the standard) use to compare their economic activities with each other, but also to compare their economic activities over time (for a detailed description, see Pošvanc 2021). The success/failure of a banking activity then determines the possible degree of accuracy in comparing the economic activities of individuals using the banking currency standard. It has to be stressed that the currency economic standard is a flow. It is constantly being created as a result of the economic activities of agents. The standard manifests itself in various rules of debt creation, banking activity rules or ways of organizing banking activity, which may have significant political influence today (fiat money or fiat banking); however, it may be based on a higher degree of market and voluntary relations (the so-called free banking theory). In this way, a social benchmark is created for the mutual comparison of the economic activity of individuals. Although this standard, as a benchmark, may change over time in specific details, it is the same in principle. Comparison over time is therefore possible even if the specific contexts of its determination are changed. This does not mean that the later (and/or politically determined) rules for creating this standard are better discovered over time than those previously used over time, and vice versa. Discovering the nature of this standard is also subject to potential adjustments and the elimination of errors over time in this area as well. It is also true that the standard is influenced over time by political decisions and its specific form is, to some extent, politically determined and is not found in the competitive process of bank interaction.[101]

2.3.6 Subjective Profit/Loss Versus Intersubjective Profit/Loss

From the economic viewpoint of decision-making and the assessment of success and error, we look at the concept of success and error from several points of view—technical, subjective, and intersubjective. The ultimate decision-maker is always an individual. However, due to the technical and intersubjective concept of success/error, we are able to

[101] However, we will discuss this in greater detail in another work aimed at describing the theory of capital and the cycle, where we describe in more detail the functioning of the standard and its impact on emerging capital structures, as well as its negative—political—influences leading to unnatural economic cycles.

understand each other; due to the formal-logical character of the concept of success/error, we can also understand some subjective parts of the concept. The economic error is always judged from a subjective point of view—it is judged by a person but based on technical objective, individually subjective and also on the basis of intersubjective criteria. All these criteria enable people to evaluate success/error in terms of spreads between Pc – Pp – Pd; this allows not only differentiation between successful and erroneous activity, but also the identification of the concept of profit and loss and the related nature of costs which have a subjective and an intersubjective character. This is because the subjective and intersubjective perception of success/error implies a subjective and intersubjective perception of profit/loss and cost. Before we show the intersubjective nature of profit/loss and costs, we will again present the views of some authors on the issue of profit and what we can consider to be costs. Following this, we will present our view. As with the success/error concept, we will use the modified theory of subjective value.

We examine the concept by asking the question, which was asked so many times before: "*why does competitive business activity not eliminate the existence of profit.*" The question, why profit exists at all, is solved by Knight, Mises, or other authors who state that profit exists in connection with the uncertainty we face toward the future. Those who know better how the future will develop (in the Mises system, for example, through *verstehen*) are better equipped and make a profit and vice versa. It seems that it is really the existence of uncertainty that implies the existence of profit. As we have shown above, the uncertainty is related to the problem of *case probability*, i.e., estimating the preferences of others. The attentive reader may again notice that the Knight or Mises's system implicitly assumes the intersubjective nature of profit. But let's take a closer look at some claims about the profit. According to Mises, the profit is derived from the action and is subjective in nature; Mises (1998, pp. 286–287) writes:

> *Profit, in a broader sense, is the gain derived from action; it is the increase in satisfaction (decrease in uneasiness) brought about; it is the difference between*

the higher value attached to the result attained and the lower value attached to the sacrifices made for its attainment; it, in other words, yield minus costs.

He also writes:

…

We cannot even think of a state of affairs in which people act without the intention of attaining psychic profit and in which their actions result neither in psychic profit nor in psychic loss. < If an action neither improves nor impairs the state of satisfaction, it still involves a psychic loss because of the uselessness of the expended psychic effort. The individual concerned would have been better off if he had inertly enjoyed life > In the imaginary construction of an evenly rotating economy there are neither money profits nor money losses. But every individual derives a psychic profit from his actions, or else he would not act at all.

It follows, from the above, that profit and loss are subjective phenomena, the origin of which is, as Mises further argues, the psychological perception of the outcome of an action. At the individual level, we should simply know whether or not our actions have seen a higher level of satisfaction. However, as we look further, we learn from Mise's writings that given the uncertainty about the future, those who do not make a mistake in estimating it are more successful; those who make a mistake are unsuccessful. However, if no one makes a mistake, Mises claims, then there can be no profit. Mises (1998, p. 288) writes:

Like every acting man, the entrepreneur is always a speculator. He deals with the uncertain conditions of the future. His success or failure depends on the correctness of his anticipation of uncertain events. If he fails in his understanding of things to come, he is doomed. The only source from which an entrepreneur's profits stem is his ability to anticipate better than other people the future demand of the consumers. If everybody is correct in anticipating the future state of the market of a certain commodity s price and the prices of the complementary factors of production concerned would already today be adjusted to this future state. Neither profit nor loss can emerge for those embarking upon this line of business.

Or elsewhere in (Mises 1974, pp. 108–109):

> *If all people were to anticipate correctly the future state of the market, the entrepreneurs would neither earn any profits nor suffer any losses. They would have to buy the complementary factors of production at prices which would, already at the instant of the purchase, fully reflect the future prices of products. No room would be left either for profit or for loss. What makes profit emerge is the fact that the entrepreneur who judges the future prices of the product more correctly than other people do buys some or all of the factors of the production at prices which, seen from the point of view of the future state of the market, are too low.... This difference is entrepreneurial profit.*

Similarly, the already mentioned Hülsmann (2000) argues that the existence of profit for an entrepreneur is related to the existence of another entrepreneur's error. He also argues that if no one made a mistake—we would be in a state of full market equilibrium—there would be no profit.[102] Profit and loss are functions of the proper judgment (profit) and realized errors (loss) of others.

However, if we compare Mises's claims from *Human Action* about the subjective nature of profit as an increase in the state of satisfaction with these claims, we see that they are in a logical contradiction. Hypothetically, if everyone estimates the future correctly, then everyone must be in a subjectively perceived profit; in his estimation, therefore, no one makes a profit. The fact is, however, that what Mises writes is equally true. The profit, in *monetary terms*, is then arbitrated to zero. It does not exist. We see that we are facing a rather interesting paradox. In the context of this paradox, Hülsmann further argues that it is the existence of error and the fact that someone is always wrong that is behind the existence of profit. However, this would imply that the market process is a *zero-sum* game; only someone's mistake is the cause of another's profit.

In the context of the above-mentioned concept of economic success/error, which we perceive subjectively and intersubjectively, these paradoxes are immediately removed. The above division of the concept of

[102] It should be pointed out to the reader that Hülsmann (2000) approaches the problem of equilibrium differently from the Mises approach. However, the conclusions about profit and loss are similar. We will address the issue of equilibrium in Chapter 3.

success/error into the subjective and intersubjective aspects implies that there is also a related view of the concept of profit/loss. It follows then, that if we theoretically knew perfectly the needs of all others and vice versa from the point of view of others, it would be possible to completely eliminate the monetary surpluses which show the intersubjective rate of profit. Assessing profit as subjective and intersubjective concepts make it possible without looking at some kind of paradox. While the intersubjective kind of profit is logically removed in a hypothetical state of mutual perfect knowledge and the satisfaction of the needs of others, subjective profit remains. According to the definition of the subjective nature of success/error, from that perspective, everyone is in subjectively perceived profit; i.e., their needs would be met by the portfolio because no one would make an intersubjective mistake (it would satisfy the correct needs of others through his/her economic activity). At the same time, he/she is subjectively satisfied, because everyone else would satisfy their needs as well. If we approach the above-mentioned division of the problem, we avoid the claim that profit is a zero-sum game and can also meaningfully explain why there would be no intersubjective profit if there is a perfect state of equilibrium.

It is necessary to look at a profit from two perspectives; the first is subjective. Mises's statements necessarily apply here. In the context of the modification of the theory of subjective value presented here, it is only necessary to add that a person subjectively perceives profit/loss by assessing the state of their portfolio today and yesterday, against the perceived amount of actual and counterfactual needs today and yesterday. If the person thinks that today's portfolio meets a given perceived combination of needs better than it did yesterday, his/her activity was profitable and vice versa. From a subjective point of view, we can assess our own activity, and we can also assess the result of the intersubjective activity of two people. The result of an activity or exchange changes the state of a person's portfolio. He or she assesses from a subjective point of view whether the result is appropriate or not in the context of perceived needs that the given portfolio has to/can satisfy. Of course, for an exchange to be successful, there must be an estimate of what the other person requires. Without attempting to identify and satisfy a suitable combination of the needs of others through a product whose properties best satisfy that combination of needs, the exchange is not possible.

However, from a subjective point of view, it is not possible to assess the success rate of one person against the success rate of another person. The fact that a person is subjectively profitable, whether in terms of their own productive activity for themselves or in terms of their productive activity which the person carries out in terms of exchange, it cannot be assessed from the point of view of the other person. Whether one person is more successful than the other is only possible if there are mutually shared criteria against which we could compare the activity of two or more people and, based on the given criteria, decide what was achieved. The comparison defined in this way makes it possible to repeat the successful activity for possible improvement of the given activity and, of course, also as a motivation to be more successful.

The space for the detection of this intersubjective comparison, as well as its source, must be sought elsewhere. If we realize that this source of profit, in the case of the ERE (Evenly Rotating Economy) described by Mises, is completely eliminated (mutatis mutandis in equilibrium in the sense of Walras), the question is, what do the given individuals experience in this case, except for repeating the same economic activities? Mises (1998, p. 709) writes about the ERE:

> *This hypothetical future state of equilibrium will appear when all methods of production have been adjusted to the valuations of the actors and to the state of technological knowledge. Then one will work in the most appropriate locations with the most adequate technological methods.*

So, what do the individuals know? In this hypothetical state, everyone can correctly anticipate the needs of the other, adjust production methods to meet the priorities of those needs, and at the same time, satisfy them based on existing technological possibilities. What then follows from this in the context of the intersubjective component of profit we have identified? Where is the source of this type of profit, which would also be eliminated in the hypothetical state of the ERE? The answer is that the source is in *knowing how one can better meet the needs of the other-one.*[103] This component of knowledge has a dual nature—on the one hand, it is about revealing the ideal combination of needs satisfied by some combination of the features of economic goods and, on the other hand, revealing a suitable combination of resources to achieve the goal.[104]

The definition of intersubjective profit as the evaluation of knowledge to satisfy the needs of others implies that the intersubjective perception of profit arises, transforms, and disappears. In the sense of the above-described principle of combining needs satisfied by a new combination of features of a good, the entrepreneur must first discover some new knowledge that leads to better satisfaction of needs, and then, must implement a plan that requires the use of some existing capital goods. This implies two things. Firstly, in the past, someone had to produce the necessary capital goods. In this way, capital goods are now being assessed on the basis of whether or not another entrepreneur's decision was correct. At the same time, this means that not everything is possible. An entrepreneur inventing a new product is *limited* by the existing stock of capital goods. It must be stressed that the term "limited" is the proper term to use as opposed to e.g., "determined," because the entrepreneur has the opportunity (knowledge) of combining the existing stock of capital goods by proposing the entrepreneurial activity. Secondly, the result of the action of the entrepreneur as described by us must be considered as useful by the consumers, i.e., they are interested in the exchange of some part of their portfolio and thereby enriching their portfolio with produced goods. We know that a person prefers a priori, a state higher than the lower satisfaction of some combination of needs determined by him/her, which is provided by some subjectively composed portfolio of economic goods. The exchange implies that the consumer gives up part of their portfolio for what he/she receives. At the same time, however, it follows that the newly composed consumer portfolio is considered ex ante as more appropriate to meet the combination of needs than the

[103]This statement has many implications in the theory of equilibrium. We will present the modification of the equilibrium concept based on the evenly rotating economy concept in a separate Chapter 3.

[104]At the same time, Kirzner's remark, that the entrepreneur does not have to be the owner of the necessary capital goods, respectively, capital resources, applies. The owner can borrow them.

portfolio before the exchange.[105] If the entrepreneur is successful, they get a share from the portfolio of others in exchange for providing a product or service. This causes the composition of his portfolio to change so that the new composition of the portfolio is considered more suitable than the previous composition. The description of this area of the process has a generally valid character that is valid for any individual and is, in principle, valid at any time, i.e., it is also valid for our predecessors.

However, for the intersubjective perception of the profit, we basically try to recognize who has better knowledge to meet a combination of the needs of others. From the point of view of intersubjective profit/loss, we need to be able to recognize one activity of one entrepreneur (equipped with some knowledge) as more/less successful as compared to other activities of other entrepreneurs. As we have shown in the description of intersubjective success/error, the standard is related to the diversification of our portfolio. The criteria are created at the same time by those who participate in their creation within the economic interactions and not by those who ignore the interactions.[106] The strategy of the diversification of a portfolio is also a priori intersubjective. It implies a *mutual* satisfaction of needs; a *mutual* satisfaction of needs is based on the diversification of the subjective portfolios of several people.[107]

In this case, it is a gradually developed tool for comparing several people with each other, who consider a higher degree of portfolio diversification as a suitable strategy for a higher degree of the satisfaction of their needs, which takes place with *each other*. In our description,

---

[105]From the individual point of view, the composition of the portfolio is always to a certain extent unique and individualized, i.e., it is subject to some community standards of a religious, cultural, family, or community nature.

[106]Nowadays, these can be various hermits or suicidal persons, but also people who think about satisfying needs *only* in terms of a higher degree of spiritual satisfaction of needs, etc. In the past, it could be groups of people who for various reasons, distanced themselves from society, i.e., groups of people who lived outside of civilizations and had their own profit standards.

[107]The strategies of hermits, suicidal persons or others who prefer spiritual strategies are based on a separation and a subjective solution to the problem of satisfying needs. The strategies of warriors, thieves, murderers are based on destruction and are not focused on a mutual satisfaction of needs. The strategies of politicians are of a special case and are sometimes implemented as the strategies of a scrounger, sometimes as strategies of warriors, thieves, murderers, and sometimes as strategies of enlightened monarchs providing also some basic services for his/her society in the form of security and the law. However, this is a problem that will be looked at in a future book.

a person is more successful if they are able to better provide for the needs of others; however, this must be somehow demonstrated. It is *not enough to know* that they have better knowledge. Their better knowledge must be somehow demonstrated. For any entrepreneur (or our predecessors), the intersubjective success is visible in the intensity of the exchange of their special product with others (other prehistoric groups), and the demonstrated outcome is the diversity of their portfolio (or the portfolio of the prehistoric group). The successful person (or a group of prehistoric people) is the one (or the group) who is perceived by other members of a society as better equipped to meet their needs compared to the portfolios that others have (or another group) have, which is the consequence of providing what others are incapable of providing. This implies that their economic activity would become interesting for others who would try to repeat it, i.e., to repeat or copy or improve their knowledge in order to meet the needs of others. Repetition of their economic activities by others also implies a reduction in the rate of how the successful entrepreneur (the successful prehistoric group) can appropriately diversify their portfolio because of the competition of others. At the same time, the repetition of activities by others implies that they can remodel their activity to a certain extent by focusing on another combination of needs, by another combination of features of their product, through another combination of capital goods or business organizations, through which the product can be placed on the market. This can lead to a situation where the successful entrepreneur (the prehistoric group) loses their knowledge advantage, or consumers (other prehistoric groups) are interested in other types of products from other entrepreneurs (different neighboring groups). It is also possible that the original product ceases to exist due to better knowledge which outdates what was previously known. With the disappearance of knowledge, the intersubjectively identified profit-assessed knowledge disappears as well.

So far, we have identified intersubjective profit/loss without money which is more applicable to our predecessors than to developed societies. While it is true that portfolios are, as a concept of the mind, comparable between individuals, the degree of their comparison is limited by the uniqueness of their diversification. At the same time, a person also strives to achieve his/her ideal portfolio which ensures the satisfaction of their individual needs; this given ideal may not be fully understandable to another person. It is clear that money as the intersubjective tool of assessment of entrepreneurship knowledge, and the expression of intersubjective profit/loss in monetary terms, offers a significant advantage over the description in a non-monetary economy. It is necessary to note that the intersubjective profit/loss represents the range of this knowledge (meaning the knowledge regarding how to meet someone's needs). However, this is only in terms of the accuracy of the expression of profit/loss, not in the ability to express profit/loss per se. Money essentially unified the way we look at and use this knowledge as a tool. Money expresses in a very precise way, the widths of spreads among our present, potential, and desired portfolios comparable to all people. This enables us to compare the activities (knowledge) which provide a better-decreased distribution of spreads over activities that provide a lower decrease of spreads. We can then imagine how we would feel if we were in the position of the entrepreneur in question. However, money provides extremely limited information, if any, with regard to the subjective view of the person in question.

The question which arises from this line of argument is whether subjectively or intersubjectively perceived profit depends on uncertainty, as Knight, Mises, or others believe. The existence of uncertainty is a condition for the existence of subjective profit. It is only a *sufficient condition* for the existence of intersubjective profit. If we removed the uncertainty from our thinking, the subjective profit would remain. Our super-humans, living in the ERE or Walrasian equilibrium, would experience a subjectively perceived profit all at once. Subjectively perceived profit depends only on the action of a person, in terms of assessing the outcome of the action as a more satisfactory state of his portfolio over a less satisfactory state in terms of satisfying his individual needs. However, intersubjective profit comes from *knowing how* to best meet the needs of others. Its necessary condition is knowledge and its sufficient condition is uncertainty related to that given knowledge.

The fact that we look at two types of profit in economics, subjective and intersubjective, allows us to elegantly explain so-called nonprofit economic activities. They precisely contain the subjective element of profit and the intersubjective element of loss. However, for some reason, there is a demand for both these elements; we do not have to examine the reason in this essay. However, the apparent existence of a demand for nonprofit economic projects meant that the community was "forced" to differentiate this nonprofit activity from profitable economic activities. Differentiation takes place at the level of the intersubjective nature of profit. This is because a nonprofit project purposefully achieves an intersubjectively displayed loss, and everyone accepts this in advance. Socially, this is how we differentiate nonprofit activities from profitable ones. Nonprofit activities are those where so-called aid is explicitly identified; profitable business activities achieve explicitly intersubjectively recognized profit. If business projects sustain a loss, the projects are eliminated—creditors stop financing the project. However, individuals can participate in nonprofit projects, but their very nature implies that in a given case, donors (resource providers) achieve only a subjective profit, which as we mentioned earlier, is acknowledged in advance. Therefore, we can identify them by another term, "donor" and not by the term "investor or creditor." From the point of view of donors, the increase in their social status or other reasons for becoming donors is incorporated into the portfolio. The portfolio of goods realized in this way brings them higher satisfaction than if they had not participated in the donation. Of course, the recipients receive what is donated. In this mode of differentiation, the economic community deals with distinguishing the activities in question.

It is also possible to look at political activities from the intersubjective standard of the profit aspect. These are equally differentiated from other economic activities so that what is to be achieved is acknowledged in advance. The division of the concept of success/error and profit/loss into a subjective and intersubjective nature raises several questions in this area. For instance, to what extent are some political actions executed voluntarily and to what extent is the politically determined economic standard of success/error or profit/loss in this area voluntarily accepted (in terms of voluntary submission to political decision-making) by others?

At this point, we can only make a few remarks on this subject; the politically determined nature of success/error, profit/loss clearly exists. However, determining what is success/error and profit/loss is different;

this is not about *market cooperation* and the participation of community members in determining how to approach the intersubjective nature of success/error and profit/loss. What is also obvious is that the character and direction of political activities are determined by political representation. It differs from the fact that in some cases, political representation is sometimes determined democratically, authoritatively, based on military force, or the monarchist-hereditary principle. What we can say at the same time about the given nature of political success/error and profit/loss, is that it is necessarily ontologically different from a market-based and voluntary standard of determining success/error and profit/loss. Political activities are based on the determination of intersubjective economic standards by some type of central authority. However, from time-to-time people accept them to a certain extent and also try to explicitly differentiate them so they are distinguishable from market economic activities. Moreover, a whole system of rules, normative standards, and institutions are built around the given activities. This is nothing more than the empirical evidence of the differentiation between political and market activities.

2.3.7 The Problem of Cost Concept: Subjective and Intersubjective Costs

The concept of costs is perceived in economic literature as opportunity costs. As Newman (2018) points out, the current perception of the concept of opportunity cost has two approaches. The first is the marginalist legacy of what Newman calls the causally realistic approach, and the second interpretation comes from what he calls the mainstream. The causally realistic approach in Menger's tradition speaks of the opportunity cost in the context of action:

> *The opportunity cost of any action, then, is the value of the highest-ranked end forgone because of the action.* (Newman 2018, p. 12)

Mises (1949): "*Costs are equal to the value attached to the satisfaction which one must forego in order to attain the end aimed at*" (p. 97). Rothbard (2009): "*'Cost' is simply the utility of the next best alternative that must be*

> *forgone in any action, and it is, therefore, part and parcel of utility on the individual's value scale*" (p. 136). (in Newman 2018, p. 23)

According to Newman (2018), the mainstream defines the opportunity cost in the context of a production trade-off, which implies either the quantitative nature of costs in terms of the number of economic goods spent, or the monetary value of costs associated with valuing the goods that are necessary to spend, in order to achieve a specific set of goals.

The problem with a causal-realistic interpretation of the definition of opportunity cost is the meaning of the statement, "the best next alternative"; i.e., what exactly must one give up in the context of needs as the best alternative, and why must it be the second most valued need that can be realistically satisfied and not the third or fourth or any other? This problem is, of course, implied by a traditionally perceived scale of needs, ranging from the most urgent need to the least urgent; this means that several levels of importance and priorities are implied in the preferential scale. However, if there is such a scale, why sacrifice the second real satisfaction of some specific need, and not the third, fourth, or any other need?[108] At the same time, the interpretation of costs implies that a person must give up something they have which satisfies the given sacrificed needs. This is because a causally realistic approach implies that an economic mean is causally assigned to a need (or end). It is not possible to sacrifice a need that we only think of psychologically, e.g., in a magical form. As such, we cannot sacrifice the need because we have no means to perform real magic. It is, therefore, a mere psychological exercise that has no real connection to action; we must give up something real, not something intangible. Therefore, the concept of costs, which is accepted within the mainstream, should not surprise us. In interpreting the concept of opportunity cost, the mainstream correctly implies the

[108]At this point, I would like to stress that I agree with the interpretation that this is "*the utility of the next best alternative that must be forgone in any action.*" This interpretation combined with the classical interpretation of value theory and the existence of some larger multilevel scale of needs suggests the question of why not sacrifice any other, less important, alternative. In the case of our modified theory of subjective value, it is quite explicit that it is "*the utility of the next best alternative that must be forgone in any action.*" This is correct due to the point that our theory implies only a two-opt preferential scale.

real spending of some quantitative number of goods, or the dollar value associated with the spending of some goods.

The modified theory of subjective value presented by us could, to some extent, combine and explain both approaches. As described above, the modified theory of subjective value is based on the perception of the sum of needs that are satisfied by the portfolio of economic goods. The sum of needs has a factual and counterfactual part. The preferential scale is only two-dimensional. The portfolio is built against the actual and counterfactual perceived total sum of needs. The opportunity costs then mean the sacrifice of satisfying some counterfactually perceived *part* (or part of the complex) of the total sum of needs represented by part of the portfolio. The goods in question were owned because they were intended to meet some potential needs but are now sacrificed in the form of costs to achieve something more desirable. This creates a basic principle that defines the concept of costs in the form of a needs-means causal relationship but does not explain the structure of costs. To explain the structure of costs, we must explain the decision process which allows part of the needs to correspond to part of the portfolio and to becomes costs. We know that a person prefers a higher to a lower satisfaction of needs provided by a portfolio; they always have a current portfolio (Pc). If the portfolio satisfies the person's needs, there is no need to change the portfolio.[109] It is changed if they start to feel uneasiness (as new combination of needs) and act to eliminate it. To eliminate the uneasiness, they mind-create a new desired portfolio (Pd); still, they will only be able to achieve some possible portfolio (Pp). As we know, this creates spreads which the person has a desire to narrow; they try to achieve as narrow a spread between Pp and Pd as possible. However, they are limited by the sum of needs that still has to be met by the portfolio. It is this limitation that has an impact on the final decision of what man is able to sacrifice in order to achieve some Pp. It is the attractiveness of the spread of Pp versus Pd and the range of the spread between Pc and Pp, which determines the ability of man to sacrifice something.

[109]We will use this state as a definition of the individual equilibrium position later on. There is no room for a deeper definition of this concept right now.

Let's explore this in terms of the extreme position of martyrs or those who make fatal sacrifices in order to emphasize a particular viewpoint. They are willing to provide not only everything they have in their possession to achieve the desired state of affairs but also their lives. It needn't be war heroes; it may be ordinary men/women (heroes for their families or community) who are willing to sacrifice everything for their children, relatives, community, be it for religious or any reason. The final needs felt at their moment of decision are to preserve/maintain a situation that is only possible to achieve if they sacrifice everything they have. It means that the spread between the desired and the possible state of things is so attractive that, if somehow forced, they will sacrifice their lives to try and achieve it. As empirical evidence shows us, it is sometimes not enough to sacrifice everything; but that is another topic.

The modus operandi is the same in situations we call normal. The entrepreneur, worker, or anybody evaluates the spread of portfolios. If they consider that part of the needs met by part of Pc could be exchanged to achieve some Pp which is closer to Pd, they will act accordingly since they will prefer to achieve Pp. It is also evident that the situation and decision are dependent on the sum and combination of needs. If the sum of needs (or its combination) is very simple (as probably our predecessors had), it has an impact on the structure of costs, its time frame, combination, and so on. More complicated plans call for different decisions and different actions, e.g., in the form of the debt exchange.

This interpretation avoids any confusion of means with needs, which often happens when explaining the opportunity costs. This is because asked result is always the satisfaction of a complex sum of needs. It is the formulation of the entrepreneurial plan as a complex of activities realized by a combination of means, where *we do not look* at the partial results of the plan to satisfy some quasi-need, which then becomes a means to achieve another kind of need, etc. On the contrary, we look at the problem in the context of a complex of costs. There are only costs as intermediate steps leading to the fulfillment of a set entrepreneurial plan. The plan does not have to be logically consistent and fixed into the particular sum of needs. With any change to the plan, we do not have to logically declare that we have abandoned the original plan and are starting to implement a completely different one. On the contrary, the modified concept of the theory of subjective value makes it possible to define a plan as a relative *complex* of means to meet the sum of needs. The significance of the sequence of their achievement, or addition or change, is subject to constant change, as required by the actual perception of the sum of needs needed as a complex to achieve the intended goal. The aim of costs is to provide a different composition of the portfolio, which, according to the human subject's ideas, should lead to a higher degree of satisfaction of needs in the future. In this way, we can actually combine causal-realistic approaches to costs as well as a mainstream perception of costs as the expense of some part of the property owned so that we have a single and consistent theory of opportunity costs.

In this way, it is, therefore, possible to explain the subjective perception of costs in the context of subjectively perceived profit/loss. However, we still need to describe the intersubjective nature of costs. These are implied in the activity which is realized in terms of the intersubjective characteristic of profit. Pošvanc (2019a) gives the example of a person who spends a lot of time on social media. Since the personal costs are subjective and cannot be compared, it is not even possible to decide from a subjective point of view whether or not the activity in question is relevant in the context of the opportunity cost. It depends on what the person considers adequate. If one person prefers to spend time on social media, the other devotes time to study and the third person devotes time to building a machine, the observer cannot decide whether someone is doing economically right or not. Not only do we not know the subjective point of view of our actors, but we also do not know the economic context in which they carry out the activities.

The situation will change if the activities in question are part of the intersubjective consideration within the economic community, i.e., whether or not they are used to meeting the needs of others in the context that spent costs will satisfy the others' needs. At this level, the economic context is determined by the intersubjective concept of success (profit) and error (loss), which results as the individual participates economically in the system, and thus takes over the standard of assessment of the activity. So, if a person builds a machine but this knowledge was not intended to meet the needs of someone else in the economic community, the profits and costs remain at his/her subjective level of judgment. However, if someone builds a machine to meet the needs of others, the intersubjective nature of success/error enables us to compare, and at the same time, decide whether his/her costs are adequate or not.

The possibility of comparison is twofold. The first option is the possibility of identifying what the implemented activity leads to—intersubjective profit or loss. The intersubjective rate of cost is determined through the alternative return that a person could achieve had they not carried out their project but devoted their existing resources to alternative economic activity instead. This allows us to identify a more successful mix of capital resources before a less successful one. Interactively, however, we can say that his/her activity is less efficient than any alternative activity on the market. Subjectively, it is still true that if a person or a business entity carries out a given activity, regardless of whether there are alternative options on the market or not, there is still room for subjective profit. The rate of intersubjective costs and profit/loss is only relative and only provides information about the intersubjective nature of the activity which is compared to another similar activity. A person's action is always ultimately decided based on a subjective assessment of his/her economic activity. At the same time, a lower rate of intersubjective profit compared to costs associated with an economic activity does not mean that there are no investors or creditors interested in that activity. Investors or creditors assess their own activities and the activities of others in the context of their portfolio and its diversification. This makes them willing to allocate resources to less profitable activities, which in turn is offset by a different degree of risk or other factors that cause changes in the perception of their desired portfolios.

The second option is the possibility of assessing intersubjective costs based on a standard defined by an entrepreneur/manager for whom we perform the given activity in an employment relationship. If someone spends time on social networks, and they only do it to satisfy their needs, we know nothing about the effectiveness and costs of the activity. However, if someone spends time on social media, instead of building a machine for their employer, we can say that they have been inefficient. However, if the person works on marketing campaigns on social media, their activity is relevant if their activity leads to the employer making the required profit. We can also compare the activities of one employee with another. If there is a second employee who also spends time on social media and the combination of capital resources (for example, of some otherwise built knowledge related to the effectiveness of marketing campaigns) leads to higher profits for their employers, we can decide that the second person is more productive and efficient than the first. The first person is not necessarily unsuccessful in terms of the activity they carry out. All we know is that one is more productive and efficient than the other. The intersubjective nature of success/error, therefore, allows us to identify the economic viability of our activities even in the context of costs. Lachmann's remark that from a subjective point of view, it is possible to perceive the activities in different ways, still applies. We can, therefore, express both subjective and intersubjective conclusions about economic activities. However, it is the intersubjective nature of costs that makes it possible to affect a comparison.

2.3.8 Other Coordinating Social Standards

Humans created many standards coordinated to facilitate mutual cooperation between people. Nevertheless, it is not the aim of this work to describe them all. However, we can mention some of them and can divide them into those which are catallactic or political. We can consider all those standards that are developed voluntarily to be catallactic. We also can consider those that are the subject of politically enforced regulations as political in nature. At this point, we will not analyze the reasons or the correctness of politically determined standards. We merely state that they exist.

Catallactic standards can be varied. They can be ethical rules of trading but can also be standards of trading on stock exchanges in terms of standardized products. They may also be standardized trading procedures, which are determined by the stock exchange owner and thus ensures intersubjective comparability of conducts for the trading participants. At the same time, product standardization does not have to take place in specialized markets only. It could also take place in the form of building a brand, quality guarantees, or the conditions for the delivery of some services which are announced to the customer in advance. It may be different types of guilds or voluntary associations which create and influence the standardized environment of products and services in some community or communities. It is also possible to talk about cultural or religious community standardization, where the identification of standards is influenced by the kind of social community, cultural or religious background. There are many examples of new types of catallactic standardization today; these can be seen with the use of new technology or smart applications; so-called sharing economy services and other products provided by specialized companies operating on the internet. They also create new types of privacy regulations, rules, and standards that lead to a greater degree of certainty regarding the coordination possibilities of market participants.

It must be stated that we also follow political standards. These take the form of various regulations, restrictions on property rights, or the personal freedoms of the individual. I think it is entirely appropriate to say that today's so-called social-democratic-market economies are of a form that could have existed on the free market as well. Protection of property, personal liberty, the enforcement of law and rules, or various forms of business standardization are present in these social-democratic communities; I think there is a general rational presumption that very similar standardization would have existed in a free society. At the same time, it is questionable to what extent they are an erroneous and incorrect determination of the direction of society; the comparison is exceedingly difficult. Perhaps because there is no competitive possibility to verify the existence of this standardization today, i.e., the verification of the extent to which the current political standardization would be identical to that applied within a free society. What would be the difference? From a scientific point of view, we can only speculate about it. However, it is empirically obvious that in the case of excessive use of political standardization, social coordination disappears and vice versa. At the same time, from the context of this essay, it should be clear that some political solutions do not have to be socially rejected and needn't have devastating effects on interpersonal coordination. From my point of view, these are some micro-political-socio solutions that would make sense and would have their place with catallactic type standards. In my opinion, macro-political-socio solutions for interpersonal coordination are already coercive. However, it is clear that seeking the optimal measure must be dealt with in other essays or works. For the purpose of what is presented here, it is appropriate to stop and focus on some other issues related to the question of the future, coordination, and the success/error dichotomy—the related questions related to the equilibration.

References

Becker, Garry. 1997. *Teorie Preferencí* [The Theory of Preferences]. Praha: Grada Publishing.

Bilo, Šimon. 2004. The Theory of Imputation: A Context of Value Spreads between Means and Ends. WWW DOCUMENT. http://www2.gcc.edu/dept/econ/ASSC/Papers2004/Imputation_Bilo.pdf. Accessed 9 Jan 2019.

Böhm-Bawerk, Eugen. 1930. The Positive Theory of Capital. *G.E. Stechert.* New York. WWW DOCUMENT. https://mises.org/library/positive-theory-capital.

Cantillo, Andres F. 2010. Shackle: Time and Uncertainty in Economics. Paper presented to St Edmund's College for the G.L.S Shackle Studentship. University of Cambridge. WWW DOUCUMENT. https://www.peri.umass.edu/fileadmin/pdf/conference_papers/newschool/Papaer_GLS_Shackle_Studentship.pdf.

Einzig, Paul. 2014. *Primitive Money: In Its Ethnological, Historical and Economic Aspects.* Oxford, UK: Pergamon Press.

Engliš, Karel. 1930. *Teleologie jako forma vědeckého poznání* [The Teleology as a Form of Scientific Knowledge]. Praha: F. Topič publisher.

Foss, Nicolai J., and Klein, G. Peter. 2009. Entrepreneurial Alertness and Opportunity Discovery: Origins, Attributes, Critique. In *The Historical Foundations of Entrepreneurship Research*, eds. Hans Landström and Franz Lohrke. Aldershot, UK: Edward Elgar, Forthcoming, SMG Working Paper No. 2/2009, Available at SSRN: https://ssrn.com/abstract=1353981.

Gillies, Donald. 2006. *Philosophical Theories of Probability* (Philosophical Issues in Science). Routledge Taylor & Francis e-Library.

Graeber, David. 2011. *Debt: The First 5000 Years.* New York: Melville House.

Hayek, Friedrich A. 1937. Economics and Knowledge. *Economica.* New Series 4 (13): 33–54. Online version on WWW DOCUMENT. https://mises.org/library/economics-and-knowledge. Accessed 22 Jan 2021.

Hayek, Friedrich A. 1945. The Use of Knowledge in Society. *American Economic Review* XXXV (4): 519–530. WWW DOCUMENT. https://oll.libertyfund.org/titles/hayek-the-use-of-knowledge-in-society-1945.

Hayek, A. Friedrich. 1952 [1976]. *The Sensory Order*. Chicago, IL, USA: University of Chicago Press.

Hoppe, Hans H. 1994. F. A. Hayek on Government and Social Evolution: A Critique. *The Review of Austrian Economics* 7 (1): 67–93. WWW DOCUMENT. https://mises.org/library/f-hayek-government-and-social-evolution-critique.

Hoppe, Hans H. 1997. On Certainty and Uncertainty, or: How Rational Can Our Expectations Be? *The Review of Austrian Economics* 10: 49–78. https://doi.org/10.1007/BF02538143.

Hoppe, Hans H. 2007. The Limits of Numerical Probability: Frank H. Knight and Ludwig von Mises and the Frequency of Interpretation. *The Quarterly Journal of Austrian Economics* 10 (1): 3–21.

Horwitz, Steven. 2010. The Sensory Order and Organizational Learning. In *The Social Science of Hayek's 'The Sensory Order'* (Advances in Austrian Economics), ed. N. William Butos. Bingley: Emerald Publishing.

Huerta de Soto, Jesús. 2012. *Socializmus, ekonomická kalkulácia a podnikanie* [Socialism, Economic Calculation and Entrepreneurship]. Bratislava: Konzervatívny inštitút M. R. Štefánika.

Hülsmann, Jörg G. 1997. Knowledge, Judgment, and the Use of Property. *Review of Austrian Economics* 10 (1): 23–48. WWW DOCUMENT. https://mises.org/library/knowledge-judgment-and-use-property.

Hülsmann, Jörg G. 2000. A Realist Approach to Equilibrium Analysis. *The Quarterly Journal of Austrian Economics* 3: 3–51. https://doi.org/10.1007/s12113-000-1025-1.

Hülsmann, Jörg G. 2002. A Theory of Interest. *The Quarterly Journal of Austrian Economics* 5: 77–110. https://doi.org/10.1007/s12113-002-1007-6.

Hülsmann, Jörg G. 2003. Facts and Counterfactuals in Economic Law. *Journal of Libertarian Studies* 17 (1): 57–102. WWW DOCUMENT. https://mises.org/library/facts-and-counterfactuals-economic-law-1.

Kinkor, Jiří. 2000. *Hayekova cesta do otroctva* [Hayek's Road into the Slavery]. Brno: Berlet. WWW DOCUMENT. https://aynrand.cz/hayekova-cesta-do-otroctvi/.

Kirzner, Israel M. 1973. *Competition and Entrepreneurship*. Chicago, USA: University of Chicago Press.

Kirzner, Israel M. 1978. Economics and Error. In *New Directions in Austrian Economics*, ed. Louis M. Spadaro. Kansas City: Sheed Andrews and McMeel.

Kirzner, Israel M. 1992. *The Meaning of Market Process*. London and New York: Routledge.

Kirzner, Israel M. 1999. Creativity and/or Alertness: A Reconsideration of the Schumpeterian Entrepreneur. *The Review of Austrian Economics* 11: 5–17.

Klein, Peter G. 2009. Risk, Uncertainty, and Economic Organization. In *Property, Freedom, and Society: Essays in Honor of Hans-Hermann Hoppe*, ed. Jörg G. Hülsmann and Stephan Kinsella. Ludwig von Mises Institute. WWW DOCUMENT. https://mises.org/library/risk-uncertainty-and-economic-organization.

Knight, H. Frank. 1964 [1921]. *Risk Uncertainty and Profit*. Augustus M. Kelley, New York. WWW DOCUMENT. https://mises.org/library/risk-uncertainty-and-profit.

Kuchař, Pavel, and Eewin Dekker. 2019. Lachmann and Shackle: On the Joint Production of Interpretation Instruments. *Research in the History of Economic Thought and Methodology* 37B: 25–42. https://doi.org/10.1108/S0743-41542019000037B005.

Lachmann, Ludwig M. 2005. Expectations and the Meaning of Institutions: Essays in Economics, ed. Ch. Donald Lavoi. First published 1994 by Routledge. Taylor & Francis e-Library. WWW DOCUMENT https://www.mises.at/static/literatur/Buch/lachmann-expectations-and-the-meaning-of-institutions.pdf.

Lawson, Tony. 2019. *The Nature of Social Reality: Issues in Social Ontology (Economics as Social Theory)*. New York: Routledge.

Lewis, Paul A. 2014. Hayek: From Economics as Equilibrium ANALYSIS to Economics as Social Theory, Ch. 9, 195–223. In *Elgar Companion to Hayekian Economics*, ed. Roger W. Garrison and Norman Barry. Cheltenham, UK: Edward Elgar Publishing.

Lewis, Paul A. 2016. The Emergence of "Emergence" in the Work of F. A. Hayek: A Historical Analysis. *History of Political Economy*: 111–150. http://doi.org/10.1215/00182702-3452315.

Lewis, Paul A. 2017. Shackle on Choice, Imagination and Creativity: Hayekian Foundations. *Cambridge Journal of Economics* 41 (1): 1–24. WWW DOCUMENT. https://www.researchgate.net/publication/304452046_Shackle_on_Choice_Imagination_and_Creativity_Hayekian_Foundations.

Lewis, Paul A., and Jochen Runde. 2005. Subjectivism, Social Structure and the Possibility of Socio-Economic Order: The Case of Ludwig Lachmann. *Journal of Economic Behavior and Organization* 62 (2), February 2007. Available at SSRN: https://ssrn.com/abstract=2534273.

Lewis, Paul A., and Peter Lewin. 2015. Orders, Orders, Everywhere … On Hayek's the Market and other Orders. *Cosmos and Taxis* 2: 1–16.

Littlechild, C. Stephen. 2003. Reflections on George Shackle: Three Excerpts from the Shackle Collection. *The Review of Austrian Economics* 16: 113–117. https://doi.org/10.1023/A:1022917509907.

Menger, Carl. 2007. Principles of Economics, trans. James Dingwall and Bert F. Hoselitz. New York: The Free Press, 1950. Online edition, Ludwig von Mises Institute. WWW DOCUMENT. https://cdn.mises.org/Principles%20of%20Economics_5.pdf.

Mentzel, Peter C. 2018. Praxeology, History, and the Perils of Historicism. In *Austrian Economics: The Next Generation* (Advances in Austrian Economics, Volume 23), ed. Steven Horwitz. Bingley, UK: Emerald Publishing Limited.

Mises, Ludwig. 1920, 1990. Economic Calculation in the Socialist Commonwealth. In *Collectivist Economic Planning*, ed. Friedrich A. Hayek, 1975, 87–130. Clifton, NJ: Kelley Publishing, and Auburn, AL: Ludwig von Mises Institute. WWW DOCUMENT. https://mises.org/library/economic-calculation-socialist-commonwealth/html.

Mises, Ludwig. 1949, 1998. Human Action. Scholar edition. Auburn, Ala: Ludwig Von Mises Institute. WWW DOCUMENT. https://mises.org/library/human-action-0/html/pp/663.

Mises, Ludwig. 1953. *Theory of Money and Credit*. New Haven: Yale University Press. WWW DOCUMENT https://mises.org/library/theory-money-and-credit.

Mises, Ludwig. 1957, 1985. Theory and History: An Interpretation of Social and Economic Evolution. Auburn, AL: Ludwig von Mises Institute. WWW DOCUMENT. https://mises.org/library/theory-and-history-interpretation-social-and-economic-evolution.

Mises, Ludwig. 1962. The Ultimate Foundation of Economic Science. New York: Van Nostrand. WWW DOCUMMENT. https://mises.org/library/ultimate-foundation-economic-science.

Mises, Ludwig. 1974. *Planning for Freedom*. Libertarian Press. WWW DOCUMENT. https://mises.org/library/planning-freedom-and-twelve-other-essays-and-addresses.

Newman, Jonathan. 2018. Contemporary Debates on Opportunity Cost Theory and Pedagogy. In *The Economic Theory of Costs*, ed. Matthew McCaffrey. Foundations and New Directions: Routledge.

O'Driscoll, Gerald P., Jr., and Mario J. Rizzo. 1996. *The Economics of Time and Ignorance*. London and New York: Routledge.

Pavlík, Ján. 1999. About the Spontaneous Emergence of the Norms of Distributive Justice and Catallactic Rules. *E-Logos—Electronic Journal for Philosophy.* ISSN 1211-0442. WWW DOCUMENT. https://nb.vse.cz/kfil/elogos/ethics/pavlik-5.htm.

Pavlík, Ján. 2004. *F.A. Hayek a teorie spontánniho řádu* [F.A. Hayek and the Theory of Spontaneous Order]. Praha: Professional Publishing.

Pavlík, Ján. 2006. Austrian Economics and the Problems of Apriorism. *E-Logos—Electronic Journal for Philosophy* 13: 1–73. ISSN 1211-0442. WWW DOCUMENT. http://nb.vse.cz/kfil/elogos/science/pavl106.pdf.

Pavlík, Ján. 2010. *Spontánií geneze jazyka* [Spontaneous Genesis of Language]. Praha: Professional Publishing.

Popper, Karl R. 1975. *Objective Knowledge: An Evolutionary Approach*. Ely House, London: Oxford University Press.

Pošvanc, Matúš. 2019a. Evolutionary Possibilities of the Emergence of Economic Calculation and Money: The Problem of the Impossibility of Socialism. Working Paper. WWW DOCUMENT. https://www.researchgate.net/publication/334084336_Evolutionary_possibilities_of_the_emergence_of_economic_calculation_and_money_The_problem_of_the_impossibility_of_socialism.

Pošvanc, Matúš. 2019b. Why I Am Not Mises' Adherent. Working Paper. WWW DOCUMENT. https://www.researchgate.net/publication/333774098_Why_I_am_not_Mises'_Adherent.

Pošvanc, Matúš. 2020a. The Theory of Interest: Revision of Austrian Approach. Working Monograph. WWW DOCUMENT. https://www.researchgate.net/publication/338595641_The_Theory_of_Interest_Revision_of_Austrian_Approach_monograph_version.

Pošvanc, Matúš. 2020b. A Brief Explanation of the Price of Money. Working Paper (March 27, 2020). Available at SSRN: https://ssrn.com/abstract=3562493 or http://dx.doi.org/10.2139/ssrn.3562493.

Pošvanc, Matúš. 2020c. Regression Theorem—The Objectivist Part of the Austrian (Subjectivist) Theory. Working Paper. WWW DOCUMENT. https://www.researchgate.net/publication/340234197_Regression_Theorem_-The_Objectivist_Part_of_the_Austrian_Subjectivist_Theory.

Pošvanc, Matúš. 2021. In Defense of Fractional Free Banking: Back to Fundamentals. *MISES: Interdisciplinary Journal of Philosophy, Law and Economics* 9 (February). https://doi.org/10.30800/mises.2021.v9.1361.

Schumpeter, Joseph A. 1983 [1934]. *The Theory of Economic Development: An Inquiry into Profits, Capital, Credit, Interest, and the Business Cycle.* New Brunswick, New Jersey: Transaction Books. ISBN 9780878556984. Translated by Redvers Opie. Translated from the 1911 original German, Theorie der wirtschaftlichen Entwicklung.

Schutz, Alfred. 1959. Tiresias, or Our Knowledge of Future Events. *Social Research* 26 (1): 71–89. JSTOR. www.jstor.org/stable/40969340.

Selgin, George A. 1990. P*raxeology and Understanding: An Analysis of the Controversy in Austrian Economics.* Auburn, Alabama: Praxeology Press of the Ludwig von Mises Institute, Auburn University. WWW DOCUMENT. https://mises.org/library/praxeology-and-understanding-analysis-controversy-austrian-economics-0.

Shackle, George L.S. 1992. *Epistemics and Economics: A Critique of Economic Doctrines.* NJ, USA: Routledge.

Smail, L. Daniel. 2014. Neurohistory in Action: Hoarding and the Human Past. *Isis* 105 (1, March): 110–122. https://doi.org/10.1086/675553.

Szabo, Nick. 2002. Shelling Out: The Origins of Money. Online article. WWW DOCUMENT. https://nakamotoinstitute.org/shelling-out/. Accessed 18 Feb 2021.

Van Den Hauwe, Ludwig. 2011. John Maynard Keynes and Ludwig Von Mises on Probability. *Journal of Libertarian Studies* 22: 471–507. Available at SSRN: https://ssrn.com/abstract=1607122.

Weiner, Keith. 2012. *A Free Market for Goods, Services, and Money.* The New Austrian School of Economics Budapest. Hungary. WWW DOCUMENT. https://keithweinereconomics.com/2012/09/05/a-free-market-for-goods-services-and-money/.

Wicksell, Knut. 1936. *Interest and Prices.* Originally published in 1898. Translation published by the Royal Economic Society. London. WWW DOCUMENT. https://mises.org/library/interest-and-prices.

3

In Defense of the Invisible Hand Concept: Modification of Austrian Theory of Equilibration and Social Ordering

Tieben (2012) shows that the concept of equilibrium has fascinated people since ancient times. According to him, however, the modern theory of equilibrium does not begin until the sixteenth century. The conclusion in Tieben (2012) implies dissatisfaction with present theories of equilibrium, in which he questions whether any realistic conception of equilibrium is possible at all. After more than 2000 years of interest and more than 400 years of more intensive scrutiny, this is an unflattering, albeit true, conclusion.

What does human intuition indicate about equilibrium? I would say that it indicates that equilibrium is a concept that should exist. Man strives to achieve some satisfaction of his needs or to have a balanced life. Man wants to be in balance with all things and people. Intuitively, therefore, there should be at least an idea of the concept of personal balance. The economic side of the problem certainly plays an important role here. Can one somehow define a broader concept of personal balance or at least the concept of economic personal balance? In the case of the existence of any effort for general or economic equilibrium, one should

M. Pošvanc, *The Evolutionary Invisible Hand*,
Palgrave Studies in Classical Liberalism,
https://doi.org/10.1007/978-3-030-71800-8_3

be able to define its principles; without the definition of principles, it is not possible to achieve any equilibrium or even discuss the concept. We can't achieve something if we do not know what it should be or look like. From this point of view, equilibrium should at least exist as an idea.

The problem is that our perception of the surrounding reality, of ourselves, and others, is constantly changing as there is no such thing as a consistent state. In human life, there is only a stream of ideas of the mind. It is not possible to cease all activity, turn ourselves off and then to evaluate who and what is in a state of balance. We face the perception of time, the flow of our thoughts, changes, and adaptation to change. Does this not, in principle, obscure any definition of equilibrium? If all our lives are streams of ideas, always heading into the future, which is ever open, can we define any concept of balance in the dynamic mode of reality and human action? Is there a structured state that we might call equilibrium?[1] Or is it such a subjective matter that, due to the openness of the future and the flow of the mind, does not have a conceptual structure and is completely different, unique, and incomparable for everyone? How it is then possible to discuss the concept? The discussion of a given concept at least suggests or even logically implies some kind of normative structure that each of us can grasp and that each of us has filled with our individual content. What then does a given structure or phenomenon which a person is trying to achieve look like?

Of course, it is not our task in this text to describe any specific form with regard to what equilibrium means to a person and what it does not. From an economics point of view, it should be a description of the concept of equilibrium and economic processes by which one arrives at one's specific content of what it means for that person to be satisfied and to be in balance. Only then can economics think about whether or not it is possible to achieve a state of social balance. It is not a description of some process of mutual coordination and the organization of society, that would lead to the maximum desired state of individuals.

This part of the book aims to present a brief outline of what, in my opinion, we can consider to be a *realistic concept of equilibrium* at the

---

[1]The terminology of the need for the existence of a structured phenomenon is taken from O'Driscoll and Rizzo (1996), who refers to Loasby (1991).

individual level and at the level of intersubjective exchange. I will also present some conceptual possibilities with regard to how to deal with equilibrium at the level of the economic community. I have to state that I am here inspired by Hülsmann (2000), who also tries to define a realistic approach to the problem of equilibrium. We will proceed by briefly summarizing some of the selected problems of the equilibrium theory described in Tieben (2012). We will present this theory in the context of the "Evenly Rotating Economy" (ERE), presented in Mises (1998). However, we will provide a modification of the concept. The definition of economic equilibrium on the level of individual equilibrium within exchange and exchange over time will follow. The possibility of the concept of equilibrium at the societal level will be described in terms of conceptual ideas. The presented modification also implies connections between the approaches to equilibrium by Mises or by Hayek's social ordering and infers several extensions of the approach of O'Driscoll-Rizzo (1996) or Hülsmann (2000).

3.1 Background and Description of the Problem

The equilibrium concept must be described in normative mode. Without the formulation of the idea of "*how something should be*," it is not possible for the human mind to discern what we are describing. Any concept of equilibrium must necessarily be based on this kind of differentiation. It is then able to distinguish various works on equilibrium while it is the discussion of the state of equilibrium that allows the description of the state of disequilibrium (O'Driscoll-Rizzo 1996). As we will see, the main problem we face is to present a normative concept of equilibrium which is, by definition, a static one in a dynamic mode. The tendency to define equilibrium in dynamic mode is not unusual within the Austrian school. Within the Austrian school, there are several concepts of equilibrium, the characteristic feature of which is the significant limitations of mechanical or static concepts of equilibrium. Mises (1998) presents the concept of the so-called ERE, we have Hayek's program described by (Lewis and

Lewin 2015) as a concept of "social ordering," Schumpeter presents the entrepreneur as a violator of equilibrium. Lachmann (following Shackle) emphasizes the element of disequilibria, which becomes an important part of the description of market phenomena. O'Driscoll and Rizzo (1996) points to equilibration and disequilibria forces in the market as interrelated phenomena where equilibria and disequilibria are part of the same process. Hülsmann (2000) introduces the concept of equilibrium based on the concept of error and success,[2] criticizing any attempt to establish some framework that the market should move toward some state of equilibrium. Hülsmann denies any possibility of some general tendency toward equilibration.[3,4] However, all attempts stress some kind of process-based concept. I will attempt to connect these approaches, showing that the tendency to some form of order or equilibration exists.

Despite the criticism of the ERE concept set out in Hülsmann (2000) and Gunning (2001), the presented interpretation here will use the modified version of the ERE presented in Mises (1998). The modification of the interpretation will also make it possible to preserve the valid elements of the ERE concept, which will allow for the linking of Mises (1998) with Hayek's social ordering program, as well as Hayek's theory of the mind (Hayek 1952). What is interesting about the concept of ERE is its character, which according to Luther (2014, p. 2), depicts the equilibrium as a "pattern behavior." The concept of the ERE was used

---

[2]Hülsmann (2000, p. 7): "*Equilibrium analysis is the method of comparing actual behavior with its counterfactual alternatives in terms of success and failure.*"

[3]Or if we paraphrase O'Driscoll and Rizzo, the crucial question remains whether the market (per se) is subject to some equilibration process or whether equilibration is defined by the process in which it arises (see O'Driscoll and Rizzo 1996, p. xx pointing to the reference to Buchanan 1986, p. 73).

[4]Tieben (2012, p. 466) gives a meaningful counter-question to Hülsmann's statement that there is no tendency: "*Why is order and not chaos the unintended outcome of the interaction between self-interested actors in the economic arena?*"

At the same time, it is obvious that the nature of the question depends on what we, as humans, (intersubjectively) consider to be chaos and what we consider to be a higher degree of order. The appearance of which is more the result of some market and social processes - chaos or order – that depends on this. However, the meaningfulness of the question is justified, despite the fact that Tieben (2012) concludes at the end of his work that "*One general lesson which emerges from this broad development in disequilibrium analysis is that the age-old view that the supply and demand mechanism secures market equilibrium, feeding the image of the invisible hand benefitting us all is long overdue*" (p. 611).

by Mises as a *mental construct* that helps to explain the processes in real life. According to Rothbard (2004, pp. 322–323), this is in principle a description of the force behind market processes. The agent's activity is headed for some *final state of rest*, which will be reflected in generally repeating the economic process. However, Hülsmann (2000, pp. 38–42) shows that the construct presented by Mises is unusable, as he writes:

> *...more generally stated, it is an impossible undertaking to define equilibrium in terms of conditions of action. There is no discernible final state of rest upon which the economy might more or less automatically "converge."* (p. 41)

Although Hülsmann's criticism is convincing, the mental construct still endures through everything; the very formulation of the construct has its own logical structure. This is mainly due to the fact that if a person achieves some satisfaction of their needs, they try to maintain and preserve this state (because that is actually what he or she wants). This implies the repetition of some activity that caused the satisfaction of given needs, if the person is not exposed to change. If we think of the given construct on society as a whole, it is logical that the result is that the economic community repeats all of the same kind of activity. But Hülsmann (2000) subjects the concept of ERE to overwhelming criticism. Gunning (2001) criticizes Mises in a similar vein as Hülsmann. He presents an interesting argument for the needs of Mises's work in connection with the ERE, namely in terms of the possibility of distinguishing between action and non-action. When using his construct, Mises (1998, p. 245) considers two basic possibilities when a person does not act: the first case is when "*all uneasiness has been removed,*" and the second case is if "*any further removal of felt uneasiness is out of the question,*" i.e., if the future perceived state of affairs is the same as the person is already experiencing without seeing any additional possibility of changing the satisfaction of needs (simply because not everything is possible). According to Mises, a person achieves this state through the so-called *Plain State of Rest*, i.e., the state when individuals perform the exchange.[5] If we proceed further with logical steps, we must imply that

[5]One of the things to note is that Mises does not describe the *plain state of rest* in the form of some individual state of a person, but *only* in the context of the exchange. In principle, Mises

we all try to achieve or head toward the so-called Final State of Rest (hereinafter "FSoR"), which, however, is just a thought construction for Mises. Mises adds to this description an explanation of the so-called ERE, which implies a third possibility of non-action, namely the existence of robotic creatures that repeat the same activities. Mises (1998, p. 247) points out that:

> *The imaginary construction of the final state of rest is marked by paying full regard to change in the temporal succession of events. In this respect, it differs from the imaginary construction of the evenly rotating economy which is characterized by the elimination of change in the data and of the time element.*

Gunning (2001) shows that the construction of the ERE can be used only in the context of comparing the behavior of automata (robots) to humans, and not as a praxeological construct to which some human action is directed. As we have already stated, a year before Gunning did, Hülsmann (2000) also argued that the ERE is not a workable construct in terms of action. Hülsmann adds and argues that there is no such thing as a coordinated behavior of market participants toward overall market equilibrium and that this is not true even under the conditions that define the ERE per se.

However, I think that it is clear from the above-mentioned conditions of non-action that Mises (1998) does not sufficiently differentiate between the concepts of the FSoR and ERE; this is also quite clear in Gunning (2001). While the concept of the FSoR is associated with the first two efforts to meet human needs which lead to a state of satisfaction and thus "inaction," the concept of the ERE, as presented in Mises (1998), describes a robotic system per se. Mises is considering *linking* the FSoR and the ERE; this is suggested when he describes that money is not necessary within the ERE. He claims that:

(1998) does not define and describe the characteristics of when an individual is in a state of *individual equilibrium* when they should not act in the sense of the two possibilities of inaction defined by him.

> *In a system without change in which there is no uncertainty whatever about the future, nobody needs to hold cash. Every individual knows precisely what amount of money he will need at any future date. He is therefore in a position to lend all the funds he receives in such a way that the loans fall due on the date he will need them. Let us assume that there is only gold money and only one central bank. With the successive progress toward the state of an evenly rotating economy all individuals and firms restrict step by step their holding of cash and the quantities of gold thus released flow into nonmonetary-industrial-employment. When the equilibrium of the evenly rotating economy is finally reached, there are no more cash holdings; no more gold is used for monetary purposes.*
>
> ....
>
> *The imaginary construction of an evenly rotating system is a limiting notion. In its frame there is in fact no longer any action. Automatic reaction is substituted for the conscious striving of thinking man after the removal of uneasiness. We can employ this problematic imaginary construction only if we never forget what purposes it is designed to serve.* (p. 250)

As we see from the quote, he describes a *step by step process* (from a plain state of rest to a final state of rest) under the condition "*a system without change in which there is no uncertainty whatever about the future*" which should finally lead into the state of the ERE which is, however, *the robotic system* with *automatic reactions* and *with no action.* I claim that this is the lack of differentiation between the FSoR and the ERE concept and it must then inevitably lead to justified criticism from Hülsmann (2000) and Gunning (2001). If we claim that the FSoR is, under the condition of "*a system without change in which there is no uncertainty whatever about the future*" an identical final state with the ERE, then it is necessary to describe *processes* that could theoretically cause the FSoR to appear to us as the ERE. We must be very careful when linking the FSoR and the ERE as thought constructs or imaginative constructions. The reason for this is that when we set unrealistic assumptions within the imaginative description, these given unrealistic assumptions relate both to the surrounding reality (exogenous factors) and human behavior (endogenous factors). But there is a difference in terms of which of the given factors we imaginatively remove and how. For the ERE, Mises (1998) requires the achievement of the so-called final price, which according to him, can be achieved only if we get rid of "*the lapse of time and of the perpetual change*" (p. 248). However, using this form of counterfactual description, Mises presupposes a thought construction related to the absence of change and time to the economic system, i.e., the ERE per se—the absence of change and time is implied to both exogenous and endogenous factors. This is not appropriate. It is true that the economic system is a separate whole (new phenomena per se) but it is at the same time the consequence of human interactions. It is necessary to distinguish between these two phenomena. It follows that if we want to use the ERE as an imaginative *human concept*, then it must be the imaginative *result of some human activity* that is repeated. If we consistently apply Mises' division of non-action to the activity of robots and to the non-action of people who do not perceive any change to their behavior because they are satisfied, we must necessarily describe two types of ERE: the robotic and the imaginative human.[6]

As Gunning (2001) shows, the robotic ERE (hereinafter referred to as the rERE) should show us the difference between a human being and a robot. In this case, we can, therefore, remove the exogenous and endogenous nature of the perception of change and time, because we apply these factors to robots and not to human beings. This is possible because the nature of the description is only exogenous, given that the robot is part of the reality and acts only as programmed (at least thus far). However, the imaginative human ERE (hereinafter referred to as the hERE) should describe the phenomena from the point of view of humans and how they achieve some form of hERE as a *result of their activities*; it must also then describe what goes on when the hERE is achieved. The outcome of these activities leading to the hERE should include a description of phenomena such as entrepreneurship. This should entail equally repetitive business activities, which in turn should cause the elimination

[6]The definition of the ERE in Mises (1998) is more or less the ERE that is robotic. The statement "more or less" is related to the fact that Mises does not sufficiently differentiate the given descriptions. Therefore, sometimes it seems to me that he is writing about hERE and sometimes rERE. At the same time, I use the term "more or less" because, to a greater extent, Mises's (1998) description seems to describe robotic "creatures" rather than humans.

of entrepreneurs' profits, the absence of endogenous changes, and the achievement of satisfaction of all members of the economic community when a person does not have to *economically act.* This is because "*all uneasiness has been removed and any further removal of felt uneasiness is out of the question.*" This state of affairs is felt by all humans. When compiling the hERE, it is only then possible to consider various imaginative assumptions of exogenous and endogenous changes, in accordance with the total knowledge of humans who should know all of their mutual needs, and so on: only then we can draw logical connections between what the given assumptions will cause and how, or see what happens by their elimination. The concept then enables us to model what we want to describe and to show the influence of real phenomena compared to a model situation. In other words, it is possible to eliminate the influence of change and the passage of time from the point of view of the system only with the robotic system as such.

As soon as we imply the use of the hERE form, which is characterized by phenomena such as, the final price, the repeating "entrepreneurs" activity,[7] zero profit, and no change in actions and the elimination of the problem of uncertainty, we must describe the hERE as the *result of the processes* which existed before reaching the hERE. In the hERE therefore, based on our imagination and our unrealistic assumptions about a given system, it can only seem to us, that uncertainty and entrepreneurship do not exist (because everybody is performing the same activity) and that we have a single price on the market with everyone coordinated. This is because in the hERE all actors repeat a certain, optimal, economic activity which they have discovered. But as we must add in the Hayek's sense, the repetitive activity would be *constantly and constantly discovered*—of course, given our imaginative assumptions. Only in this way is it possible to maintain the goal of studying the phenomena in question with a realistic outlook, so that the mental construct with reality could be compared.

[7]It would still be entrepreneurship discovery. However, entrepreneurs would discover the same mix of people's needs and would use the same (ideal) mix of production factors again and again. The fact that the entrepreneurs in question repeat the same does not imply that they are robots. The emphasis here is that this would be the result of their discovery. It is, of course, an imaginative construction.

Therefore, the imaginative construction of the hERE would be described as the *result* of the actions of human beings (but not robots). This would result in the elimination of uncertainty because of the mutual knowledge of individuals, the discovery of an equilibrium price, of a natural interest rate (spread), ideal economic processes, and all relevant economic projects through the repetitive activities of entrepreneurs. However, this state can theoretically be achieved as well in a different way; it is enough to assume the total, but limited knowledge of primitive beings (the term used in a non-pejorative way). Their limited knowledge would always lead to the same results in terms of their "primitive actions," only in an extremely limited form of variants. Both systems would thus be the result of either beings with mutual omniscient knowledge or beings with primitive and, therefore, precisely limited knowledge. It would then be true that all activities would be repeated by everyone; that activity would respond only to exogenous changes in the environment if we allowed exogenous changes in the description of the construct. It means that, if the exogenous changes occur, they would be immediately incorporated into the plans of those individuals so as to re-establish a state of the hERE that would last until some exogenous change re-emerged to which individuals would adapt. This would be a dynamic method of describing the hERE, which would only appear as the rERE (because of repetitions of activities). At the same time, this method would show us that there is still a fundamental difference between the hERE and the rERE. This is the nature of beings who act within the systems in question and the fact that the hERE would be the result of coordination by human beings while the rERE would be an IT-programmed structure. At the same time, it shows us that in the case of the hERE, the given phenomena are always the result of some economic activity and the mutual interactions of individuals and not the result of assumptions derived from the imaginative construction of the hERE.

It is in this context that we will introduce the theory of equilibration. We will also focus on other problems related to the existing theories of equilibration which are relevant in the context of this text. Across the theories of equilibration, it is possible to observe a literal obsession with the description of the coordination phenomena based on the concept of price. However, the price is always the result of processes—whether through equilibration or disequilibration. All the phenomena that we have to describe in order to define any equilibration theory, must be described before the emergence of the price; the given processes lead to results that we observe empirically in the form of the price. Paradoxically, from this point of view, the concept of price is the last thing that should interest us in equilibration theory. Related to this description is the second observable problem of the many equilibrist theories. In the worst-case scenario, they describe either a static state of the acquisition of goods and services which manifests itself in an equilibrium static price, or at best a dynamic movement of goods, or services, or acts of exchanges. Again, what do these results represent? They represent intentions and plans. At the level of intentions and plans, it is necessary to provide a relevant description of the mechanisms and processes that lead to these results. It is too late to describe the equilibration processes based on the equilibration results (if we paraphrase and modify Shackle). Any arrangement of relationships, any equilibration, or disequilibration, ergo, its processes, must take place beforehand; it is these processes that need to be described and their operation clarified. Other significant issues often discussed are the questions related to the transition between equilibrium and disequilibrium, the existence of any tendency to equilibration, or the question of whether a permanent state of disequilibrium is a natural state of affairs.

3.2 Individual Equilibrium

Many of the processes behind the principle of market equilibration (the problem of grasping and estimating the future, the problem of entrepreneurship discovery, the concept of economic error), were described in Chapter 2. We will use the modification of the theory of subjective value in this part as well; the modification states that a person satisfies the sum of needs by the sum of goods (the portfolio). As we already know, modifying the application of the causal link between the sum of needs satisfied by the sum of goods (the portfolio) over time makes it possible to avoid value heterogeneity, which is related to the diverse perception of the value of specific goods. Over time we can prefer one structure of the portfolio over another, given that it is an identical concept and a person compares the structural composition of the portfolio. A person's intentional actions are, therefore, concerned with the intended state of affairs of these goods (the real goods portfolio) to satisfy his/her combination of needs. At the same time, a given state of affairs either exists or does not exist in reality; accordingly, needs may or may not be met. Given that in all circumstances the sum and combination of needs are required and that the mind can compose an infinite combination, there can always be an unsatisfied combination of any qualitatively and quantitatively combined needs. However, it is always a person who formulates the combination of needs in question; though a person is not limited in terms of limiting their needs, he/she can limit themselves. This does not mean that the individual will consider every combination. The infinite number of combinations of needs only implies the infinite possibilities of combinations and the possibilities of satisfying them. However, this does not imply that each of the given combinations of needs has to be formulated, and not each formulation will be assessed or satisfied by *the* action and will transform into a good, real, economic good portfolio.

Based on the modification, it is also possible to define a real concept of individual equilibrium. We will speak of individual equilibrium as a state of *economic in-action* that is achieved, according to Mises (1998, p. 245), when uneasiness related to the satisfaction of needs is not felt (the first option) or further satisfaction of needs is not possible (the second option). Thus, Mises clearly implies that there is an individual state of equilibrium. But how to describe it? Obviously, Mises doesn't say we're going to be robots, or we're going to die or vice versa. We will continue to be humans, but the difference would be that we will either not feel an uneasiness associated with meeting our needs, or it will not be possible to satisfy some needs further (according to the knowledge of men). This implies a dynamic future-oriented state of perceived rest (or peace) that persists. Basically, it is a dynamic state of affairs.[8] In the context of the modified value theory presented here, we will argue that individual equilibrium is a state in which an individual has created an

[8]The phrase "dynamic state" in economics can give the impression of a logical paradox, where the term "dynamic" expresses some process that implies change and the term "state" expresses something static or fixed and unchanging.

individual portfolio of goods that does not force them to pursue any *economic* activity—whether their own or through exchange—aimed at changing the existing portfolio composition. Thus, a person remains very human (he/she doesn't transform into a robot) and acts in the sense of satisfying some envisioned needs over time. These are satisfied by the portfolio. We can call this *an individual state of economic rest*. This is not a state of inaction in the sense of not doing anything. Inaction would only apply as a result of death or the aforementioned robotic state. It is a subjectively assessed level of satisfaction with the economic portfolio a person has created, which satisfies his intended needs over a given period of time.

The described structure has a dynamic and temporal character that lasts. Given that the portfolio has a relational character, it is possible to define its marginal state and thus differentiate satisfactory and unsatisfactory states; the structure of the portfolio provides this information. An equilibristic portfolio has a particular structure whose parts are under change. People consume goods because the relational structure changes toward the marginal limit (a dynamic variable). However, until the portfolio reaches a given imaginary marginal threshold (a static variable), a person does not need to act economically in the sense that their needs are either continuously being satisfied or are already satisfied, so there is no reason to act economically. The situation is caused by the widening spread between the desired and current portfolio structure. The spread begins to form in the case of the net consumption of goods from the portfolio. However, from a subjective point of view, that perception may be negligible at first; only if the spread widens does that person begin to perceive it as problematic, as it begins to engage economically. We do not describe any static state of affairs at the same time. On the contrary, we describe a dynamic state of affairs. The perception of the range of the spread between the current and the desired portfolio structure can be caused from an individual point of view by both exogenous and endogenous factors. Something may cause that individual to act and respond with a new composition of portfolio, or the combination of needs may change so that the spread begins to widen and the individual begins to perceive that the portfolio is not satisfactory. Not any change in the portfolio causes the perception of the spread to become problematic for an individual. At first, the spread is only *relatively* problematic and only becomes really problematic when it causes a feeling of uneasiness and consequently motivates action. This means that it is only a subjectively perceived *significant* marginal change of the structure of a portfolio that causes a state of uneasiness, which subsequently causes a person to act economically in order to regain an equilibristic state of affairs that could have a different structural character derived from the factual combination of needs. This occurs because the equilibristic structural character of the portfolio is derived from the factual combination of the needs of the person in question. Basically, the perceived structure of factual needs coincides with the idea of the structure of goods, which are, in reality, used to satisfy a perceived combination of needs. Paradoxically, we can therefore say that the structure defined in this way describes a dynamic state, where the *state* implies something immutable or fixed, and *dynamics* imply something that is subject to process and change. This is a conceptual definition of the individual state of equilibrium, i.e., the definition of the structure we require.

We now need to return to Mises (1998) and his description of the ERE and the FSoR. It is quite important. As we mentioned above, Gunning (2001) uses this description to differentiate robots from humans. We have suggested that based on Gunning's (2001) view, we must differentiate between the rERE and hERE. However, it is necessary to describe what occurs when hERE is achieved. We know that Mises stated that humans would repeat all around the same economic activity. However, due to the differentiation between the rERE and the hERE, we know that some kind of outcome is necessary. If each individual achieves the FSoR, we will have the hERE. This means that we need to explain the FSoR, in terms of what lasts and what goes on during this state—and it is quite a tricky state. We have to claim that when a person does not act, it does not mean that he/she is dead or in a vegetative state. If the person is not in a vegetative state, dead or a robot, he/she acts; this is quite a logical inconsistency. In essence, it is. However, if we use Hayek (1952), and the interpretation of Hayek by Horwitz (2010),[9] and we combine it

[9]The reader should be reminded of the section "2.2.3 Modified theory of subjective value".

with our claim that: "individual equilibrium is a state in which an individual has reached an individual portfolio of economic goods that does not force them to pursue any *economic* activity, whether their own or through an exchange, aimed at changing the existing portfolio composition" it will not be as logically paradoxical as it at first seems. Let's provide an explanation.

Horwitz (2010, pp. 274–276) uses the analogy of routines and the rules of the firm with brains and minds. I am not sure if he realizes how important his analogies are, but basically, he describes, mutatis mutandis, the very state of equilibrium we define at the level of the individual. He writes (p. 275, bold added):

> *Mental rules link the sensory stimuli that come into the brain to the actions that the organism takes based on them. How the mind classifies those stimuli determines how the organism acts upon the external world. … people have "activities" or goals that they wish to achieve, whether* ***conscious or automatic*** *(e.g., breathing or other non-conscious activity), and they have "resources" that go into the process of achieving those goals in the form of their perceptions of the world around them.* ***The mind's rules of classification are, in essence, routines that guide the organism's behavior by turning stimuli into action on the external world.*** *The classification process is a matter of "faced with this set of sensory inputs, what is the best model of the current world and what does that imply about how to react, given the goal at hand? … Firms process inputs to outputs in a similar fashion.*

Horwitz describes conscious *and* automatic actions based on the rules of classifications which are routines that guide our actions *based on resources*. What else can we add? If we combine this approach with our structure, we are able to explain equilibristic actions. It is an *automatic or routine action* based on goods (resources) in the equilibristic portfolio. It is different from human *economic* action which is very intentional. This one is *the* choice; it is a demonstration of a more preferred state of affairs to that which is less preferred; it is motivated by the model-based concept conceived in the mind compared to the map-based concept by man which leads into uneasiness and is followed by action focused on eliminating uneasiness. However, automatic—routine action is action in which a man is satisfied with the given conditions. The structure of that condition is only described by the portfolio when a marginal change of the portfolio (the state of affairs) is not relevant to the man. The needs, in a subjectively given period of time, are met by the means; otherwise, planned needs will be met by automatic actions. It is a state of mind in which the map-based structure of the mind provides us with everything necessary in order to fulfill the needs, based on the acquired resources (the portfolio) within the subjectively given time period; it is a thymological-praxeological state when a man discovers some state of affairs he is satisfied with and the resources he has (the portfolio) which enables him to enjoy this state. It is because the future-oriented model character of the mind arrives at the same conclusion which is provided by the map character of the mind; the map character provides automatic responses to the planned state of affairs. In other words, the model-based structure conceived by the mind coincides with the map-model structure.[10]

Automatic action or some form of automatism is very much a part of our lives. Breathing is not the only action that is considered an automatic action (an example given by Horwitz). Automatic action refers to all activities not consciously or intentionally performed, such as driving a car, just relaxing around the house, watching TV, eating, or chatting. There are many other societal, religious, and cultural routines, which we practice in the same way, e.g., praying, greetings, casually talking, and so on. It is necessary to state that automatic actions usually start as intentional. It is a matter of fact that we must make a choice; however, the choice leads us to a (subjectively given) state of affairs defined by us when an individual performs some automatic actions. It has to be also stated that some of us are more successful at achieving this state. Everything depends on the subjective evaluation of the model-map coincidence. I think that there are also many intentional actions, that we try to transform into automatic actions. For example, when we make a deal over time and decide about principal, interest, and other conditions of the deal, relying on the legal system to achieve the planned state of affairs. The deal, the legal system, each one provides us with the flexibility to

[10] I think that this is possible to apply, mutatis mutandis, to the problem of the firm as well. Horwitz (2010) also provides another analogy of the model/map vs. the budget-plan/balance sheet of the firm. It is also, mutatis mutandis, applicable to the individual.

make other decisions and not to control this agreement for every second of its duration. A similar example could be a deal between entrepreneur and worker. Both examples are based on the deal relying on conditions that enable them to function within the boundaries of the deal as well as focusing on other factors or features, e.g., the worker is able to act in the interest of his/her family, and the entrepreneur can focus on other aspects of the business. Yes, it often happens that the deal is not fulfilled, or the conditions are broken by one of the parties. This only provides us with information for intentional action in order to improve or re-arrange the desired state of affairs. When the conditions of a deal are broken, it results in a state of disequilibrium. Intentional actions are then focused on in order to re-arrange the desired automatic actions of a person, which leads to the desired state of affairs (described as "it should be").

In principle, from the point of view of the individual, individual equilibrium is a state in which he/she is indifferent to intentional action, which would lead to a different compositional structure of his/her portfolio since the present composition of the portfolio satisfies the combination of needs perceived by the individual. As Block (1980) shows, this situation must be thymological in nature. This state of affairs has, on the one hand, a thymological (historical) character in that it arose sometime in the past and is continuing. At the same time, it has a praxeological (purposeful) character—it is a part of the person's action, although an automatic one. The person continues to act automatically, based on the given state of the portfolio—he/she is satisfying his/her current needs. The individual does not request an intentional change. Thus, they continue to act, but from the economic point of view, they do not carry out any intentional economic activity that would lead to the achievement of any other desired composition of the portfolio. From an individual point of view, the composition of the portfolio is then optimal.

We can imagine the situation for a subjectively given period of time e.g., a weekend. If I assume that the composition of my needs should consist of some form of relaxation, spending time with family, or engaging in hobbies, during the week, I would prepare the composition of the portfolio so that on Friday, I will be ready to implement my plan with the composed portfolio that I will start using. In the short term, I will therefore be in the "*individual state of economic rest.*" My spread will only start to widen on Sunday; if I have estimated the composition of needs and the composition of the portfolio for the weekend well enough, and if I correctly planned the steps in order to achieve the plan for the weekend, I would automatically follow each part of the plan. Yes, it could happen that some parts of the plan would not be fulfilled as planned, which would result in disequilibria, and force me to intentionally solve the problems (e.g., that an all-inclusive service is not provided in the hotel as expected or arranged), or, it could also be that some parts of the plan will not be fulfilled, but I can choose to ignore them (e.g., the coffee in the hotel is quite disgusting but I can tolerate it), and automatically act to fulfill the remaining parts of the plan or to intervene. The range of individual equilibrium depends on model-future oriented predictions (needs, plans) and map-present oriented automatic/conscious actions. It means that disequilibria could happen anytime, e.g., on Saturday morning, when I find out that I have not anticipated something or that I must arrange something else at work. This is given by another subjectively perceived need, e.g., the satisfaction of a client whose needs I should satisfy immediately because whether I would be able to satisfy my needs again after the weekend, depends on him/her. This state is, of course, empirically individualized. Here we must realize that the degree to which a person is satisfied/dissatisfied depends on the very combination of needs defined by the individual. Empirically, therefore, satisfaction is theoretically achievable by limiting one's infinite combination of needs (as we stated above, we can be ignorant of some changes of plans).[11] Likewise, the ideal personal portfolio could be absolutely unattainable for an individual as a constantly evolving new form of a combination of needs which could cause him constant uneasiness until his/her death. The state of individual rest may be achievable for one at the end of life, or in some limited time horizon, it may be unattainable for another due to the constant perception of some uneasiness that he/she is trying to eliminate by their actions. Empirically, it depends on the individual.

[11]This does not demonstrate that this is the only way that equilibrium is empirically achievable. It is only possible to demonstrate that it is also a combination of needs that determines the degree of individual satisfaction.

3.2.1 Current vs. Desired vs. Possible Structure of the Individual Portfolio

It must be stated that a person's actions, plans, and intentions are focused on building a portfolio; a person has only one portfolio, which reflects reality. However, as stated above, the portfolio is also a mental construct. Basically, we formulate in our minds a combination of needs and the idea of economic goods (the portfolio). This is the principle of value imputation. Following their ideas regarding their portfolio, a person tries to achieve a real combination of the elements of reality we call economic goods, which reflects their idea of the portfolio in their minds. The idea of the portfolio and the structure of the mind reflects what is in the reality of our surroundings. If we use the terminology of Hayek (1952) and we take inspiration from Horwitz (2010), we can say we are on the level of a map-based construct of the mind. However, the *idea* of the structure of the portfolio has a contra-factual character. It means that the idea of the structure also reflects aspects of reality, which a person does not have. These aspects are in the form of an idea or wish; this idea may or may not reflect reality. For example, I may have an apartment; however, I wish to have a house that may or may not exist. It is also possible to wish for something that does not exist. Meaning, I may wish to possess a magic wand or a telescope, which would enable me to see behind the horizon of the universe. So, I can somehow imagine these items to be real. I can imagine that I might have Harry Potter's wand or a telescope. But existing wands and telescopes do not have the correct combination of features, and therefore do not exist in the form I wish them to exist in, nor does present knowledge support this combination of features. There is no practical possibility of realistically constructing a magic wand. The idea of the structure of a portfolio can, therefore, have some counterfactual components, which do not reflect reality. That does not mean that this counterfactual part of the portfolio cannot be realistically constructed in the future. Still, despite our current level of technical and expanding knowledge, the fact remains that not everything is possible. These contra factual parts are formulated by the model-based structure of the mind and are focused on the future. A person's action is then focused on making the intended structure of the mind a reality.

From an individual point of view, a person always has a current portfolio (hereinafter "Pc"); the current portfolio coincides with the actual economic goods in the person's possession. This indicates some degree of satisfaction of the person's needs. There is also another counterfactual structure—the structures of the desired portfolio (hereinafter "Pd"), which can be anything. There are no restrictions on the Pd in the form of an idea. However, the restrictions on the actual economic goods of the Pd are primarily related to the fact that not everything is possible, both in terms of the combination of needs that can be formulated, and the technical possibilities of satisfying those needs.[12] Anything can be desired, and any combination of needs can be formulated, thereby creating an unrealistic combination of needs; e.g., being in the Bahamas and on Mt. Everest at the same time or, knowing how to create real magic or how to see beyond the visible boundaries of the universe. It is not technically possible to satisfy this combination of needs, either because of natural laws or the formulation of the combination of needs, which is simply unachievable. A person must therefore decide between the desired and the possible structure of his/her portfolio (hereinafter "Pp"), which he/she compares with the structure of the Pc while striving for the optimal composition of the portfolio; i.e., to make the spread between the structure of the Pd, the Pp, and the Pc as narrow as possible. From the individual point of view, the time aspect of the individual effort to achieve the narrowest possible spread between the given portfolio structures is equally important. It also determines a realistic perception of individual equilibrium. The spread between the structure of the Pc, the Pd, and the Pp are identifiable. This is because the concept of the portfolio has a relational character. The idea of the Pc which coincides with a combination of real goods gives us a starting point, while the idea of the Pd, and the Pp gives us the required benchmark. This causes the existence of the degree of difference between the Pc and the Pd and the Pp, which is qualitatively and quantitatively identifiable for man.

[12]Even the very structure of reality (its elements) creates certain inherent limitations on the combination of parts of reality; e.g., in the form of only a certain possible mutual combination of the elements of reality (some chemical elements by nature do not react with others) or limitations given by some physical laws (the speed of light), or the very nature of reality (e.g., the expansion of the universe).

At the same time, the formal-logical concept of the portfolio is applicable over time—the idea of the portfolio remains the same, even though its composition or morphology changes over time. Both qualitative and quantitative compositions of the Pc can be monitored, compared, and evaluated over time to give some idea of the Pd or the Pp. What does this spread look like? I think that it could be in the form of the missing parts of the portfolio. However, it could also be a particular combination of goods, which may result in the other parts of the Pc being sold (parts of the portfolio become goods within other portfolios) or abandoned (goods will be transformed back to general parts of reality). It could be in the form of an implicit or explicit wish—meaning that one can only mentally speculate about some of the economic goods. The modification of the theory of subjective value also makes it possible to determine the reasons for perceived changes between the factual and counterfactual structures of the portfolio in question. Those changes occur between the perception of some combination of factual needs (Nf), and real counterfactual (Nrc) and unrealistic counterfactual needs (Nuc). The Nf were created by the model structure of the mind sometime in the past. Past actions were focused on in order to bring about the present state of affairs to meet these needs. However, today, the situation could be different. The perception of the Nf against the Nuc will affect the spread between the structure of the Pc and the Pd. The perception of the Nrc by the Nuc will affect the spread between the structure of the Pd and the Pp. It is obvious that given the subjective nature of the theory of value, in principle, we cannot speak with specificity about the consideration of needs, as we do not know what specific combination of needs a person prefers. We only know that a person prefers a higher to a lower satisfaction of some particular combination of needs. It follows that if the structure of the Pc satisfies some perceived sum of the Nf, the Nrc, and the Nuc, a person is in a state of individual economic equilibrium and then he/she acts automatically. As mentioned above, this could happen if we sufficiently limit the time aspect of satisfying the sum and combination of the Nf, the Nrc, and the Nuc, respectively because of some psychological reasons the Nrc and the Nuc coincides with the Nf even in a longer subjective time frame, e.g., for hermits, Buddhist monks, or for people who limit themselves because of religious, societal or cultural reasons, and also, because of their age or other personal reasons. It has to be stressed that the individual economic equilibrium doesn't mean that if some rich men, whose portfolios are quite robust and are in some kind of long-term equilibrium, decide to gradually consume their Pc and no longer economically engage. They are in individual equilibrium if they do not intentionally act to re-arrange the state of affairs into the equilibrium. Theoretically, however, if they are prepared to accept that not everything is possible and if they are uninformed about marginal changes, their actions could be only automatic; this means that they would be in equilibrium. For some subjective reason, their Pc = Pp = Pd already satisfies some of their perceived, most suitable combination of the Nf, of course, without achieving all possible combinations of satisfying their needs in general, which could be formulated in the context of the Nrc and the Nuc.[13]

However, if a person perceives that the structure of the Pc does not satisfy his/her perceived Nf and expected Nrc, he/she must act economically and eliminate the perceived state of uneasiness. The change in the perception that the structure of the Pc does not satisfy the needs is based on the change in the perception of a combination of factual and expected counterfactual needs. The change in the perceived combination of needs is based either on some marginal change in the portfolio that ceases to satisfy the factually perceived combination of needs or on a change in the perception of factual and expected counterfactual needs. The counterfactual needs become factual this way. A person, of course, prefers some structure of the Pd which, under ideal circumstances, would satisfy all combinations of needs (Nf, Nrc, Nuc). However, this is not achievable either in terms of subjective factors (insufficient knowledge), objective factors (not everything is objectively possible), intersubjective factors (catallactic rules which imply the boundaries of others), or political factors (something is enforced by power). That is why a person

[13]Let us remember that the very possibilities of combination only allow an infinite combination of needs, which, may never be assessed or satisfied. We are unable to assess everything and to have in mind any combination of any needs. Our thinking has also some limitations, and of course there are also some limits that reality has (so far) prepared for us, e.g., the impossibility of living forever. It doesn't mean that some current Nuc or Nrc would not be satisfied in the future as well, when the knowledge of men (economic and other knowledge) will increase.

ultimately (in action) prefers (or tries to achieve) only some form of Pp composition which only corresponds to a certain combination of Nf and expected Nrc. A part of the needs in the form of Nuc remain unsatisfied, but potentially still in demand. An individual chooses the structure of the Pp because the spread between the Pc and the Pd is wider than the spread between the Pp and the Pd. In other words, a person prefers the structure of the Pp to the Pc, because the Pp is closer to the idea of the Pd. The composition of the structure of the Pp can be diverse. In principle, there can be an infinite number of combinations of economic goods within Pp. Therefore, the question of which structure of the Pp one chooses is inappropriate. It is, of course, decided for such a Pp, which on the one hand is achievable and, on the other, has a spread that appears to be the narrowest possible against the structure of the Pd. A person aims to have the narrowest possible spread between the structure of the Pp and the Pd; it is only for such a Pp we can declare from an individual point of view that a person thinks about a given portfolio because it satisfies the needs more, and at the same time can be composed (either by exchange or by one's activity). If the Pp does not narrow the spread and does not bring it closer to the Pd, man would prefer to continue to prefer the existing Pc.

3.3 Market Equilibrium in the "Here and Now" Exchange and the "Debt" Exchange

After describing the individual state related to the definition of the equilibrium process from an individual perspective, we can proceed to the description of equilibration based on the mutual interaction of two or more individuals within the society. We need to explain how to achieve equilibrium in exchange. It has to be stressed that voluntary exchange is only a tool to improve the state of affairs of two or more individuals. The description presented here follows Mises's terminology used in the sense of "*plain state of rest*"; *at the same* time, we will explain the slightly paradoxical statement by O'Driscoll-Rizzo that any market equilibration also has a disequilibration component[14] and that economic learning takes place against the background of mutual economic interactions.

3.3.1 Barter/Money Exchange—Here and Now

What happens when you exchange an economic good X, owned by Alice for a good Y owned by Bob? There will be an X/Y price from Alice's point of view and Y/X from Bob's point of view. The price is the result of at least two evaluation processes—one from Alice's point of view and the other from Bob's. The description of the creation of price is as follows: Assuming that we have three people in the market, Alice, Bob, and Charlie and Alice owns the current portfolio of goods PcA composed of economic goods (20X, 2Z, 5M), Bob owns the current portfolio of goods PcB composed of goods (20Y, 2 K, 7R), and Charlie owns the current portfolio of goods PcC composed of goods (20Y, 2T, 5R). Suppose Bob and Charlie are identical twin-brothers and produce a homogenized product Y and Alice offers product X. Suppose further that Bob offers 10Y and demands 10X for it and Bob offers 10Y and demands 11X for it, and Alice comes to the market with an offer 5X for 10Y. All participants show their expectations and intentions. It is beneficial to mention that the X/Y exchange implies that Alice, Bob, and Charlie, for some reason, want to incorporate these goods into their portfolios to meet their combination of factual and expected counterfactual needs.

So, we have the following situation on the market: Alice requires some PdA (15X, 10Y, 2Z, 5 M), Bob requires some PdB (10Y, 10X, 2 K, 7R), and Charlie requires some PdC (10Y, 11X, 2T, 5R). The reason Charlie demands 11X in exchange and not just 10X like Bob, is related to the fact that Bob and Charlie have different portfolios regardless of the reason. It

---

[14]O'Driscoll and Rizzo (1996, p. xxvii) "*In facilitating these changes the higher-level pattern equilibrium ensures maximum market coordination. Maximum coordination, however, does not necessarily mean a state that is fairly close to full or exact coordination* (Rizzo 1990, pp. 25–27). *This is because to attain the highest possible degree of coordination we must have (adaptive) change which itself involves a certain amount of discoordination. The very process of coordinating must involve dis-coordinating. Thus, encompassed within an overall pattern equilibrium there is a system of market interactions that endogenously produces a certain degree of disequilibrium—a disequilibrium that is vital to generating whatever degree of market coordination we do in fact enjoy.*"

may be because of a past decision related to the fact that Bob thinks the given combination is more advantageous for him than the one Charlie has, regardless of the fact that they are identical twin-brothers. We can also see in the market that there is a price spread between the product X and Y, while the order book looks like this:

5X – 10 Y.........
10 X – 10Y
10 X – 11 Y.

The exchange cannot exist in these circumstances. When will the exchange take place? Only if Alice is willing to provide 7X for 10 Y for some reason and Bob is also willing to provide 10 Y for 7 X. Why would the situation change from their point of view and the exchange occur? It may be because Bob and Alice judged that the exchange was ultimately beneficial to them. We know then that they decided they would prefer some possible structure of their potential portfolios (Pps). From Alice's point of view, this may be because she has lately enriched her Pc with a W good, which means that her ideal combination of the PdA portfolio will be (13X, 10Y, 2Z, 5 M, 1 W) and becomes more preferred than the originally required ideal PdA. From Bob's point of view, the reason could be that K was a debt that he had to repay, which "forced" him to accept Alice's terms. Thus, Bob prefers PpB (10Y, 7X, 1 K, 7R). Charlie stays with his PcC given that the price change, in the form of 6 X for 10 Y, would cause the resulting PpC portfolio to widen the perceived spread between the PpC and the PdC much more than the existing spread between the PcC vs the PdC. The reason may be that Chalie's combination of goods (20Y, 2T, 5R) allows him to continue to sufficiently satisfy his needs more than the combination in the form of the PpC.

The final price of 10Y/7X was, therefore, based on the evaluation process related to the narrowing of Alice and Bob's portfolio spreads. We see that the past price of X and Y plays no role in this process. We also see that in this case, the price spread has *narrowed* in the market. We can also assume that both Alice and Bob are happier than they would be without an exchange when Alice reached her PdA and when Bob narrowed the perceived spread between the new PpB and the desired PdB. We can also assume that Charlie is just as satisfied under the current circumstances as he would be in others, because his combination of goods in the form of the PcC is better than the PpC, although worse than the PdC. Mises calls this moment the *plain state of rest*, which brings a greater degree of satisfaction for Alice, Bob, and even Charlie than any other possible state, but a lesser degree of satisfaction than any other *desired* state.

The origin of the X/Y price is not described in terms of the existence of any past X/Y price Alice or Bob may have offered previously. It does not matter what the price of X/Y was in the past, whether it was exactly the same, or whether it was 72X/15Y, or 1X /3Y. The price depends on preferences and evaluations between the structure of Pc and the Pd of market participants and the resulting value assessment of their composition of the Pd against the Pp. The creation of the price informs Alice, Bob, and Charlie about the narrowing of the price market spread of goods X and Y by market participants. However, it is information about the narrowing of the spread between their portfolios, not information about the price per se, that the market participants are better off than they would be under other circumstances. The price on the market only informs us that this has happened. If the X-Y price spread remains on the X-Y market after this particular exchange, the situation provides additional information in the form that there is still room for market participants to increase perceived satisfaction in the form of their *desired* state of affairs. We know this because the existing price spread informs us that there is still room among the remaining market participants to narrow the spread between their individual portfolios under the conditions as defined by the bid-ask prices. In the case of a further narrowing of the price spread of the exchange of X/Y goods, this information tells us that the exchange of the given goods further causes a higher coordination of market participants whose spreads between their individual portfolios are narrowed precisely due to the X-Y exchange. Consequently, the opposite follows. In the event that the price spread in a given market widens, goods X and Y are traded less under the given price conditions; the situation implies a decreasing demand for one of the goods, X (or Y) under given price conditions. The decreasing demand could be because some combination of other economic goods in the portfolio of a person operating within the

X-Y market causes the demand for X or Y to decline. At the same time, the properties of X (or Y), in combination with other goods in a participant's portfolios, may lead to the exclusion of X (or Y) in the participant's portfolio. In this case, the bid price for the good X (or Y) disappears, depending on which good people do not want to include in their portfolio. The price spread is extended to the extent that one of the goods becomes unsaleable unless some combination of the properties of X (or Y) indicated by the entrepreneur offering the goods changes. The second possibility is that the demand for goods exists, but participants demand another change in the exchange ratios (the prices of goods). The reason must be a re-evaluated change in the composition of the portfolio in question, which implies that a participant of the exchange is not willing to dispose of one of the goods under conditions that were previously maintained on the market. The entrepreneur offering the product must adapt to the new situation, either by changing some combination of the characteristics of a given economic good that will make it more attractive again under new price conditions or by changing the combination of factors of production-related to the production of a given economic good. This would make it more affordable and would make his personal portfolio less sensitive to the combination of factors of production (in other words, it would decrease the costs of production).

It is, therefore, not the past price, but the spread, that gives entrepreneurs operating within the X-Y goods market information on their plans and how to adjust those plans. The past price only informs us that the spread has narrowed compared to the past and that the exchange has taken place. At the same time, it is clear that if the spread within the X-Y market narrows to the point where it is intersubjectively insignificant for the exchange participants, there is a *practical* equilibration in the X-Y goods market. It is necessary to emphasize that the possible perception of the insignificance of the width of the spread by participants of the exchange, (before the spread does not significantly narrow or expand significantly) informs us that there are some circumstances in the market (e.g., informational) that cannot be completely eliminated. From an intersubjective point of view however, there is still market equilibrium—participants experience a *practical plain state of rest*; from the point of view of the observer, e.g., social scientists, the X-Y market may still appear out of the equilibrium, i.e., the price spread in the given market still exists and is not completely eliminated. This is a correct and logical statement. However, from a practical point of view, this remains unnoticed by market participants precisely in certain circumstances, which are obscured to the social scientist as an observer. In principle, the point is that the use of an additional unit of any economic good from the portfolio of exchange participants within the X-Y market, the aim of which would be to eliminate the disproportion in question, appears to be unjustified; costs, i.e., spending the unit of economic goods X from the portfolio (e.g., in the form of acquiring particular information), would not bring additional profit in the form of a marginal unit of goods Y, which someone wants to include in the portfolio (or inversely from the point of view of other participants in the market). If the price spread in the X-Y goods market does not change, the additional marginal exchange is insignificant from an intersubjective point of view. The X-Y market participants signal that the additional exchange does not bring about the additional required narrowing of the spread of participants' portfolios. Revenues related to the implementation of the additional exchange would not exceed the costs associated with the implementation of the exchange. Of course, this does not mean that this will not change in the future, or that some market participants will not take advantage of the situation with the existing spread on the X-Y market.

With a zero-price spread, which means that the bid-ask coincides, there is a single price in the X-Y goods market; at the same time, this implies a complete market equilibrium in the X-Y goods market. This type of full equilibration must also be distinguished from the exchange in the market in the form of a momentary clash of the inter-individual bid-ask price in the realized exchange in the market. An inter-individual match of bid-ask prices eliminates the spread on a given market at a given moment and between given market participants. In this respect; in this case, we can say that the bid-ask clash caused the narrowing of the spread in the market, which led to a higher degree of coordination between the participants and thus one part of the whole market. However, the presence of other market participants caused the continued existence of a spread on the X-Y market, which implies that other participants consider the conditions set by them (displayed in the order book) to be more appropriate.

Here we face the problem of deciding what is and what is not a market equilibrium in the X-Y market. From the intersubjective point of view of the actors of the given X-Y commodity market, we know that narrowing the spread implies a higher degree of coordination and approaching equilibrium, while the opposite situation is related to the widening of the spread. We also know what maximal states are. The maximum of disequilibria is if the spread cannot be changed in the absence of a bid price on one of the X-Y goods market when the given market disappears. In this case, the entrepreneur who loses the bid price on his product must leave the market. The maximum equilibration is when the spread is eliminated in such a way that only one price is visible on the market, meaning the final price which is described in the dynamic mode, i.e., a non-existent or zero spread on the current market, which takes place over a period of time. A non-existent spread on the barter market is a situation where each offer of good X is purchased for Y, and vice versa, and a zero cardinal spread occurs if one of the goods is money; whereas, if Y is also money, every price offer of good X is bought for Y.[15] However, everything between the two states is relative in terms of equilibration for an observer, such as a social scientist (not a market participant).[16] We can also say about the given process that a narrowing spread means a higher degree of equilibration and vice versa.

Given that this is a dynamic process—the market is open and current information is practically permanently considered—we can only express specific findings with regard to the degree of equilibrium. This is because only when changing the spread, are we able to see the degree of current coordination or discoordination as it narrows and widens ahead. Only the dynamics of the process provides us with the required information which can be evaluated ex post, in terms of how market participants

[15]Money and currencies allow us to express a given spread in cardinal and comparable units. The issue of how these goods acquire these properties can be found in Pošvanc (2019).

[16]Essentially, the X-Y market participants perceive market equilibrium from a practical point of view if it is not economically sensible for them to further eliminate the market spread for any reason. However, from the point of view of a social scientist who perceives the existence of a price spread, this may not be the case.

were indifferent to its change at that point in time. At the same time, the extent of the spread range implies the degree of their intersubjective interest or lack of interest in coordination or the subjectively perceived cost circumstances that prevent the spread in question from being narrowed or eliminated altogether. The degree of the equilibration position of the X-Y market is then proportional to the degree of the width of the price spread on the given market.

To assess these circumstances, some related facts must exist, such as, the intersubjective standardization of the conditions with regard to how trading is formally carried out, what trading rules are, what trading practices are considered ethical or unethical, what is meant by product X, and what is meant by product Y. Today, in developed markets, these conditions of standardization are usually determined by owners of the exchange places and political regulations.[17] If one of the products X or Y is money (i.e., currency), their value standardization is determined by the related banking and financial markets as shown by Pošvanc (2019, 2020b, 2021). This value standardization related to the determination of the price of money or currencies is then used only implicitly in the commodity markets. These rules also impact the criteria, thereby determining how far or close the equilibrium commodity markets are to equilibrium.[18]

[17]Rules could be set by owners of first marketplaces in the past, or through the agreements between the participants of the exchange.

[18]From this point of view, we can evaluate some developed markets today, where an almost zero money spread is empirically apparent, as practically equilibrium markets. These are e.g., forex markets or certain commodity markets (metals, crops) traded on stock exchanges with related derivatives markets, etc. In terms of the theory presented here, a significant degree of coordination is achieved in these markets. The reason is the standardization of these markets, which allows us to eliminate, *practically and in principle*, any degree of information and knowledge asymmetry.

On the contrary, some less developed markets, which have practical problems, e.g., with the standardization of the product (e.g., real estate), with the standardization of trading processes (local markets), with the standardization of bid-ask pricing, etc., have to be considered as less balanced markets due to the natural wider bid-ask price spreads. I think that an interesting technological solution to these problems can be e.g., the tokenization of these markets through various crypto technologies in the future.

3.3.2 Individual and Market Equilibrium and Disequilibrium

We know for certain that any exchange narrows the price spread in the X-Y market, leading to a higher degree of equilibrium in the X-Y market. We also know that any exchange does not mean that the X-Y market itself is in equilibrium, nor does it mean that there are players in the individual equilibrium operating in the X-Y market as well as in other markets with other economic goods. How then to describe the above-mentioned problem of transition from equilibrium to disequilibrium and vice versa? Since we describe a very dynamic phenomenon, we have to deal with these incidents of transition from equilibrium to disequilibrium. It is already clear from the above that we are dealing with two possible views if we speculate about market equilibrium. The first view is connected to market players (the subjective view) and the second is connected to the logical and theoretical approach of social scientists (the intersubjective view). The first opinion is from the point of view of market players; it is also a satisfactory state of affairs when an *existing price spread* exists. Equilibrium may appear to exist from the subjective point of view as there is no additional economic knowledge that could eliminate the spread. It is also a more advantageous situation for any market player (market players such as Charlie) because their individual spreads between the possible and the current portfolio are relatively narrower (although not ideal—otherwise they would not set bid-ask prices) than the spreads that would arise if they exchanged under less advantageous conditions. However, with regard to the second opinion, the intersubjective view (also known as the point of view of the social scientist),[19] the market situation can still be a disequilibrating situation with the existing spread. The (intersubjective) equilibrium in the market can occur from the point of view of market participants as well as for the social scientist only if the price spread is zero or there is no spread.

Both views differ in their description; let us begin with the intersubjective considerations. If there is no spread, then the social scientist as well

[19]This equilibristic situation, an intersubjective one, has its own ontology, so, it is not surprising that it is a different comparison to a very individual view of the situation.

as any market participant must logically imply local market equilibrium. This is a situation in which the intersubjective equilibrium coincides with the subjective equilibrium of market participants *in this particular* market. Based on activities of other markets, market participants could still be in individual disequilibrium if they do not achieve their Pp or Pd structures. This implies that in other Z-W, market participants are in the same position as Charlie in our example given earlier. i.e., there are still some price spreads in the given markets which are created by market participants due to their perceived individual spreads between the Pp and the Pd structures. Although they achieved the maximum possible degree of coordination on the X-Y market, this market only contributed to the narrowing of their individual spreads between the Pp and the Pd structure. If it were true that the price spread on X-Y was eliminated and at the same time all market participants reached a Pd structure, only then would it be true that the same thing happened in other Z-W markets.

Let us assume that there is still a price spread on the X-Y market. Some market players did not even reach their Pp structure while still having their Pc structure. It means that the Pc structure is more preferred than any achievable Pp structure (they could still have a Pp structure if they decided to take other bids or asks than they would like to have). The reason is that the Pp structure would be achieved by the market player only by having to give up more goods or acquire fewer goods than expected. At the same time, it is true that then the Pc structure satisfies his/her needs more than the Pp structure, regardless of the fact that they are trying to achieve the Pp structure (however, the Pp is not achievable due to the idea of the other players in the market, which reflects the opposite situation). Here we must realize that though the given situation is created by individual spreads between the Pd, the Pp, and Pc structures, the outcome is not directly influenced by the personal situation of a particular participant in the market. The outcome is also dependent on the ideas of other market participants. It means that when a market participant looks at the order book where information about bid and ask are collected, the participant is able to recognize an alternative state of affairs (with Pp) which is different from what the participant expected when they entered the market with their bid or ask. The participant can evaluate marginal change if he/she takes the bid or ask, which is different than first expected. The market participant would take some bid or ask only if the marginal difference is not significant for them. While the Pd structure is something a person desires, the Pp structure is something he/she knows can be achieved; that is the difference. Basically, the participant knows that this state of affairs is possible to achieve, otherwise he/she would not participate in a given market.

Both views of equilibrium, subjective and intersubjective, imply "spring-tensioned" states that require some kind of action on the part of the actors, which should, but need not, release the tension. We can imagine this as interacting "springs," the complete relaxation of which can only occur if all actors in all markets achieve their individual Pd structure (we will get to this idea at the end of this chapter). Their stretching and loosening are related to an individual assessment of the differences or spreads between the Pd, the Pp, and Pc structures of one market player in the context of other market players. Thus, it should be apparent that the disequilibrium component of equilibrium lies in the difference between the possible Pp and the desired Pd structures of Alice, Bob, and Charlie, as well as their potential ex post evaluation of the exchange acts based on new market information. Any thought Pp structure changes into some Pc structure (i.e., the portfolio that a person has which satisfies their needs) later in time; given that a Pp structure is some kind of plan and a Pc structure happens as the consequence of some action. I mean here that Pc always refers to time t and Pp refers to time $t + 1$, which then becomes the time in which we re-assess the suitability of the portfolio—meaning here that it becomes the new time t. At the same time, a person can still strive for a Pd structure, which exists, though a person may limit the formulation of any idea of the Pd and may intentionally require only a Pp structure. The reason for the potential existence of a Pd structure is that although not everything is possible, anything can be formulated as a need.[20]

[20] From this point of view, we can formulate needs that are not at all possible due to the nature of reality (at least in the context of today's knowledge). One can e.g., formulate a truly unrealistic need in the form of: "To fly tomorrow with F. A. Hayek at a speed higher than the speed of light to the edge of the universe." However, this need will remain unfulfilled, given that the very structure of reality makes it impossible for us to satisfy it. However, the possibility of its formulation is essential knowledge for a person to be able to differentiate between possible and unrealistic needs and a portfolio aimed at satisfying his needs.

The reason for changing the spread is always the agent. He/she assesses and interprets economic information when he/she evaluates his/her Pc against Pd or Pp structures, on the basis of how he/she perceives the existing combination of goods within the portfolio against the desired or possible combination of goods to satisfy his/her actual and counterfactual needs over time. Changes in the perception of the combination of needs and their satisfaction by the portfolio subsequently cause changes in the interaction of market actors. The disequilibria component has its origin precisely in the relationship between the desired, possible, and current portfolio of the agent. Though the agent may feel the satisfaction of current needs with the current portfolio of goods, if the spread between the current, potential, and desired portfolio begins to change at the individual level, either because of the change of the portfolio per se or because of a change of the combination of needs, the agent enters individual disequilibrium which requires his action to re-establish the individual equilibrium. This is reflected in the interaction with other agents in the market. The person then comes to a market identified by him/her, where he/she is looking for means to re-compose their portfolio in order to increase the satisfaction of their needs, while also having to offer something in interaction with others in the form of goods, work, product, services, or money. This causes a new offer which generates some kind of local price spread between the demanded and the offered goods to enter the market. The market in question serves as an environment for given individuals operating within this market to narrow their individual spreads between their current and potential/desired portfolios. As a result of operating on the market, the nature of the price spread on the given market also changes; it may narrow or widen. What kinds of individual disequilibration and subsequent market disequilibration can occur, and what happens then?

In the illustrative example described above, it is only Alice who has achieved individual equilibrium in an exchange within the X-Y market. This is because she also operated in the market where the W good is produced/traded (she also ended her activity in that market). The new combination of goods with respect to the good W added to her portfolio, caused her to achieve her Pd structure via an exchange on the X-Y market, which she considers satisfactory and has no reason to change the achieved Pd within the subjectively set time horizon from t to $t1$. We assumed this, at least in the illustrative example. A change in the perception of the Pd structure that does not meet her needs may come at a time when she finds that her combination of goods in the portfolio no longer satisfies her combination of needs and she is forced to act economically again to achieve a Pd/Pp structure. At the same time, Alice's feelings of uneasiness do not necessarily occur after the planned $t1$. The given moment can also come before the expiration of the planned time $t1$, i.e., earlier or later than Alice planned to use her portfolio. Let us remember that an achieved portfolio does not mean that Alice is in a vegetative state between time t and the time she begins to feel uneasiness. Alice only assumed that the achieved portfolio would satisfy her needs for time t to $t1$. However, as her needs are gradually met, she may change her view of her combination of needs. This change may cause her to find that her ideal Pd structure becomes a Pc structure or current portfolio of goods that she perceives as unsatisfactory. In other words, Alice changes her plan in the form of a re-formulation of a new Pd structure, which she compares with the existing Pc. Then her individual spread will be widened. She then tries to remove by action, the individual disequilibrium that occurs, i.e., by trying to narrow the spread between the Pc and Pd structures. We can say that she is attempting to reach by action the newly defined Pd structure.

Bob and Charlie provide a second example of an existing individual disequilibrium. While Bob exchanged his goods in the X-Y market, Charlie assessed the situation as more advantageous for him not to exchange goods in the X-Y market under the given conditions. Bob has reached a potential portfolio, and Charlie has stayed with his Pc. However, both evaluate the situation individually and are not fully satisfied, given that they are trying to achieve a Pd structure that they have not yet achieved. Bob only reached a Pp structure, and Charlie was left with a Pc; they must therefore continue to look for ways to best meet their perceived needs by trying to achieve a Pd structure. Although there has been a higher degree of equilibration in the X-Y market, Bob's and Charlie's existing and persistent *individual* disequilibrium causes them to continue to operate economically in other markets or in the X-Y market, which dynamically further changes spreads in those markets where Bob and Charlie are active.

From an individual equilibrium point of view, it may be that Charlie, (for example, given that we assume he has no debt as Bob has) by operating within the X-Y market and possibly in other markets, finds out that achieving his Pd structure is not possible. Let's say that Charlie wanted to fly to the Moon while having lunch with F.A. Hayek, who is dead. He finds out (learned) that his Pd structure is not technically feasible; the knowledge causes him to abandon the combination of the given needs. This alters the pressure on the spread between his Pc and Pd structures. Thus, knowledge can cause Charlie to change his view of unrealistic counterfactual needs. If he chooses realistic factual and counterfactual needs, he can also achieve his Pd structure. Thus, learning and knowledge affect individual equilibrium and disequilibrium.

3.3.3 The visibility of the invisible hand of the marke—the tension from equilibrium to disequilibrium and back to equilibrium

It is, therefore, either the ex post evaluation of Alice's portfolio or the evaluation of spreads between Bob and Charlie's achieved and desired portfolios, which cause the X-Y or other markets within which they operate, to dynamically change that lead to either a higher range of equilibration or disequilibration. Let us now focus on the transition from market equilibrium in the X-Y market to the disequilibrium of this market, showing that the dynamics inevitably cause market participants who are re-attempting to achieve some kind of individual equilibrium causing the market (more precisely, the market's participants) to re-equilibrate.

Suppose entrepreneur Bob (who is motivated e.g., by a debt) differentiates a combination of features of a good Y in that manner that he will offer some Y′. Let's say that the combination of the features of a given new product means that Alice will not need W, and at the same time, Bob's production costs Y′ are significantly reduced. This causes Charlie, who continues to produce Y, to lose any bid on his Y products. It does not matter whether we look at the given situation as the emergence of a new X-Y′ market or as the collapse of Charlie's activities in the X-Y market, each causing the demise of the X-Y market. Markets in which commodity price spreads arise are only a means of meeting the needs of their participants. Whether or not there are given sub-markets in equilibrium, depends on the assessment of the actors in the given markets in the context of their individual satisfaction of needs by the appropriate composition of some portfolio. What happens in a given market is the result of an individual assessment of the spread between any Pc and Pd structure of participants in that market.

Essential for the description is the information that Charlie loses a bid on his products; it does not matter whether we perceive the situation in terms of the absolute disappearance of the X-Y market and the emergence of a new X-Y′ market. This does not change the fact that Charlie's product Y is not marketable for X. The spread for his Y cannot be eliminated by reducing the price of X-Y, because Y′ is too advantageous for Alice. In addition to the advantageous price of X/Y′, there is the fact that Alice does not need to operate in the W's product market. How can we assess this situation? Is it a dis-equilibrist act of a Schumpeterian entrepreneur (Bob) or is it a higher degree of market equilibration?

Although it does not seem so, some form of individual equilibration will appear in the minds of all the actors. The situation is clear with Alice and Bob; this is a win-win situation where a higher degree of their individual equilibration is caused by the exchange of X /Y′, which also narrows the existing spread in the X-Y′ market. But what would be the resulting situation with Charlie? Charlie gains important information and knowledge. It's not only that Charlie can now buy a super-product Y′ from Bob, to meet his needs in a more effective way. If Charlie does not change the production of product Y, he will get into an even deeper individual disequilibrium. The existing portfolio of economic goods focused on the production of Y—while Y is no longer in demand—is caused by widening the spread between his Pc and Pd structure. How? It costs Charlie to produce something that no one wants; part of his Pc is focusing on the production of Y. Continuing this activity would cause an even wider spread between the structure of Pc and Pd. This widening of the spread in the example above (assuming that Y will lose any bid because of Bob's innovation) pushes him to act in such a way that he seeks knowledge, based on which he is able to re-arrange his individual equilibrium. This takes place again based on some idea-structure of the Pd or Pp, which he tries to achieve. If Charlie is sufficiently attentive, he will duplicate Bob's knowledge as he tries to disable Bob's activity so that he achieves his Pd. Based on this reasoning, we see that competition is not a prerequisite for the functioning of markets. Rather, the competition arises due to a change in the spreads between the individual Pc and Pd of market participants.

Of course, Charlie may not be sufficiently attentive and may continue to strive to produce Y. However, the result will only be a widening of the spread between the structure of Pc and Pd. Until he is forced to pay attention to the situation, he will face a fatal result in the form of the consumption of all his resources by which he meets even his most basic needs. Bob's work and Alice's demand also provide Charlie with very important information related to his lack of knowledge of what satisfies the needs of others through Y. It is not Bob's fault; it is Charlie who has not been attentive enough and whose knowledge is insufficient to meet the needs of others. Markets only provide and convey information.

The market is not in disequilibrium if the bid for Charlie's Y product is lost. Charlie did not have a guaranteed demand for his Y. The loss or reduction of the bid price for Charlie's product Y is information for Charlie that affects his individual disequilibrium. By reducing or eliminating the bid on Charlie's product Y, other market players narrow their individual spreads between their Pc and Pd, thereby increasing the rate of their individual equilibration. Because Charlie never had a guaranteed bid for his products, he only receives information that his individual spread between the Pc and Pd will widen if he is unable to respond operatively to the loss of his knowledge of meeting the needs of others through Y. Thus, the activities of others are not disequilibrating in nature. Disequilibration can only be triggered by Charlie's ignorance of the information provided. If Charlie's unawareness of information somehow persists, then his individual structure of the Pc is probably not disturbed from his subjective point of view. Charlie demonstrates that the composition of his portfolio also includes combinations of goods that compensate for the absence of a bid price on Y; then again, it may be that

Charlie, finds a strange satisfaction in producing a product that no one wants. That satisfaction is subjectively justifiable.

3.3.4 Debt Exchange

When exchanging over time, the same description of the situation applies as in the case of exchanging here and now. However, by inserting "time" into the exchange, we see new phenomena, which impact the perception of the structure of Pc, Pp, and Pd (these structures are compared over time) and perceptions of spreads between given portfolios. It follows that time has an impact on individual and market equilibrium, (intersubjective) equilibrium, and also encourages market participants to discover new kinds of markets that are formed around the following phenomena: production of some alternative Y′ in comparison to existing products on the market, interest, maturity, collateral and the legal claims of creditors, time preference related to the portfolio (savings), diversification of the creditor's portfolio, the production (capital) structure of the debtor and the evaluation of this capital structure (the plans of debtors).[21]

Suppose that Bob producing Y′ enters into a debt exchange in order to produce an economic good that will have an attractive bid price and it is probable that the demand will be huge. Bob assumes that this decision will allow him to achieve his desired structure of the Pd as quickly and efficiently as possible. The combination of new features of economic good Y′ is made possible based on resources obtained to expand a capital structure (e.g., to build a factory, buy machinery, improve marketing, etc.). The liability, therefore, becomes part of his Pc.[22] Due to the intersubjective and time nature of the debt exchange, there is also a creditor,

[21]These are the main phenomena related to debt exchange. Given that the phenomena affect the process of debt exchange, they affect the widening and narrowing exchange spread. The impact on the debt exchange spread and the fact that these are different types of phenomena means that some actors in the loan market subsequently specialize in the given phenomena and create specialized markets around.

[22]It is necessary to stress that not only does the entrepreneur have the balance sheet and the plan (budget), but every person also has them. It is interesting in this respect to link the concept of the balance of sheet and plan with the concept of the map-model concept of mind, presented in Hayek (1952), which is implemented by Horwitz (2010). I think that the balance sheet—the plan analogy, also describes quite accurately the dichotomy of a combination of the

e.g., Lucy, who incorporates her claim into her structure of the Pc against Bob. The structure of the portfolio as a map-concept of mind enables us to explain the possession of a product which is not already in existence—meaning, a dichotomous relationship of claim and liability as some intersubjective structure, which is incorporated into the map-model of minds of both human subjects who enter the debt exchange at once. This part of the structure is also maintained by legal conditions and the legal code of the economic community.

Lucy must have some real Pc, the composition of which is such that if she gives up part of her portfolio to Bob in the form of good F until time $t1$, the satisfaction of her needs will not be endangered, otherwise, she would not have entered the exchange. This way, Lucy shows a time preference, which is related to the depletion of the Pc at time t; the time preference cannot be related to a particular good, it can be related only to the concept of the portfolio per se. Lucy also perceives a structure of the Pd, which will be at time $t1$, enriched by her economic activity (if Lucy is still working), as well as by compensation in the form of 100 units of Y′ from Bob, which he secures with a commitment. Suppose the compensation is not in the form of money, but Y′. This means that the compensation implicitly includes interest. Lucy and Bob agreed on the time structure of debt from time t to $t1$—i.e., they identified maturity. They also identified rules related to what would happen if Bob were unable to fulfill the obligation at time $t1$. Let's say that Lucy, at the same time, is able to also lend money in the form of commodity M to David, who operates in the M-Z market, where he wants to break through with the Z′ product. Suppose Lucy agrees with David on the second set of maturity terms ($t2$), but she does not ask him for collateral, nor does she agree with him on any legal terms. However, Lucy stipulates that her payment be made in the form of compensation or the enrichment of her future Pp at time $t2$, in the form of principal 100 M, and interest in the form of 10% M (assuming M is money). Finally, in another possible scenario, supposing Lucy doesn't want to lend anything to Charlie, and

sum of goods (portfolio), which are acquired and produced to meet some combination of the sum of needs (individual ideas, as something should be).

Alice is already looking for the Y′ and Z′ products in which she is interested, how then would Lucy, Bob, Charlie, David, and Alice examine the principles of the situation?

3.3.5 Lucy's View

Lucy considers her composition of real Pc. She is willing to support the project of Bob and David, but not Charlie. The reasons may be as follows: Perhaps Bob and David promised Lucy better compensation for her future structure of Pp1 at time *t*1 and Pp2 at time *t*2. It doesn't matter if Lucy demands compensation in the form of principal and interest of 110 M from David or 100 Y′ from Bob. At the same time, Charlie could offer something disadvantageous or uninteresting, which either does not narrow her spread between the existing structure of the Pc and the desired Pd or possible Pp later in the future in a significantly short time frame. Perhaps because Charlie offers the project only with respect to time *t*3, which is too late for Lucy for some reason or what he offers causes, from Lucy's point of view, inappropriate diversification of her future structure of the Pp.

The second possibility is that Lucy gives up a good F to Bob and 100 M to David, which means that her remaining Pc′ (without F and 100 M) still satisfies her needs and the Pc′ does not jeopardize the satisfaction of her needs since the spread between the Pc and Pc′ is not so wide as to interfere with satisfying Lucy's needs. However, Charlie could have demanded a product that widened the spread between the Pc and Pc′ too much for Lucy. In this way, Lucy expresses her willingness to postpone the time preference associated with the immediate satisfaction of her combination of needs through the Pc, of which F and 100 M were parts.[23]

[23]At this point, it is worth noting that Lucy demonstrates a time preference in the context of postponing the satisfaction of a combination of her needs, comparing the two states of the structure of the portfolio today and later. Lucy demonstrates that the future composition of her portfolio is a more preferred state, while Lucy does not jeopardize her current perceived needs with an impoverished current portfolio. Lucy is able to make a comparison over time due to the fact that the portfolio concept is a homogenized, time-comparable concept and, at

An important and significant qualitative change from the exchange here is that in the event of an agreement with Bob and David (in the loan market) and a disagreement with Charlie, Lucy would create a structure of her Pp that is more favorable to her than any other Pp′. It follows then, that even if Charlie offered some favorable interest or collateral for a loan from Lucy, the exchange would not have to take place, because it

---

the same time, has a relational character, i.e., Lucy can compare the marginal change within the structure of the portfolio over time.

An interesting and related question is the empirical comparison of time preferences between e.g., children and the elderly, or nationals of the Nordic European states vis-à-vis African states (see Wang et al. 2011), or the time preferences of people during and after the war. What is the reason that some have higher and others lower time preferences, respectively, that some prefer higher consumption rates and lower savings, and others prefer more savings over higher consumption rates? We know that people with higher time preferences prefer to meet their needs immediately or as soon as possible. They formulate and strive to achieve their structure of Pp (potential Pd) in terms of the highest and fastest degree of the satisfaction of their needs. However, the opposite is not true for people with lower time preferences. People with lower time preferences *do not try to* satisfy their needs a priori less and later. People with lower time preferences satisfy their needs through differently composed portfolios. This is the difference between people with higher time preferences. They may show a lower time preference because their actual structure of the Pc is considered by them to be optimal for satisfying their currently perceived factual and expected counterfactual needs, and at the same time their composed Pc does not endanger the satisfaction of the given perceived needs. If the composition of their Pc were such as to jeopardize the satisfaction of their needs within a subjectively assessed time continuum, they would also increase their time preferences. Their higher propensity to save (or allocate savings in the productive activities of the other) is possible because it does not endanger their perceived current and expected counterfactual needs through their Pc in the subjectively assessed time continuum.

So, what do time preferences depend on? They depend on a different formulation of a combination of needs and a different way of satisfying a given combination through a portfolio (a combination) of goods. Therefore, it is the cultural, social, religious, age-based, situational, or temporal context on which the perception of time preferences of given individuals depend. Given the eventualities, on the one hand, they cause differences in the formulation of specific combinations of the needs of a person belonging to a group of people. Equally important is the economic approach to how to meet needs through the composition of a person's individual portfolio.

Therefore, we see e.g., in children's high time preferences. These are associated with children's views on the formulation of their "naïve" combination of needs and children's limited knowledge related to their satisfaction. Prisoners' time preferences are related to the limited possibilities of combining the satisfaction of their needs with the composition of the portfolio. The difference in time preferences across nations mentioned in Wang et al. (2011) is also related to the different approaches to the combination of needs and ways of satisfying them. However, this is not a priori a valid conclusion for every individual with a given cultural, social, or religious background; there could be Germans with high preferences and Italians with low preferences. The difference among individual time preferences arises precisely in the individual approach to the formulation of a given combination of needs and the economic ways of satisfying them.

is for some reason a combination of compensation from Bob and David that Lucy considers more preferable, while Charlie's project could disrupt this optimal combination, even though it may seem advantageous to Lucy; it is the combination of all the projects that Lucy decides on, and it is not the genuine level of Lucy's interest in Charlie's individual project.[24]

The second qualitative change is a degree of legal certainty that Lucy both requires and acquires. In the case of Bob's failure, Lucy demands collateral, but not in David's case. The difference may be in the credibility of debtors. The consequence of this certainty is that there are two additional possibilities for Lucy. The first is that Lucy can continue to trade her receivables, or she can exchange them with Charlie or Alice. The second consequence is a more specific idea of the structure of the Pp composition to occur at $t1$ within Bob's vision and at $t2$ within David's vision. Also, the legal certainty that their portfolios would be diversified in the event of the success or failure of Bob's and David's projects. The degree of certainty allows Lucy several options.[25] As time flows toward $t1$, $t2$, Lucy has the flexibility to adjust her idea of the structure of the Pp. This is because both Bob's and David's commitment can be traded and offered to Alice or Charlie. Lucy can also mediate a possible settlement of liabilities between Bob and David if such liabilities and receivables exist. Of course, she evaluates all potential possibilities in the context of her individual equilibrium when she strives for the narrowest possible spread between the structures of the Pc and Pd. As debt exchange allows a greater degree of flexibility in decision-making and adaptation over time, this would have a positive effect on generally narrowing the spread of creditors between their Pc and Pd.

[24]This is also the reason why some projects are preferred even with offered lower interest rates from the borrower. The creditor does not necessarily prefer high-interest rates. The creditor assesses the overall diversification of his Pp compared to some idea of Pd; it is the spread that is decisive. Accordingly, the profitability of a project approaches the individual view. In other words, it diversifies the investment portfolio. A project with a low-interest rate, therefore, compensates for the higher risk associated with a project with a higher interest rate.

[25]The degree of certainty has evolved throughout history from simple community rules to societal rules, which are now highly coordinated and interconnected in this area. The described possibilities that Lucy can use are, in principle, very simple tasks that we see in practice in the banking system today.

At the same time, Lucy's activities influence the events in the loan market. First, she affects the discovery of interest rates and, second, she affects the discovery of time preferences of players in the loan market. Lucy and Charlie, therefore, become marginal creditors and debtors in the loan market. From Lucy's point of view, the last opportunity was to support, in her opinion, one of David's meaningful economic projects. Charlie's project either increases the time preference associated with endangering her needs by the Pc′, or the combination of Bob's and David's projects in her idea of the Pp is ideal and ideally diversifies her portfolio, while Charlie's project disrupts this notion or Charlie does not offer attractive interest rates. In the loan market, actors such as Lucy look for a marginal debtor, and market players such as Bob and David and Charlie must also look for a marginal lender. The spread in this market is not just about interest rates. The spread on the loan market is influenced by several of the above-mentioned factors such as interest, maturity, legal circumstances, diversification of creditors' portfolios, and the attractiveness of borrowers' projects.

3.3.6 Bob and David's View

Bob and David received resources from Lucy at time *t* that they will use to fulfill their commitment, with the advantage that they can immediately use the given resources, since their structure of Pc is immediately enriched and becomes the Pp. At time *t*, they only acquire some Pp due to the fact that their portfolio also includes a liability to Lucy, which they need to eliminate later.[26] The resources from Lucy compress their spreads between the structure of the Pc and Pp, and assume that by implementing the given project they will also compress the spread between the structure of the Pp and Pd. The production of Y′ and Z′, which they are able to realize with Lucy's resources, when their obligation to Lucy is settled, and that in the future they will achieve some structure

[26]We suppose here that Bob and David are not sadists who are satisfied with the torment associated with the existence of some debt and some consistent punishment that would result from the non-payment of their obligations. However, if they were sadists, then, from their subjective point of view, it would be a satisfactory state of the Pd, which they would achieve precisely through punishment for the non-fulfillment of their obligations.

of the Pp which is the closest possible state to their desired Pd. This implies that Y′ and Z′ must be products that will receive their bid price in the future, comparative to Charlie's product (Y). At the same time, Lucy provides resources because she estimates that a given combination of product features will ensure their future marketability and demand from Alice.

Let's suppose that Bob and David can produce Y′ and Z′ based on the resources from Lucy. The difference between them is that David obtained commodity money M from Lucy and Bob a particular good F. Since the money is not used to produce the Z′, David has to buy capital resources for M in the capital resources market; these resources are necessary to produce the Z′. David operates in the market of factors of production and capital resources. These factors of production were made in the past by other members of the economic community, like Alice. Alice is now examining whether her economic activity at time *t*-1 was meaningful. If David buys Alice's capital goods, Alice repays her past debt, and let's say she's so successful that she attains her structure of the Pd. David thus acquires capital goods for the production of Z′, which, from his individual point of view, means that he reaches his structure of the Pp. Bob has already achieved it by acquiring the F. This is the way the price spread narrows in the capital resources market. There is, therefore, a greater degree of coordination between David and Alice. Alice reaches her structure of the Pd and David his structure of the Pp.

If David and Bob are successful, they will be in the same position as Alice (achieving entrepreneurial success). Bob and David will be able to sell their products in consumer or capital markets. In the future, they can eliminate their obligations to Lucy or to the person to whom Lucy sold her claims. At the same time, their activities narrow the spread in the given markets, which implies a higher form of coordination in the given markets and the loan markets. The success of future activities shows that Lucy was able to discover both the right level of interest rates, her time preferences, and the diversification of her portfolio. The chosen parameters were, therefore, relatively successful. Relative success results from the fact that in the example given here, we cannot assess the degree of a given success because of its intersubjective character. This can only be identified by comparing the *monetary* success of other players in the loan market who also influence the identification of interest rates, time preferences, and the degree of diversification of the portfolios of savings holders (meaning real economic goods).

But what happens if David fails in his actions? This we will find out later at time *t*2. We know that David, from an intersubjective point of view, created a business mistake which caused a problem for Lucy. And we know that the resources produced by Alice, which were allocated to the production of Z were successful at the time of their purchase but were allocated to a project where David was unsuccessful. It is clear that from the individual point of view of David and Lucy's desired portfolio, their individual spread widened, resulting in an individual disequilibrium. From an intersubjective point of view, David's failure has an impact on the higher degree of disequilibration in the loan market. Because of David's failure, Lucy has to change her plans with her current Pc as she faces a widening of the spread between the structure of the Pc and the Pd. Lucy, therefore, either changes the time preferences related to the Pc′ (it happens at time *t*2) or changes her view of her new idea of the Pd (at time *t*2). At this point, she creates a different combination of projects to support her further operation on the loan market or changes her assessment of interest rates offered by those looking for her resources for their new projects (at time *t*2). In the loan market, the spread widens, and the position of a marginal borrower and marginal creditor changes.

How much the spread in the loan market changes depends on how much David compensates Lucy for her loss and the level of his project's failure. The failure rate is again relative and depends on a comparison with other players in the loan market. As we know, Lucy didn't ask David for collateral or some form of compensation. Her spread between the structure of the Pc and the expected Pp, therefore, widens in proportion to David's intersubjectively assessed failure rate. David's spread is also affected by the failure rate, which is not fatal, given that Lucy didn't ask him for collateral at time *t*. These circumstances affect the spread of the loan market, spread between the marginal lender and the borrower. While the unsuccessful David can continue to try to convince the new creditor, Lucy must deal with the new situation in a more difficult way. Theoretically, David can be quite positive about the situation because he can try to sell capital goods used for the production of the Z′ at a discount rate on the capital goods market since he did not promise Lucy any collateral. If Lucy had asked for collateral from David, Lucy's losses would not have affected her individual spread between her Pc and Pp so significantly and David would then find himself in a more difficult situation.

The emergence of a business error requires the identification of new knowledge on how to meet the needs of other members of the community. This new knowledge comes to the loan market in the form of potential new projects. Educated by the failure of David and the success of Bob, Lucy reformulates some of her ideal structure of the Pd by looking for optimal projects, thus trying to again narrow the spread in the loan market. It is, therefore, Lucy's search for new knowledge on meeting the needs of others which will push the loan market back to a higher level of equilibrium, and which will affect the elimination of David's error. Also, if Lucy asked David for collateral, it would be David's spread between his structure of the Pc and Pd that would make the mistake necessary to correct by David's new actions. Thus, Lucy and David's individual spreads and the circumstances of the agreement at time *t* had caused what will happen at time *t*2. The learning process is possible to identify with regard to the background of this story. Actors learn about their mistakes, as well as learning to adapt to the given mistakes.

The last question related to Bob's error is whether Alice's products, used in David's project, are an economic mistake or not (Kirzner 1978 question, see also Sect. 2.3.5 of this book). It could be that if Lucy did not support David's project at time *t*, David would not buy resources from Alice. Let's say that Lucy supports Charlie's project, but Charlie doesn't need Alice's products. It would be Alice who would suffer a loss. And Charlie could and may not continue to be successful. We do not know. Lucy's decision to support David, however, caused Alice to correctly estimate the demand for her products at time *t*-1. It is David who subsequently made a mistake and not Alice. We do not know the alternative history in this case. In light of the example provided, we can only state that in the past, Alice's knowledge of meeting the needs of others was correct.

The last remark in this context is that the circumstances of debt exchange also open new, separate, and specialized markets focused on the issues of debt maturity, collateral market, the market for the risk mitigation of various projects, etc. There are professionals who specialize in the assessment of debt-related phenomena. Their decisions subsequently affect events in the economic community. In principle, these are professionals who compete with Lucy, and today we see them on the market in the form of banks and financial institutions.

3.3.7 Charlie's View

Charlie is a bit of a failure in our scenarios. His idea of creating a certain capital structure was not successful for Lucy. His structure of Pc can only be changed to some Pp, or Pd only by his own activity. However, by the outcome of his activities on the loan market, Charlie is informed that Lucy (possibly other players in the loan market) does not find the parameters of his project's offer interesting and is not interested in using their resources for the activities proposed by Charlie. The spread between his structure of Pc and Pd informs Charlie that he must take a different path and learn how to satisfy the needs of others to enable him to fulfill his own targeted structure of the Pd. By participating in the loan market, Charlie also provides information to other actors that Lucy was not interested in his project, thus she is identified as a marginal debtor in the market.

Would the loan market be on a higher equilibrium if Lucy made a deal with Charlie? The market is at a higher equilibrium if Bob's and David's projects are supported; the market spread is narrowing with the support of these projects. Charlie's project either remains without a bid price or the bid for his project is uninteresting. If Charlie does not have a bid for his project, the spread on the loan market cannot be eliminated. The project is likely to be unworkable either due to a lack of savings, or an inappropriate time preference associated with Lucy's portfolio. Lucy would jeopardize her needs, or would cause an inappropriate combination and an extremely risky portfolio diversification for Lucy; existing evidence suggests that the project is unrealizable, e.g., if Charlie plans to produce a longevity elixir.[27] However, if we incorporate the failure of David's project into the scenario, the given failure will cause a relatively widening spread in the loan market sometime in the future, but only a relative widening spread. Why? It could happen that Lucy (and other market players) may in the meantime acquire new and extensive resources to relativize the significance of David's error in the overall view of our illustrative situation; i.e., although Lucy could have a higher level of resources with David's success, a different time preference related to her portfolio, or a different portfolio diversification, Lucy continues to act on the loan market because David's mistake was not so significant in the context of other market projects.

3.3.8 Alice's View

Alice comes out as the "winner" of the whole story. However, it is because she correctly guessed, in the past, how to meet the needs of others. In our example, she correctly estimated David's needs; only her successful estimation gave her the opportunity to operate on the market with Bob and enjoy the new complexity of Y′ products. With the inclusion of Y′ products, her portfolio allowed Alice to narrow her spread between the structure of Pc and Pp, and to achieve, let's say, some structure of the Pd.

3.4 The Final State of Rest (FSoR) and the Human Evenly Rotating Economy (HERE)

Let us now move from the description of these individual illustrative situations to the social impacts. If the individual FSoR of every member of the economic community manifests itself for all people in the economic community at the same time, they will achieve the hERE. Basically, every

[27] However, if we look at history, people were willing to invest resources in these types of alchemical projects as well. See e.g., Glick et al. (2005).

member of the economic community will achieve the preferred structure of their Pd at once. Thus, it would be a kind of state of the maximum quantity of an individual's Pd (Σ_{max}Pd), which would also imply that for a certain period of time, the given individuals would act only automatically and would repeat and practice some kind of automatic actions. This is, of course, a mental exercise aimed at identifying the causes, consequences, and interplay of some conditions. The traditionally recognized conditions to achieve this state of affairs for all individuals in an economic system is to remove uncertainty and change. I claim, however, that these two conditions are only *sufficient conditions* for a given mental exercise. The necessary condition is related to the removal or restriction of our knowledge or cognition. The impossibility of achieving hERE or some state of manifestation of the Σ_{max}Pd of individuals in an economic community is related to the fact that in reality there is the possibility of an individual formulation of an infinite combination of needs and at the same time, an infinite combination of resources to satisfy them. This implies a modified theory of subjective value. This is the *necessary condition* for the real impossibility of achieving something like hERE or the FSoR for everyone at the same time. A potential infinite combination of needs satisfied by an infinite combination of resources implies several serious and related claims concerning the reality, economic ordering, and disputing of some ideal state of affairs of an ideal social order.

First, the infinite possibility of combining needs implies that even if we are enlightened, omniscient beings, the possibility of an infinite combination of needs prevents us from satisfying them. This shows us the important characteristics of man and human coexistence. Even in the case of enlightened and omniscient beings, we are not able to fully satisfy the needs of all beings, i.e., to achieve some FSoR of all beings simultaneously. It means, and here we follow Hülsmann (2000), that even enlightened and omniscient beings are not able to eliminate the principle of entrepreneurship and the discovery of an endless combination of needs, which also implies the existence of this specific entrepreneurial knowledge and the existence of (intersubjective) profit[28] even if everyone

[28]The concept of intersubjective profit is defined in Sect. 2.3.6. Intersubjective profit is an economic representation of an entrepreneur's knowledge to satisfy the needs of another human

knows about everyone's needs for everything simultaneously. Therefore, even in the context of the hERE, it is not possible to reach $\Sigma_{max}Pd$. We also see the reason for Mises's claims (Mises 1998) about the impossibility of removing the so-called *originary interest*, or the so-called *natural rate of interest.*[29] Given that there is an infinite possibility of combining resources, there will always be some economic projects that cannot be implemented. This implies the existence of an originary (natural) interest rate spread even in markets where omniscient people operate; i.e., even omniscient people could still choose more attractive and endless offers with regard to economic projects (another combination of resources) where they could direct their savings, which in turn, implies the existence of a *natural interest rate.*[30]

It is also true that the coordination and elimination of spreads (i.e., the tendency to equilibrate) is a natural part of human activity in the community and will exist as long as people need to meet each other's needs. Likewise, the coordination has no specific endpoint; nor will we get rid of disequilibrium. This is an integral part of economic processes, given the permanence of the existence of a spread between the individual structure of the Pp and Pd at the level of the individual, which inevitably causes disequilibrium at the societal level.

Second, the endless possibility of combining needs in the form of some $\Sigma_{max}Pd$ of all people, implies that the only way to satisfy all needs at the same time is to ensure a state of the hERE, which lies in the formulation of some limitation of $\Sigma_{max}Pp$. Simply put, a state of

---

subject. The difference with regard to subjective profit can be imagined if one looks at the situation of the Wallras equilibrium, where everyone correctly satisfies the needs of others and entrepreneurial activity removes the specific knowledge of an entrepreneur. At a given moment, the intersubjective profit is eliminated (it is arbitrated to zero), but the subjectively perceived profit continues to remain in the form of the satisfied needs of everyone.

[29]The reader must be reminded that Wicksell (1936) or Mises (1998) were not able to define this concept and describe exactly what it means. A relevant critique of Mises's approach to interest can be found in Hülsmann (2002). The concept is described in section 2.3.2 and the solution proposal to the problem can be found in Pošvanc (2020a).

[30]The issue of zero or negative interest rates expressed in money or currencies on some financial instruments has a different character than the issue of natural interest rates. A zero or negative interest rate is related to a trade-off within the portfolios of financial entities that receive a given interest rate on some financial instruments. You can examine the problem in greater detail in Pošvanc (2020a).

the hERE can only be achieved by limiting knowledge or by limiting combinations of needs. At this point, it is possible to identify the attractiveness of some ingenious but, at the same time, socially dangerous ideas related to socialism, communism, fascism, or any dictatorial social arrangement. In the case of sufficiently conscious individuals or a sufficiently conscious leader in the community, it seems theoretically possible for each person to give up his or her ideal achievement of the structure of the Pd in favor of the common good, and, on that basis, the promised paradise on earth should occur. It is more than obvious why these theories must be called scientifically naive and, at the same time, socially dangerous. Logically, they imply the necessity to limit the needs of man either voluntarily in the name of a vision of a "better" society formulated by someone else, or without discussion and based on coercion. However, any involuntary determination of any social Σ_{max}Pp, in the form of the limitation of possibilities with regard to the combination of individual needs in the form of Σ_{max}Pd, implies a socially worse situation than would be the case under other voluntarily accepted conditions. This reveals why any centrally planned economy is always relatively less economically efficient than any voluntary economic community organization. Any political limitations of the discovery of market processes must naturally lead to a lesser range of the satisfaction of the needs of a given economic community. Any different discovery process of meeting needs of members of any economic community than market-voluntarily one implies either reducing business activity or reducing people's needs which, in turn, only leads to a relatively lower possible combination of resources and a reduction in meeting the needs of members of a given economic community. We should not be surprised by the conclusions of socio-anthropological researchers who indicate that the hERE may have existed in our predecessors, namely, in some "primitive" communities. The lower level of individual self-awareness of our predecessors could indeed have had an impact on the existence of a lower degree of the combination of needs and thus lower requirements in terms of the portfolio of goods of our predecessors. This implies a lower level of self-awareness of individuals in a given community, which further implies a low level of the individual combination of needs in the form of ΣmaxPd.

It may also seem to these researchers that present "primitive" communities and their members show a higher degree of satisfaction compared to modern societies. However, this is only a question of the gradually emerging Ego of these individuals. An emerging Ego gradually created a higher degree of the combination of needs (as the knowledge of these individuals increased), which inevitably led to the higher complexity of thought processes and the effort of satisfying, as much as possible, the newly created combinations of needs with new business activities. From this viewpoint, the possible demands of some social anthropologists or their political supporters to return to such social arrangements from our modern world are fully unacceptable.

Third, there are interacting forces between the market (voluntary) and political (involuntary) constraints influencing the individual satisfaction of some desired needs of the individual. As we can see, there are differences if the formulation of an individual structure of the Pd and the Pp is left to the individual and to the voluntary cooperation of individuals within the community or if the formulation is left to a political decision-maker such as a dictator. Voluntary communities must necessarily narrow the spread between individual structures of the Pp and Pd. This follows from the nature of the market discovery process, which is focused on the endless discovery of new combinations of resources aimed at meeting the combination of needs. In contrast, tyrannical communities must widen the spread by definition. In this case, we are describing two borderline situations at their maximum; there are communities that are not in these borderline situations. It is, therefore, clear that there is some trade-off within these communities on an individual and social level. In principle, we can divide political decisions into two types. The first type of decision (let's call it the decision of the enlightened ruler) mirrors decisions that would be made voluntarily by people themselves. These are decisions that narrow the spread between the structures of Pp and Pd at the individual level. From the point of view of the enlightened ruler, these are decisions that are reflected in the catallactic social rules. These are rules that have been followed precisely because they have enabled individuals to realize the widest possible degree of the discovery of the right combination of resources aimed at combining individual needs.

The second type of decisions (let's call them the decisions of the tyrannical ruler) are decisions that people would not voluntarily make because these decisions would widen the spread between the individually perceived structures of the Pp and the Pd; the tyrant must use violence in order to implement these ideas. However, this second type of decision may also have a lower intensity compared to the decisions of a more moderate tyrannical ruler (let's call it the social-democrat's decisions). They would naturally impact the widening of spreads between individual structures of the Pp and Pd compared to voluntary market situations. However, part of those decisions copies a voluntary market situation which has a positive impact on spreads between individual structures of the Pp and Pd, which in turn, improves the situation of members of the given community in question. It is also true that some of the social-democrat's decisions favor one group of their supporters and other decisions support other groups. It is also true that the decision of social-democrat does not have to have some kind of fatal impact on the individual's spreads, even for those individuals for whom their individual spreads between structures of the Pp and the Pd widens, due to the social-democrat's decision. In other words, the widening spread will be withstood by these individuals because the increased costs are too high.[31] At the same time, the more the decisions of social-democrats move away from the decisions of the enlightened ruler toward that of a tyrant, the more people in the community become dissatisfied, or their spread between structures of the Pp and Pd widens and vice versa, which causes some (also unexpected revolutionary) actions. It is thus clear that life in a community is subsequently influenced by both the degree of volunteer opportunities that meet the needs of individuals and the degree of political influence. The given forces influence the resulting perception of the social order by the given individuals. The complexity of political-economic social coexistence should be, therefore, obvious.

[31] From this point of view, it is not necessary to think of some kind of violent uprising. It is equally relevant, for example, to consider *all* the costs associated with the decision to move from a comparatively worse jurisdiction to a relatively better one, where an individual may consider that the restrictions may worsen his or her state of affairs, but not so much as to make it advantageous to move.

3.4.1 Formulation of the Concept of the HERE

In case we would still like to imagine hERE, it can be based on the following assumptions. First of all, we must necessarily limit the possibility of an infinite combination of needs and their satisfaction with an infinite combination of resources. Otherwise, it is not possible to compile a given mental construct; we must limit our knowledge. This is a necessary condition for the construction of this mental construct. Then it will be true that there is an ultimate possibility of combining needs that can be met by a final combination of resources. Let's say that a given restriction on a given economy is imposed by a tyrannical demigod. Only in this way is it possible to achieve some kind of the hERE. In this way, we automatically limit the possibilities of the scope of knowledge and possibilities of mutually satisfying needs. Other preconditions for the existence of the hERE would have to be some kind of idea sharing and dissemination of information within the system and knowledge related to the mutual satisfaction of needs.

As such, the hERE occurs when each member of the community reaches his/her individual equilibrium, the FSoR, i.e., the preferred structure of his/her Pd and begins starts to act automatically. At the same time, it is not possible for hERE to be sustainable. It is only possible, since under the given conditions, people automatically get into a state of the hERE which they are able to maintain only for a certain period of time; subsequently, the state of the hERE would be disturbed again. Dis-equilibrist tendencies cannot be removed at the individual or the community level; they can *only be mitigated* (not eliminated) by limiting the knowledge of a combination of needs and resources. They could be eliminated only in the case of predefined possibilities of given combinations. However, this would get us to the rERE state, i.e., the state of robots. What can be defined in the context of the hERE is that any dis-equilibrist individual tendency will eventually be eliminated, given the assumption of the limited possibilities of combining knowledge and an ideal way of sharing the information. Then this would mean that the economic system would always get into some state of repetitive activities. This allows the assumption of limited knowledge, which would reduce the formulation of the combination of needs and their satisfaction by a restricted structure of the Pd, as well as the assumption of the ideal sharing of information.

This would result in virtually zero price spreads in all markets for all products in which community members are interested in including into their individual (knowledge-limited) structures of the Pd. Zero spreads would imply that each exchange participant would set a given product price for its bid and ask price.[32] However, we could not eliminate the natural interest rate; there would always be a Charlie and his project that would not be supported. This implies that the number of possible projects offered which would be supported would generate a perception of the natural interest rate. A natural interest rate and related time preferences would be generated on the market for individual supported projects, which would then be repeated. These result in an interactive process of discovery, with the interest rate always being discovered in its same form for identical types of projects, as well as time preferences and other legal contexts in the loan market. However, even in the hERE, it is not true that all kinds of combinations of needs and all kinds of combinations of their satisfaction are realized; i.e., not all projects are implemented and some projects do not have a bid from the creditors. This is because we have *only limited knowledge*. We didn't remove it; if we removed it, we would describe only the rERE instead of the hERE. The natural interest rate has no reason to exist in the robot system since robots are programmed and not humans. As we can see, the given thought concept shows us that the importance of interest is related to the importance of knowing how to satisfy people's needs over time, meaning here to have knowledge about the allocation of existing resources into promising projects. The more we limit knowledge and move toward the

[32]Assumptions about the FSoR imply the existence of a single price that lasts thymologically and it is also a quasi-praxeological concept. The reason is the zero spread, which is permanent in time, and at the same time has a uniform expression of price, when bid and ask are equal. This is a quasi-praxeological concept because we assume the existence of quasi-praxeological assumptions about the mutual coordination of individuals. At the same time, from the point of view of the theory of equilibration, the *final price* is not interesting at all. All coordination and important equilibration processes took place long before the *final price* was reached. The final price also does not provide any relevant information for further coordination. It only provides information that final coordination was reached.

robotic or animal world, the more the concept of interest is lost until it gets to the point when it is completely lost (the point when consciousness evaporates). Robots and animals only repeat what they have been programmed to do or that which they are predestined to do by natural selection.[33]

Of course, if a temporary state of the hERE is reached, it would seem to the observing social scientist that the system in question is not subject to any change, given that the participants in the system would always repeat the same economic activity. How would we get to this state? Entrepreneurship activities within the hERE are not eliminated. The entrepreneur would always and under all circumstances arrive at *only* the same conclusion in this system of repetition of the economic activity. Market participants are then, in principle, aware that they have discovered all possible technological limitations in meeting their mutual needs. In hERE, *it only seems* that entrepreneurs do not carry out any activity. They perform exactly the same and repetitive activity, otherwise the hERE would not occur. As for the intersubjective profit, it is clearly eliminated in the hERE, and only the subjectively perceived profit in the form of an "individual state of rest" remains. A new business opportunity and a new potential space for intersubjective profit in the hERE would arise as soon as one of the members of a given community became disequilibrated, which would trigger the need to remove some potential spread in the market and create room for new entrepreneurial activity or a new combination of knowledge to be discovered.

With this explanation, we come to the penultimate interesting topic in connection with the description of the imaginative state of the hERE—the question of money. Mises (1998) rightly states that there is no reason to use money in the rERE. It is a programmed robotic system in which robots perform programmed actions; a pre-identified set of input data causes pre-identified combinations of actions that become a pre-identified data set for another robot, that will again react in a pre-set mode. Although it is clear that Mises thinks of this construct as the result of some human action, as we have shown above, the description of the

[33]It is possible to speculate, based on this conclusion, that there was point when our predecessors were only unconscious animals. The point in time when the concept of natural interest was fully absent.

rERE is possible only in a robotic way in which money is not theoretically necessary.[34] However, the hERE system we describe is different. Is money (or currency) needed in this system or not?

As Pošvanc (2020b, 2021) shows, money is a construct that was developed as a new abstract layer of thinking, and knowledge was needed to express more precisely economic plans and projects over a period of time (debt exchanges). The motivation for the emergence of this mental layer, which grasped reality, laid down the simplification of the system of primitive debt exchanges in the economic mini-system of our predecessors, when the complexity of primitive debt exchanges within some community or communities reached its limits. Money basically enabled better orientation. If we imagine the description of the hERE presented here, it follows that money will be used in a given economic community depending on the degree of the restriction of knowledge. If the knowledge is highly limited, the community will never be motivated to use the money because, for such a community, there is no reason to reach the complexity of mutual relationships. Limitations of knowledge will prevent this. Conversely, if the tyrant-demigod has not imposed significant restrictions on the knowledge of the individuals in the hERE, they will utilize the concept of money and they will invent money or its equivalent. Even the degree of complexity of the knowledge is related to whether a banking system will be created. In the hERE, the following proportionality would apply. A higher degree of knowledge in terms of the satisfaction of needs that the tyrant-demigod allowed in the hERE, would mean that more people in a given community must tend to be more abstract in the organization of mutual economic relations. The community would, therefore, naturally discover money as well as other superstructures for the monetary system in the form of a banking system and its various products, and vice versa. The mental construct of the hERE shows us that the reason for the creation of money resides in the increase of the robustness of economic knowledge related to ways of satisfying the mutual needs of individuals in the economic community. Money arises as a consequence of the need to simplify previously

[34]However, as we will see below, the existence for some *token-based numeraire,* which has its price derived from money or currency has its justification in the rERE.

created complicated systems of *planning* by individuals over a period of time.[35]

The last problem created by these hypothetical model-constructs, which we will describe here is the contrast between the use of numéraire and money in the concept of the rERE (Mises 1998, p. 250). For the sake of clarity, let us change a further description, the designation of the rERE as a robotic system (RS), which is a programmed autonomous command system in the form of "if-so conditions", programmed by human minds. We can imagine such a system in reality in the form of certain elements of a company (in the future, possibly a whole company), or some production line, or other automated components of a production process. From this point of view, the role of the RS is also clearly defined to serve the needs of people who use the systems in order to fulfil their economic plans. However, each system encounters the robustness of possibilities in terms of mutual relations and their combinations and interconnections of commands in the form of "if-so".[36] If the complexity of the relationships in some RS encounters program deterministic constraints, it is necessary to create a new RS. The activities between given robotic systems are then coordinated, based on a human decision and an assessment of the situation; it is the assessment of the situation between each RS that is problematic to define predictably, in a deterministic manner. Entrepreneurs thus create RS1, RS2...RSn, which act independently and use human decision-making to coordinate their otherwise autonomous actions. If we imagine the full automation of a given decision-making process from RS1 to RSn to coordinate each activity of RS, it is possible to consider the use of numéraire—a token.[37] The token will provide

[35]When dealing with the problem of economic calculation Mises (1920) is, therefore, correct to focus on the problem of more complicated production structures that are possible based on the monetary calculation. However, he did not provide the description of nonmonetary calculation principles and the description of the transition process from nonmonetary to monetary calculation. For more details, see Pošvanc (2019, 2021).

[36]The problem is simply described by Song (2018) while describing the problems related to the implementation of the so-called smart contracts. In principle, this is a problem of the complexity of programming subsequent deterministic processes of individual, separate robotic systems.

[37]The positive information in this regard is the existence of crypto-technologies, which make it possible to secure an information consensus related to the transaction history of some native token of crypto-technology (e.g., Bitcoin). In principle, an immutable information consensus on

an economic (monetary—human action derived) incentive for particular autonomous RS to perform or not to perform some activities for which the RS is pre-programmed, based on the visions of the owner of autonomous RS in connection with the visions of other owners of separate RSs. The numéraire-token provides incentive and information from RS1 to do something not-directly connected to RS2. After performing the activities in RS2, the sensor and the programmed software assess the state of RS2 based on which decision process is started toward RS3, which again receives information via a numéraire-token for the repeated implementation of the internally programmed production.[38]

In terms of the contrast between the RS (rERE) and the hERE, we can also consider the hERE whose members still have limited knowledge of the tyrant-demigod. In this case, it is possible to think that people living in this hERE can, through their own, though limited knowledge, build a complex chain of interconnected robotic systems and automate the entire production process. The state of limited economic information about everything within the economic community, which is transmitted through the numéraire-token, then allows them to coordinate all industrial activity, which will deterministically be carried out by RSs. It is, again, clear that this kind of interpretation is only possible in the hERE whose members have limited knowledge of the tyrant-demigod. The limited knowledge here implies a finite set of defined relationships between the various parts of the production process performed by RSs. In reality, the programmability of the RS chains and the existence of a complete determination of automated relationships between

the transaction history, when the price of a given token is expressed in money or currency terms, can then automatically transmit economic information related to a potential subsequent deterministic instruction to perform some automated activity within numbers not-directly connected to RSs.

[38]An example from the future can be the following idea: An autonomous truck (RS1) arrives at a wheat warehouse (RS2), where a robotic mechanism performs a token transaction (from RS1 to RS2) for the autonomous wheat warehouse. This causes RS2 to release an adequate amount of wheat, based on the information transmitted by the transaction, overseen by some sensor and so-called oracle software. After the truck is loaded, the RS1 transports the wheat to the autonomous bakery (RS3), where a transaction is performed again (from RS3 to RS1), which causes the wheat to be unloaded in a bakery (RS3) that bakes the exact number of bread based on the token transactions within some so-called smart contracts between consumers and the bakery. Subsequently, RS3 delivers the bread to the consumer via a drone (RS4) based on pre-executed orders based on a smart contract between the consumers and RS3.

RSs although interconnected by numéraire tokens are limited, due to the infinite possibilities of combining resources that prevent knowledge of the absolute determinism of production processes. In other words, a complete degree of automation of the production process through the RSs and its coordination through a numéraire, always "encounters" a higher degree of complexity associated with an ever-increasing possibility of the complexity of production processes. This implies the infinite necessity of the existence of a planning and decision-making mechanism in the form of an assessment of given situations by man. This also implies the absurdity of the argument about replacing every activity in the economic community with some robotic systems.

The illustrative hypothetical model-constructs presented here are basically infinite and depend on the range of presuppositions with regard to the limitations of our knowledge. However, I think that this kind of disputation enables us to discuss many economic issues. Both the theory of equilibrium and the theory of individual equilibrium are connected with/to the concept of indifference. It is another area where the Austrian school present their own genuine approach. However, as the reader will see, it is possible to connect the Austrian school perspective about indifference with the mainstream schools of thought, in order to improve the whole picture about the problem of indifference. And this is our last task, presented in the last part of this book.

References

Block, E. Walter. 1980. On Robert Nozick's on Austrian Methodology. *Inquiry* 23(4, Fall): 397–444.

Glick, F. Thomas, J. Steven Livesey, and Faith Wallis. 2005. *Medieval Science, Technology, and Medicine: An Encyclopedia.* New York: Routledge.

Glick, F. Thomas, J. Steven Livesey, and Faith Wallis. 2005b. *Medieval Science, Technology, and Medicine: An Encyclopedia.* New York: Routledge.

Gunning, J. Patrick. 2001. The Praxeological Concept of Equilibrium. *Working Online Paper,* August 27. WWW DOCUMENT http://www.nomadpress.

com/gunning/subjecti/workpape/log_equi.htm. Accessed on 30 November 2020.

Hayek, A. Friedrich. 1952, 1976. *The Sensory Order*. Chicago, IL, USA: University of Chicago Press.

Horwitz, Steven. 2010. The Sensory Order and Organizational Learning. In *The Social Science of Hayek's 'The Sensory Order' (Advances in Austrian Economics)*, ed. N. William Butos. Bingley: Emerald Publishing.

Hülsmann, G. Jörg. 2000. A Realist Approach to Equilibrium Analysis. *Quarterly Journal Austrian Economics* 3: 3–51. https://doi.org/10.1007/s12113-000-1025-1.

Kirzner, M. Israel. 1978. Economics and Error. In *New Directions in Austrian Economics*, ed. M. Louis Spadaro. Kansas City: Sheed Andrews and McMeel, Inc.

Lewis, A. Paul, and Peter Lewin. 2015. Orders, Orders, Everywhere … On Hayek's The Market and Other Orders. *Cosmos and Taxis* 2: 1–16.

Loasby, J. Brian. 1991. *Equilibrium and Evolution*. Manchester: Manchester University Press.

Luther, J. William. 2014. Evenly Rotating Economy: A New Modeling Technique for an Old Equilibrium Construct. *The Review of Austrian Economics* 27: 403–417. https://doi.org/10.1007/s11138-013-0242-8.

Mises, Ludwig. 1949, 1998. "Human Action. Scholar Edition." Auburn, Ala: *Ludwig Von Mises Institute*. WWW DOCUMEN.T https://mises.org/library/human-action-0/html/pp/663.

O'Driscoll, P. Gerald. Jr., and J. Mario Rizzo. 1996. *The Economics of Time and Ignorance*. London and New York: Routledge.

Pošvanc, Matúš. 2019. Evolutionary Possibilities of the Emergence of Economic Calculation and Money: The Problem of the Impossibility of Socialism. *Working Paper*. WWW DOCUMENT https://www.researchgate.net/publication/334084336_Evolutionary_possibilities_of_the_emergence_of_economic_calculation_and_money_The_problem_of_the_impossibility_of_socialism.

Pošvanc, Matúš. 2020a. The Theory of Interest: Revision of Austrian Approach. *Working Monograph*. WWW DOCUMENT https://www.researchgate.net/publication/338595641_The_Theory_of_Interest_Revision_of_Austrian_Approach_monograph_version.

Pošvanc, Matúš. 2020b. A Brief Explanation of the Price of Money. *Working Paper*, March 27. Available at *SSRN* https://ssrn.com/abstract=3562493 or http://dx.doi.org/10.2139/ssrn.3562493.

Pošvanc, Matúš. 2021. In Defense of Fractional Free Banking: Back to Fundamentals. *MISES: Interdisciplinary Journal of Philosophy, Law and Economics* 9 (February). https://doi.org/10.30800/mises.2021.v9.1361.

Rothbard, N. Murray. 2004. 1962, 1970. Man, Economy, and State. Auburn, Ala. Mises Institute. WWW DOCUMENT. https://mises.org/library/man-economy-and-state-power-and-market.

Song, Jimmy. 2018. The Truth about Smart Contracts. *Online Article*, June, 11 WWW DOCUMENT. https://medium.com/@jimmysong/the-truth-about-smart-contracts-ae825271811f. Accessed on 4 June 2020.

Tieben, Bert. 2012. *The Concept of Equilibrium in Different Economic Traditions*. Edward Elgar Publishing.

Wang, Mei, Marc Rieger, and Thorsten Hens. 2011. How Time Preferences Differ: Evidence from 45 Countries. Discussion Papers 2011/18, Norwegian School of Economics, Department of Business and Management Science.

Wicksell, Knut. 1936. Interest and Prices. Originally Published in 1898. Translation published by the *Royal Economic Society*, London. WWW DOCUMENT https://mises.org/library/interest-and-prices.

4

The Problem of Indifference and Choice: An Answer to Nozick's Challenge to Austrians

The text was originally published in the New Perspectives on Political Economy Journal; Vol. 17, no. 1 year 2021. Here presented text is a modified version. The author would like to thank the issuer for the permission.

The concept of indifference and indifference curves was criticized by Rothbard (1956, 1997). In principle, the representatives of the Austrian School accepted the solution he proposed. Indifference cannot be identified in the choice as indifference is not part of the choice. On the contrary, the choice is necessarily based on strict preference and there is nothing about which to be indifferent in terms of choice or action (within praxeology); indifference can only be a psychological concept when we consider whether a person is indifferent to something in terms of his/her preferences. The primary discussion within circles of the Austrian school[1] was initiated by Nozick (1977, pp. 370–371,

[1]The whole genesis of the Austrian discussion on the topic can be seen at the beginning of Block (2012).

M. Pošvanc, *The Evolutionary Invisible Hand*, Palgrave Studies in Classical Liberalism, https://doi.org/10.1007/978-3-030-71800-8_4

taken from Block 1980), who identified the following problem in the methodology of the Austrian school:

> *Austrian theorists need the notion of indifference to explain and mark off the notion of a commodity, and of a unit of a commodity. . . . Without the notion of indifference, and, hence, of an equivalence class of things, we cannot have the notion of a commodity, or of a unit of a commodity; without the notion of a unit ("an interchangeable unit") of a commodity, we have no way to state the law of (diminishing) marginal utility.*

Block (1980, p. 423) considers this kind of criticism to be one of the most brilliant and creative ways to criticize the methodology of the Austrian school. Nozick has identified contradictory statements in two arguments of the Austrian School. If Austrians reject the concept of indifference associated with making decisions and making choices, then it is necessary to reject the law of diminishing marginal utility and vice versa. In principle, the problem we face is a homogeneous assessment of economic goods. According to Nozick, logically, homogeneity is necessary for the validity of the law of diminishing marginal utility when an additional unit of economic good necessarily satisfies our needs less than the previous one.[2] However, homogeneity collides with the logical conclusions of the subjective theory of value and the associated problem of choice. Choice implies that a preference exists for one economic good (e.g., good A) over another (even physically the same economic good A, or a different one, economic good B). It should be pointed out here that it is completely irrelevant if a "chosen A" is physically identical to another physically identical A[3]; what matters is the value determination.

[2]The law is inevitably practiced in time. Therefore, the aim of our work is focused on this time-context.

[3]Wysocki and Block (2018a) argue that any good A differs from the other good A at least in terms of its location in the space. It follows logically, according to them, that the selection of a particular good A is always a unique choice in this respect. Wysocki and Block's argument (2018a) implies that there is (in principle) no identical economic good, given the fact that each economic good has its unique position in space. It is true that the item/good indeed has a particular location in the space, but the choice is primarily about the value determination from an economic point of view and not about the location of items/goods in the space. We see different valuations of economic goods *because of the agent*, not because of the location of items/goods. Theoretically speaking, if there is any possibility of having two items/goods at the

This means that if I choose A, then that particular A is for me subjectively more significant in terms of value over (although physically the same) another A, or as (a physically different) B. However, this means that the selected good (A) cannot be considered as having the *same value* as any physically identical A or any other B. However, if choice causes value heterogeneity related to the good it contradicts the possibility of applying the law of diminishing marginal utility. We have nothing to apply it to (no similar or homogenous good). The choice causes there to be no second or third unit of the good to be preferred over the first. We have only discontinuous value perceived goods over time.

The theory of indifference states that there is no such strictly preferential character of our valuation of goods. According to this theory, we are in an optimal position when we are indifferent between goods A and B. In that case, we should actually perceive in value terms that the economic good A as well as B satisfies our needs *identically*; therefore, we are able to recognize the given goods as value homogeneous. According to Nozick, the concept of indifference implies that we can identify the same class of goods. However, this contradicts the fact that we make a particular choice and select a very specific good (*the* A), which is therefore considered heterogeneous. We must prefer it based on certain criteria and, therefore, we choose it. The proof is that we did. The choice is the very basis of this action that Rothbard (1956, 1997) defines as the concept of so-called demonstrated preferences. Nozick claims, however, that without the assumption of indifference, the law of diminishing marginal utility does not apply. And he's right. So, we are facing an interesting logical paradox where both sides of the debate seem to be correct.

The following procedure is required to show the possibility of linking the two approaches to the problem. First, I will present a more detailed approach of the Austrian school to Nozick's challenge; it will be necessary to make some methodological comments on the Austrian approach. This will make it possible to identify the root problem of the Austrian approach. I will present the basic argument which will enable us to satisfy the legitimate claims of Nozick to value homogeneity while maintaining

exact and same location in the space, there is still room for the agent to choose one particular item and make it *the* specific economic good to meet his/her needs.

a logically consistent view of the Austrians' approach to the problem of choice. The solution lies, as the reader may suspect, in our modification of the theory of subjective value. As we already know, the value causality between needs and goods is not applied to the dichotomous relationship of the *need-good* which must necessarily cause value heterogeneity over time due to the different value context. The value causality is presented at the teleological level of thinking, whereas the dichotomy is applied to the conceptual level of thinking in the form of a *combination of the sum of needs*, which is satisfied by a *combination of goods (a portfolio)*. This makes it possible to identify a value-homogeneous concept or a mental construct, which can be applied over time. Since the portfolio is always a structure composed of specific parts, it is not a problem to maintain the desired homogeneity at the level of a portfolio and, at the same time, to preserve the diction of a strict choice. This will allow us to formulate a consistent response to Nozick's challenge. The answer has several implications which will already be directed to the connection of both seemingly logically contradictory approaches to the problem of indifference—the Austrian approach and the mainstream approach.

4.1 Reactions to Nozick by the Austrians

Block (1980) has tried to solve the problem. He is trying to preserve the valid parts of the concept of demonstrated preferences[4] based on a strict preference promoted by Rothbard (1956, 1997) and to respond to Nozik at the same time. Block must show that choice is actually made on the basis that "I want *this* good A!", so, I don't decide that I want both A and B because I know that both A and B will meet my needs in the same way but eventually, I opt for A (a weak preference). At the same time, he must

[4]It should be noted that Rothbard's definition of the *demonstrated preferences* is not very happily named. The very concept of demonstrating a preference implies that economic science is able to identify, along with the demonstrated preference, some non-demonstrated preferences. However, economic science obviously doesn't know what is not demonstrated. The only point it can say about the situation is that a choice has been made, and that someone preferred good A over another good at that time; but which one, or any indication of a "lack of preference" remains only as a secret on the individual level of the acting individual. See also Stroukal (2014).

maintain the law of diminishing marginal utility, which implies a homogeneity of goods. Block (1980) comes up with a fresh solution where he explains the homogeneity of the good on the thymological level—outside of the action. He claims that the person making the choice related to a unit of good A (using the example of an ounce of butter) must, by definition, decide based on the evaluation of a *particular* unit of an economic good. Until then, he perceived it as a part of a homogeneously assessed stock of the economic good (100 ounces of butter). He gives an example of a butter vendor who perceives 100 ounces of butter as a homogeneous good, to which he is indifferent (outside of action and choice; he judges butter from a psychological—historical perspective—thymologically). However, if he/she sells the x-th (e.g., 72nd) ounce of butter to his customer, he perceives it specifically as an independent economic good, for which he receives a *specifically* perceived sum of one dollar from the customer while continuing to perceive a homogeneity of the good in the form of 99 ounce of butter. In this case, this specifically perceived 72nd ounce of butter (as good A) is less preferred than 99 ounce of butter (good B) for the obtained good—one dollar. In other words, Block claims that we are indifferent to 100 ounce of butter until we decide otherwise. As he later remarks (Block 2009) he leaves the indifference at the level of thymology; in the absence of action, i.e., within the psychological-historical motives of why we make decisions. In doing so, he ensures that the law of diminishing marginal utility is maintained with regard to its applicability to the butter supply, while at the same time maintaining the strict choice on the basis of preference and not indifference.[5]

The topic has been discussed by several authors. However, it is Hoppe (2005) who criticizes Block (1980) in the context of the Austrian discourse. He points out that the concept of indifference is an epistemological category that is indispensable for the classification of the objects of reality. We must be aware that classification is also necessary for the conduct of the action; at least to be able to distinguish one good from another or for the identification of resemblance. He accuses Block of a

[5]As the reader will see below, Block (1980) is very close to the solution proposed here. A small modification of a given example from 100 ounce of butter to a portfolio (a stock of any) goods owned by an individual will allow us to anchor the concept in a time continuum.

vague and psychological interpretation of the character of indifference. Hoppe points out to Mises, who explains that: "*Quantity and quality, are categories of the external world. Only indirectly do they acquire importance and meaning for the action. Because everything can only produce a limited effect, some things are considered scarce and treated as means. Because the effects which things are able to produce are different, acting man distinguishes various classes of things. Because means of the same quantity and quality are apt always to produce the same quantity of an effect of the same quality, action does not differentiate between concrete definite quantities of homogeneous means*" (Mises 1998, p. 119).[6] Accordingly, Hoppe further points out that the heterogeneous nature of the good (butter) cannot arise by any division of a given group of objects of reality, i.e., 99 ounce of butter and 1 ounce of butter. It can only arise if exactly the 72nd ounce of butter (exactly that one and no other) is attributed by some separate character. Only then can we speak of a heterogeneous (other) good that is different from any ounce of butter. Hoppe goes on to say that the problem of indifference is more in the description of our actions. If we imply in the description of an action that I am indifferent to the blue and green sweater, and finally I choose one of the sweaters, it only means that we are mistaken in the description of the choice, where my choice was simply focused on the sweater itself (not green or blue) while I chose a sweater instead of a T-shirt (or anything else).

There was another discussion between Block with Barnett (2010), and Hoppe (2009). Their interchange is characterized by Wysocki (2017) as a discussion of the dual nature of what the term "choice" means for both authors. Hoppe perceives choice in the context of strictly given preferences of classificatory different goods, while not denying the existence of indifference as a psychological relationship between equally assessed options. However, at the same time, he claims that if one perceives this psychological character of indifference (blue-green sweater), then our description of action and choice must be different. Choosing sweaters

[6]For the sake of completeness, here is the full quotation from Mises (1998, p. 119), where Mises adds: "*But this does not imply that it attaches the same value to the various portions of a supply of homogeneous means. Each portion is valued separately. To each portion, its own rank in the scale of value is assigned. But these orders of rank can be* ad libitum *interchanged among the various portions of the same magnitude.*"

must be based on another categorization of action: I prefer a sweater over any T-shirt. According to Wysocki (2017), Block is attached to specific circumstances, which lead a person to choose a *particular* good. It is a necessary praxeological explanation of what happens when we choose, leaving the concept of indifference in the thymological field of analysis as a necessary psychological-historical explanation of the law of diminishing marginal utility.

At this point, it is appropriate to identify some of the problems facing both Block and Hoppe. Block's relatively elegant solution implies that the law of diminishing marginal utility has a one-off nature in the context of action. Based on his explanation, the law would always be applicable only to particular temporal circumstances. In other words, it is applied to good A (100 ounce of butter), then comes action and choice at a given point in time. We exchange one ounce of butter for a dollar—and we are done. Consequently, the law must be applied to another good B (99 ounce of butter) given the fact that the choice of replacing a particular ounce of butter for a dollar should have caused the butter owner to perceive the butter as two goods, the specific ounce of butter (good A), which he has exchanged, and the remaining 99 ounce of butter (good B). Block's solution, therefore, lacks a wider application in the time continuum.

Hoppe is unaware of the implicit value aspect of Block's reasoning; his remark on the classification of objects of reality is inaccurate. It is clear that Mises (Hoppe) considers only the physical properties of goods.[7] We have no reason to claim that means (goods) of the same quantity and quality are apt *always* to produce the same quantity of an effect of the same quality *in terms of value*, which is *attributed* to goods.[8] Logically

---

[7]It must be stressed, based on previous footnote 6 where I left the remaining part of Mises's citation, that Mises value approach in the citation has a different character to the one we asked for. He is focused on the different valuation of different parts of the supply of economic goods. We are focused on the *value causality* between needs and means.

[8]The primary problem is that Mises' (Hoppe) interpretation implies the immutability of valuation. Once recognized, causality related to the need-to-good relationship must be "always" the same. There is strict causality of satisfying needs with the same good at the physical level of course. Water satisfies thirst. Sofa satisfies the need for sitting or lying. However, the value context by which we attribute value to economic good necessarily changes over time. And it is the question of value, not physical properties, which count in economics. Let's take the example of a sofa. The sofa serves the same person who bought it for sitting or lying, but also

speaking, an economic good of the same kind and quality may not exist at all if we look at the good from the point of view of valuation. This is because the value context in which given (otherwise physically identical) goods are evaluated necessarily changes. For example, buying a fireplace, sofa, dog, or relaxing music; their physical properties imply their use, but in value terms, their use may be perceived as different since they satisfy different needs over time. The objects may all bring relaxation as in the form of sitting in front of the fireplace, which is associated with stroking the dog and listening to music, but later can be used to maximally engage the female attention for sex, and a day later the fireplace can be used in the context of heating and the dog used for hunting. Value effects are simply different and are constantly adapted to fit new plans that the owner of the objects of reality may have. Hoppe's (Mises) arguments in this section lack the value context that Block (1980) implicitly assumes. As we will see in a moment, the value context is explicitly brought to the discussion by Machaj (2007). In other words, Hoppe, in an epistemological sense, omits to explain the *value-perceived homogeneity*. It is precisely the value homogeneity that we should apply to the law of diminishing marginal utility; otherwise, we would have to assume the existence of some *objective utility of goods*, which must always be perceived in the same way.

Wysocki (2017) draws attention to the ambiguous perception of choice by both authors. In the context of our approach, it is necessary to add that both authors lack the temporal, continuous aspect of choice. The choice is not inevitably focused on a particular moment when it is made, but it is focused on the future. This is "required" by Shackle (implicitly also by Mises[9]). In other words, the choice is merely

for sitting/lying while relaxing, watching TV, relaxing in front of the fireplace, or maybe for working... and also, if I know that it is made from wood, it could have a heating effect if I decompose it, etc., etc.,... Purchased water can be used for drinking; but also for bathing, or as garden irrigation. The value context in which a person uses physically the same economic good can be very variable. At the value level in terms of physically similar goods, there is not *always* the same effect of satisfying needs. However, Mises (Hoppe) writes: "*means of the same quantity and quality* ***are apt always to produce the same quantity of an effect of the same quality****, the action does not differentiate between concrete definite quantities of homogeneous means.*" See also the Sect. 2.2.3.

[9]Unfortunately, Mises' requirement to focus on the analysis of economic phenomena in the future has a dichotomous character. Mises derives much of his analysis of economic phenomena

the implementation of a plan to remove the perceived state of uneasiness toward the future. It is in this value context (the context of needs and the plan for their satisfaction) that it is necessary to explain both the realization of the choice, and at the same time, our ability to apply the law of diminishing marginal utility. It is precisely from the satisfaction of needs that the value characteristics of goods and their epistemic economic classification should be derived. However, there must also be a value-classification character, not only a physical-classification character.

It is Machaj (2007) who draws attention to the necessity of the value-based character of goods derived from how we subjectively perceive that some goods meet subjectively perceived needs. Machaj gives an example of a physically identical wedding ring which would have a different meaning for a fiancée if she got it from her fiancé than if she got it from a complete stranger. In other words, *it is not* (only) the physical characteristics of the goods on which the homogeneous perception of the goods is dependent, in terms of the context of action and evaluation. Machaj then defines value homogeneity as follows:

> *...two objects are homogenous if they both can serve the same end. If so, it follows these are two units of the same supply, because they are capable of satisfying the particular need. From the point of view of an actor's particular need, they are homogeneous and interchangeable or equally serviceable. It does not have anything to do with psychological considerations or psychical characteristics, but rather with the possibilities of action. Now, this point cannot be demonstrated through action, and cannot be observed in action. But as we emphasized before, economics is not only about actions, but also about different possibilities of acting toward the satisfaction of human needs.* (Machaj 2007, p. 234)

Machaj is followed by O'Neill (2010); In the discussion following Machaj, O'Neill brings interesting observations which are based on the concept of so-called weak preference. O'Neill, as well as Machaj, point out that our primary interest should be in need assessment, claiming that:

from the past. Shackle is much more consistent in this respect. See, for example, the criticism of Mises' procedure of analysis and methodology in Pošvanc (2019b).

> *...we are indifferent between two actions when we judge that there is no difference in the magnitude of the satisfactions of needs obtained from those actions (the actual needs may be different, but the magnitude of the satisfactions from these needs must be equal). Similarly, we are indifferent between two goods when we judge that there is no difference in the magnitude of the satisfactions of needs that depend on our command of those goods.* (O'Neill 2010, p. 72)

O'Neill is aware that, according to Machaj, we do not evaluate goods. He claims that we evaluate our needs, which we satisfy with goods. Only in this way can goods have some value; on this basis, he brings the element "*no worse than*" into the analysis. Since it is primarily through an assessment of identified needs that we seek appropriate action, some of our actions may be assessed as 'not worse than' some other results, but since they remain counterfactual, we ultimately reject them. The so-called strict preference concept is then a subset of this modus operandi, where sometimes the outcome of the action is necessarily assessed as "*better than.*" Machaj (2007) was criticized in Block (2009) and O'Neill (2010) was criticized in Block (2012). Machaj and O'Neill were also criticized in Wysocki (2016). In principle, criticism is fixed on one issue. Both Machaj and O'Neill imply decisions based on indifference between goods. This is because two, even physically heterogeneous, goods can satisfy the same need. It depends on the subjective judgment of the person in question. Subjective judgment indeed counts, but at the same time, it is correct and logical that once someone chooses the good A that satisfies the need, it must at the same time be true that he prefers it over something else. We still face the same paradox: If there are strict preferences related to the choice, how do we explain the validity of the law of diminishing marginal utility?

Although Machaj and O'Neill are criticized, in my opinion, their contribution to the debate is very important. Machaj and O'Neill bring a much-needed subjective value aspect to the discussion. According to them, the perception of subjective value is derived from the perception of human needs; it is the point that needs are prioritized, which consequently brings value to economic goods. The action is aimed at the elimination of perceived uneasiness. The perception of the priorities of needs implies the preference of one good over another; that ascribes the value. Only this relationship can then be imputed into some good(s) that already satisfy the perceived need(s).

Wysocki (2016) enters the discussion with this very important question: Under what condition does the law of diminishing marginal utility apply? He states that since the law is conditional, it necessarily implies the prerequisite of having the same good concept. What does the concept of the same good mean? Wysocki and Block (2018a) define, first of all, the difference between goods and economic goods. They write that the difference between things and goods has already been identified by Menger, who has made a condition of existence for economic good as follows:

a. existence of need
b. existence of causality between a given need and a thing that is, a causality we know that this item satisfies that need
c. the ability to control those things.

According to them, the *good* exists if there is at least one person who identifies causality between one's own need that is met by the identified object/part of reality. According to them, an *economic good* exists if the above-mentioned conditions occur for the existence of the good (meaning man, need, and knowledge about the causal relationship "need – good"), and at the same time it applies[10]:

[10] I am not sure whether Wysocki and Block (2018a) realize that in their elegant and absolutely clear interpretation of the distinction between items, goods, and economic goods, they explain that scarcity is not a necessary condition for action. On the contrary, based on their interpretation, the concept of scarcity must be inferred from the action. This is a premise that is wrongly interpreted within the Austrian school. It is interpreted in the form that scarcity is a necessary condition for action, i.e., that without the world being scarce, we would not act.

Cf. with a very gritty and not quite obvious explanation of this statement in Pošvanc (2019a, p. 18), where Pošvanc explains the connection between action and the grasping of reality. At the time of writing, Pošvanc (2019a), in which, inter alia, the author claims that scarcity is not a necessary condition for action, the author was not aware of this much more elegant explanation by Wysocki and Block (2018a).

> *(economic good exists if) its marginal utility is greater than zero. This means that the good is able to satisfy some other human need or satisfy more completely the need previously attended to.* (Wysocki and Block 2018a, p. 134)

Based on these clearly defined and classified phenomena, they come up with the following statement, which I will quote in its entirety:

> *The concept of homogeneity (or, equivalently, the same good) must be prior to the law of diminishing marginal utility because this law assumes it. That is, this law applies only when it considers homogeneous units of the same good. What is more, the relation between human action and homogeneity is very complex indeed. This is because of the fact that a person treating homogenous units of a given commodity as the same good cannot ever demonstrate this in action.*
>
> ...
>
> *the same good is a concept which is clearly prior to any action. Therefore, it belongs in the category of transcendental concepts– it provides us with a way of construing human agency, and it cannot by any means be inferred from the data of particular human acts. In other words, the notion of the same good gives us Bedingung der Möglichkeit for formulating the law of diminishing marginal utility. It is due to the concept of the same good (not being manifested in action itself) that we can better make sense of human action. The same is true about the concept of human purpose. After all, human purpose does not manifest itself in human action. The former is rather assumed a priori to make sense of the latter.* (Wysocki and Block 2018a, pp. 135–136)

Wysocki and Block (2018a) point out that by definition, a choice must always be based on a good that we prefer, at least from the point of view of the location of the good, since physical and homogeneous things cannot be in the same place at the same time. Subsequently, they approach the definition of the same good, whereby they still remember that the action per se does not enable us to identify whether one has economically used consecutive or different units of a given commodity.

For them, physical equality is *only a sufficient condition* for defining the same good. They consider Machaj's value condition (*the same end is served by the same good*) to be too roughly defined, depending on how the need is defined. Machaj's value condition would mean that once we define the need as "*to satisfy any need,*" it would actually be true that everything is the same good because everything that is identified as a good satisfies a need. Going to the other extreme, two physically heterogeneous goods, although they can satisfy the same need, are nevertheless physically different. This factor makes it quite tricky to describe the goods as the same. There is one more problem they face—it could be that an additional unit of some goods, e.g., a second beer relative to the first, can satisfy the given need more than only one beer. What this implies is that in the context of the equality of the assessment of goods, we must also take into account that physically divisible goods must sometimes be perceived as a single good. For example, one good = 2 beers, which is preferred to another good = 1 beer. Rothbard (1956, 1997) argues similarly.

Of course, Wysocki and Block (2018a) still realize that they must inevitably respond to this ingenious point, the challenge that Nozick (1977) puts forward most aptly, in footnote 30 of his work. They quote Nozick (Wysocki and Block 2018a, pp. 138–139):

> *However, on p.122 he [Mises] says, "All parts – units – of the available stock are considered as equally useful and valuable if the problem of giving up one of them is raised." Here, then, we do have indifference. Yet a choice will be made, perhaps at random. One particular object will be given up. Yet, the person does not prefer giving up this one to giving up another one. Therefore, choice entails (at best) weak preference; it does not entail strong preference.*

It is clear that, on the one hand, they must explain a strict preference, but with a homogeneous good, which necessarily implies an identical possibility of satisfying the perceived need. They present the following solution (Wysocki and Block 2018a, p. 140, use the example of the ring, since they respond to the example given by Machaj; bold added):

> *Homogeneity is defined as a physical identity but the equal serviceability of the units of the same good cannot be demonstrated in action. It is necessarily true that only one particular ring [good] will be eventually picked up, thus*

> *showing the actor's strict preference for the chosen unit. So, no contradiction arises.* ***Those weddings rings [goods] are equally serviceable prior to the act of choice and this is what makes them a supply of the same good before an actual choice is made.***

Wysocki and Block (2018a) complement this explanation in Wysocki and Block (2018b), which takes on even clearer contours. It is in this work that they focus on how their concept is related to the formulation of needs (ends). It is the specificity of the definition of the needs, which creates the list of these needs in question. It is evident that a need, which is too specifically defined, would identify any good as heterogeneous, and a too generally defined need would make any good homogeneous. They write (Wysocki and Block 2018b, p. 404):

> *First of all, we posit that whether two items represent the same economic good always depends on how a given economic actor envisages his ends. This, in turn, implies that there can be no inter-subjectively correct answer to the question of whether two physical goods can be subsumed under the category of the same good. For the answer thereto is always contingent upon the way of referring to an actor's ends.*

The argument is probably best explained by their example stating that the difference is when we define the end (need) in the form: "*going to the cinema with a woman*" and in the form, "*going to the cinema C, with a woman W, by route R.*" The first example implies that we can satisfy the end in any cinema, with any woman, and we can get there by any route, i.e., the means of *fulfilling the end* may be more variable. However, the second example of the end implies a more specific form of the good—namely *the* cinema C, *the* woman W, and *the* route R. This implies a very important finding (Wysocki and Block 2018b, p. 406; bold added):

> *… whether any given pair of goods are in the same supply depends on how a given economic actor frames his ends. A pair of items would thus constitute the same economic good* ***relative*** *to one way of describing ends but not from the other.*

Thus, Wysocki and Block (2018b) finally give a more complete picture of what the same good means[11] and leave it in the thymological area. In my opinion, it is a pity that Wysocki and Block (2018a, b) do not use their knowledge of relativism associated with the economic perception of the satisfaction of needs with goods over time. They would avoid the criticism presented here. So, what, in my opinion, are the problems of their approach? They can be summarized as follows:

1. The concept of an economic good based on a premise of marginal utility higher than zero implies a cardinal perception of utility; that concept implies that the good has utility per se.[12]
2. Goods, economic or otherwise, are not useful per se. The usefulness is attributed to goods—it is not a given. It is, therefore, always derived from the valuation of an agent. Without the agent's valuation, the goods would be regular items. Valuation, as Čuhel-Mises (Mises 1998) rightly shows, is only possible in the more-less relation; and as Rothbard (1962) notes and Bilo (2004) stressed, this is possible at the level of needs, which are then imputed into goods.
3. This implies: any value concretization of the good that occurs over time will cause the good per se to be non-homogeneous in value terms. I think that we must simply accept this. It can't be bypassed.

[11]We can also say that they come with relativism. Wysocki and Block (2018b) use subjective relativism related to the definition of goods, which is very similar to the modus operandi in explaining some economic phenomena over time, presented here.

[12]This footnote was not included in the original text. It should be noted that my criticism is possible with respect to point one, in that Wysocki and Block base the concept of evaluation within the commonly used premises of the Austrian school and the established nature of evaluation in the Čuhel-Mises version "more versus less"; meaning here that we are able to evaluate something only as more or less valuable. By that logic, this context must prevent the cardinal application of a utility greater than zero outside the monetary economy; it is money which brings the cardinal consideration into play. It is precisely the context presented in this work in the form of a portfolio that allows us to apply the concept of evaluation "more versus less" and the derived concept of cardinal marginal evaluation at the same time, where the overall utility and its change is applied to the concept of a portfolio. The change with regard to the point of view of valuation in the context of the portfolio enables the perception of marginal utility higher than zero even outside the monetary economy. In other words, Wysocki and Block are intuitively correct but they need the full range of the argument presented here, as well as the proposed modifications in order to claim the existence of a marginal utility that is greater than zero within the Čuhel-Mises's diction about valuation in the mode of "more versus less."

Evaluation in time continuity necessarily implies the possibility of changing the value perspective of *particular* goods per se.

4. The law of diminishing marginal utility is the law of logic and mind. It must be a part of the actor's modus operandi. The presupposition of the existence of a homogeneous good as a prerequisite for a given law, when the law is applied to the concept of an economic good is a circular argument (a *pettito principi error*). This is more explicit when Wysocki and Block (2018a) define an economic good on the basis that it has a marginal utility higher than zero, while at the same time assuming the existence of that good as a condition of the existence of the law of diminishing marginal utility.
5. In terms of my last reservation, I am not quite sure because Wysocki and Block (2018a, p. 136) are unclear. They claim that "*physical sameness is a sufficient condition for two economic goods to be the same economic goods because physically identical economic goods necessarily serve the same list of (correctly perceived) ends.*" This is similar and already criticizes Mises's assumption, (see above), that "*means of the same quantity and quality are apt always to produce the same quantity of an effect of the same quality, the action does not differentiate between concrete definite quantities of homogeneous means*" (Mises 1998, p. 119). However, in the footnote, Wysocki and Block (2018a, p. 136, footnote 14) write that: "*We hesitate to say that, but it can be the case that this 'correctly perceived' scenario is not necessary at all.*" As we have explained above, Mises' premise is not correct, and their hesitation, in my opinion, is therefore not appropriate. In other words, they should stop hesitating and reject Menger-Mises's interpretation of economic causality. Menger-Mises's premise implies only a physical connection between needs and goods, but this is inevitably contrary to the fact that in economics we "engage" in valuation. Nozick's challenge must, therefore, be explained on the value principle valid over time.

Based on the above, I consider that Wysocki and Block (2018a, b) still have not responded to Nozick's (1977) expressed position on the problem of indifference. Their proposed solution has logical inconsistencies. It is necessary to eliminate all reservations and prove that both strict preference and the validity of the law of diminishing marginal utility are part of the solution.

4.2 The Indifference Problem Solution: A Proposal

It is evident that Wysocki and Block's (2018a) approach to the argument in explaining the law of diminishing marginal utility is circular. As Pavlík (2004, 2006) shows, the circular nature of the argument implies that the concept to which the argument relates must be explained differently—in a more abstract way, by a Hegelian crossing of the circle or by changing the paradigm of its perception. And since the law is valid, and it is equally correct that choice causes a preference to be expressed, *it is necessary to abandon the assumption that the law is based on the assessment of the homogenous good* per se. The proposed solution presented here will be based, therefore, once again on the already presented modified theory of subjective value. As we know, the modification of the theory states that the *combination of needs* is met through a portfolio (the combination of means). At the same time, the mental concept of the portfolio has an overlap with reality in the form of a real accumulation of goods. The value perception depends on the content of the need. The content of the need is always a combination of some perceived needs.[13] If the perceived need is "*to relax on the sofa while listening to music,*" the need will be met if the person has in his possession "*a sofa, music carrier with music and music player.*" From a physical point of view a sofa has a positive effect

[13]A reservation was expressed in one anonymous review to this approach with the statement that it is possible to define a solely non-combining need and a corresponding good. I am not so sure about this reservation. I believe that we are only able to define either a very abstract need, which implies a combination of other needs or we can define only a very particular combination of some needs. Let's consider these two examples: (a) abstract need exemplified by "to live a happy life" implies endless combinations of needs over time which could be met by any combination of goods and (b) to define some particular need per se, we need to show some combination of description, e.g., such as "eliminating thirst to stay alive and continue reading." This implies some specific good which has some combination of specific features, e.g., water which must be safe to drink, is clean, fresh, etc. I think that the reason lies simply in the fact that a man holistically grasps himself over time as a conscious being who can define a chain of reasons in terms of why he needs this or that.

on the need, i.e., relaxation; and still has the same effect in this physical sense (one can lie on it and relax) but, without the other goods, the combined defined need is not met. The economic *value causality* between needs and means is, therefore, a more complex perceived phenomenon.

How, then, is it possible to formulate the answer to Nozick (1977) on the basis of these presuppositions? All of the above arguments and the modification of the theory of subjective value leads us to apply the law of diminishing marginal utility, not to the concept of the homogenous good, but to the portfolio and its marginal changes. The portfolio is the desired homogeneous concept. Thus, homogeneity is "ensured" on another layer of grasped reality—the mental concept of the portfolio. This allows us to use the law continuously over time and it is possible to solve the problem of a one-time application of the law as Block's (1980) proposal implies. The law, which is based on the prioritization of a combination of needs, is like the mental law applied to another mental concept of the portfolio. Čuhel-Mises "more/less dictum" is assessed in terms of a higher/lower satisfaction of needs by the portfolio, which consists of goods. Therefore, we can have a strict preference for goods as well as portfolios. It means that in terms of goods per se, we continue to apply a strict preference. Additionally, the choice is always associated with the strict preference of a portfolio as well. However, the statement does not affect the validity of the law. We can perceive at the same time that the marginal change of the portfolio due to the withdrawal/incorporation of economic goods from/to the portfolio will occur. The law is also our modus operandi in the continuum of time. As follows: Enriching a portfolio with a particular good is preferred until we perceive the satisfaction of a perceived (even in the context of an expected counter-factually perceived) combination of needs; on the contrary, the portfolio is deprived of a particular good until the satisfaction of the factually perceived (even in the context of a counter-perceived) combination of needs is jeopardized.

4.3 Implications

In principle, the concept relates to the valid parts of Wysocki and Block (2018a, b). As these authors rightly point out while assessing the physically identical characteristics of a good, the homogenous value perception of the good in the context of demand and supply, which is possible on the basis of the relativization of needs. However, we have abandoned the application of the law of diminishing marginal utility to the economic good. Relativization allows us to identify, over time, a homogeneous value concept, i.e., a portfolio where the problem of applying the law of diminishing marginal utility no longer exists.

In my opinion, the definition of an economic good given by Wysocki and Block (2018a, b) needs to be modified and extended. It is possible to do so by the realization that we examine the good through several, mental-like layers of perception of the world around us. In other words, Menger's definition of good conditions must be enriched with other conditions, mainly from the teleological and normative fields of mental perception. What does this mean? We could use Engliš's terminology to explain this. Engliš (1930) claims that we perceive the world through a causal (Kantian "as is") and teleological and normative system of thinking (Kantian "as it should be"), over which the formal-logical system operates. If we apply this distinction to the perception of economic goods, then three different views are needed to define the economic goods.

We perceive goods at the level of the *causal layer* of thought in terms of their physical properties, which creates one content for the idea of the causal relationship of the satisfaction of needs. It is necessary to agree with Wysocki and Block (2018a) that this kind of categorization is a sufficient condition for identifying the same kind of good. It is at this level that we can imply the validity of Menger-Mises' (used by Hoppe 2005) dictum that goods of the same kind and quality will always satisfy the identified needs with the same intensity. And at this level, the Menger conditions for the definition of a good can be fully applied in the form of:

a. the existence of a need

b. the existence of causality between the need and the thing, i.e., the causality with which we know that this item satisfies that need
c. the ability to control the thing.

The second view of the notion of the needs-goods relationship is made at the teleological level. It is necessary to enrich the Menger conditions based on the new knowledge of how we value goods. In principle, it is a more detailed description of the above-mentioned condition (c). The economic value causality has the character of a relationship where *Σ Ends are satisfied by Σ Means.* From an economic point of view, we can then create a distinction between an economic good and other goods as follows. Meeting the needs is possible with goods and economic goods. There must be some knowledge about the good and the economic good, meaning that it satisfies a complex of needs in terms of the physical-causal character of the relationship. A good becomes an economic good if one wants to include it in their portfolio. Otherwise, it is what Mises (1998, p. 90) calls *the general conditions of human welfare.* It is the intention of a person to include a good into the portfolio (to economize the good). This implies that a portfolio enriched by good is greatly preferred to a portfolio without good. At the same time, the assessment of the portfolio is influenced by the law of diminishing marginal utility. This means that the portfolio will be enriched by the given parts of goods as long as there is a perception of both actual and expected counterfactual needs that can be satisfied in continuity over time with the new portfolio composition. And, of course, vice versa. The portfolio will be deprived of some selected goods until the satisfaction of a person's needs is at risk from the point of view of the person. In other words, the needs at risk would become factual if a marginal change in the portfolio causes such a change that would make the satisfaction of needs impossible.

The third kind of insight is created based on normative rules that imply different forms of standardization and possibilities for the mutual understanding and comparison of subjectively perceived content from other layers of thinking. At this point, we must disagree with Wysocki and Block (2018a, p. 404), who claim that there is no possibility of the intersubjective comparison of goods. They write "… *we posit that whether two items represent the same economic good always depends on how a given economic actor envisages his ends. This, in turn, implies that there can be no inter-subjectively correct answer to the question of whether two physical goods can be subsumed under the category of the same good.*"

I believe it is the other way around. Whether a good can be categorized intersubjectively as the same good is recognized by the "agreement" of at least two people.[14] This also implies an intersubjective categorization option. At the social level, even a wider version of this standardization in the form of money or standards of the trading of goods exists.[15] At the same time, this normative standardization does not imply that we cannot (like Lachman) interpret an economic perception of goods ultra-subjectively (Lachmann 2005). The agreement (standard) *only allows* the mutual understanding of what does or does not constitute the same good. For example, having a standardized ounce of gold, we understand what an ounce of gold means, what it looks like, what we do when we trade it, how we use it in debt relations, what its purchasing power is, and so on. We know all of this regardless of the possibility of an ultra-subjective interpretation of the enrichment/depletion of a portfolio by an ounce of gold. This triple-division also meets the epistemic demands of Hoppe, where differentiation, respectively categorization is based on:

a. physical characteristics (causal field of classification)
b. economic perception of a good and its composition into a portfolio (teleological field of classification)
c. normative rules, i.e., intersubjective social standards (normative field of classification).

We also avoid circular arguments related to the law of diminishing marginal utility. This is because the sequence of interpretation is as follows: firstly, the perception of the complex of needs, from which the law of diminishing marginal utility is derived. The complex of perceived

[14] As is shown in Chapter 2 we, as individuals, have created some economic and normative standards. The above-mentioned relativism we use to mitigate the uncertain future and our very subjective view of the world is thus open for this coordination and understanding of each other. They enable us economic coordination and an economic understanding of each other. These normative concepts eliminate the trap of subjective relativism.

[15] Clearly not only market and voluntary relationships and agreements among people (e.g., some stock exchange rules) affect the normative determination of the definition of good, but also politically initiated regulations or politically normative rules.

factual and counterfactual needs that are satisfied by a portfolio of goods (the sum of goods) implies that one can differentiate between an item (an object of reality), a good (an object of reality that could satisfy some complex of needs), and an economic good as an object of reality to be used economically to satisfy some complex of needs. The differentiation is possible along these lines.

The object of reality is a part of reality (an item) or a part of the general condition of human welfare (good) when the complex of needs does not imply its inclusion into the portfolio of goods. Concerning items and goods, there may or may not necessarily be the knowledge that something satisfies a need. In the case of some items, we do not know that this object could possibly satisfy some needs; e.g., uranium two centuries ago. In the case of goods as a general condition of human welfare, we need not *intentionally* think about the need-good relationship because we have an abundance of supply of a particular good; however, we know that this object could satisfy some needs. It, therefore, means that the good is not subject to any intentional perception of the change of the satisfaction over the dissatisfaction of needs, it is merely good in the form of a *general condition of human welfare* (such as water in an area where there are abundant freshwater supplies and a person drinks when he/she needs to, or goods such as air or sunshine, which are in abundance). Although goods like sunshine or air are used by people, the needs satisfied by these freely available goods are met automatically without the need to prioritize them.

However, everything changes depending on the person's reason for including goods into a portfolio. It is precisely through the inclusion of good into the portfolio that we can assume that the good is perceived as an *economic* good.[16] The good ceases to be part of the general condition

[16]There is also an interesting question about how our predecessors started to differentiate among items, goods, and economic goods. It is impossible to reconstruct or describe this process empirically. At this point, we have at hand only the method of logical historical reconstruction (theoretical conjectural history); see method description e.g., in Pavlík (2004) or a brief outline in the Sect. 2.2.2. If we imagine our predecessors as pre-humans with a lower level of awareness (e.g., intellectually being on the level of children aged 2–3 years), we can imply the existence of some *quasi*-needs. I use the term "*quasi*-needs" because if they were not fully aware themselves, it was not possible for them to become intentionally aware of what *the* needs are and what are explicitly the goods that meet those needs. The need implies the intentionality of thinking.

of human welfare and becomes an economic good. The differentiation (mental as well as logical) enables the concept of a portfolio. And this is because the law of diminishing marginal utility is applied to the portfolio, not to the good per se. If an economic good is included in or withdrawn from the portfolio, it implies that the action connected with the good in question changes the perception of the marginal utility of the portfolio. Thus, the concept of an economic good is the result of an action, not a presupposition of the law of diminishing marginal utility.

The portfolio of goods conceptually allows the mind to differentiate between an economic good, a good in terms of a general condition of human welfare, and what is an unusable object of reality—an item. The differentiation between an economic good and a good in terms of a general condition of human welfare depends on whether the good is intentionally included in the portfolio or not. This is the only way we actually can distinguish one from the other. The differentiation between a general condition of human welfare and an inapplicable object of

---

Rather, there had to be some instinctive (naturally controlled) processes where the quasi-needs were met automatically, and the surrounding objects of reality were not perceived as some economic goods, but either as the general condition of human misery-welfare or the ignored objects of reality. It can be assumed that our predecessors did not fully realize what scarcity meant; even to perceive scarcity we need to assume the intentionality of mind. Thus, they could have felt only physiologically (not consciously) their dissatisfaction connected with some vaguely perceived quasi-need; we see this today when we observe very young children—they feel either misery or welfare. However, the physical durability of the objects of reality also allowed for accumulation and hoarding. Hoarding is not a strange or rare activity; we see it in nature as well. So, it is possible to presuppose some kind of instinctive activity. The accumulation could have been focused on any object of reality; not only useful ones. Meaning anything that causes attention or interest in the personality of the "post-animal-pre-human" being. These individuals could have also accumulated things that were not necessarily limited (i.e., they were the *general condition of human welfare*). However, they probably also accumulated the physically limited objects of reality (they could not have been fully aware of scarcity). Instinctive hoarding is, therefore, the way they could have created incentives for the emerging Ego to differentiate between the objects of reality and economic goods. The incentive to differentiate here may have been not only the subjective perception of the necessity of goods, but also the perceived usability of goods from other members of the group, or when they had to face any change in the combination of needs caused by environmental change or some elementary economic social activities within the group (e.g., exchange, or liability repayment). To admit some possible attacks with regard to this argumentation, it has to be stressed that the assumption here is some kind of instinctive activity in the form of the hoarding of the objects of reality.

I also wonder how our economic concepts (need-means, the law of diminishing marginal utility, costs, revenues, time preference, etc.), which we use to grasp our economic reality and which have a conscious mind character, develop in children's, not fully conscious, mind. This could be an interesting stimulus for some further research.

reality—an item—is also done through a definition in terms of whether a person assigns them to his/her portfolio. We are fully ignorant of many items. These are objects of reality which bring us nothing (e.g., one particular insect or bacteria or some unnoticed star in the Andromeda Galaxy). They are not, however, general conditions of welfare. The general conditions of welfare are used by us; however, we need not incorporate them into the portfolio. But we are aware, a good in terms of the general condition of human welfare can become an economic good by changing the combination of needs (from time to time). It is because we can know explicitly that it satisfies some of our needs, e.g., water in the desert if we have moved there from the rain forest, or fruits from the rain-forest trees when we move to the savanna, or the air under the water, or sunshine in a cave, and so on. The difference is, therefore, based on the intentionality of putting something into the portfolio (while the portfolio implies that we meet some combination of needs in terms of the portfolio). The human mind can differentiate all these options based on the portfolio concept, which satisfies the sum (the combination) of needs. The attentive reader observes that the concept of the portfolio coincides with the private property concept. And it is no coincidence. As Engliš (1930) states, the teleological and normative order of thinking is the decomposition of the Kantian "as it should be" (it is the sphere where we see the intentionality of the mind). It is also no coincidence that the definition of good presented here is the decomposition of Menger's condition to have the ability to control the item. The attentive reader would also recognize that a precondition to all of this is human intention.

4.3.1 Implications Within the Austrian School's View of the Problem of Indifference

We can solve several of the problems mentioned above based on the proposal presented. First, I think it is a relevant response to Nozick (1977). We have maintained the law of diminishing marginal utility and the concept of strict preference. The law is applied to the concept of the sum of needs satisfied with the sum of goods (the portfolio). The strict preference is applied around goods.

There is no problem explaining why 2 beers over 1 are sometimes preferred (example of Wysocki and Block 2018a) or 4 eggs over 3 (example of Rothbard 1956). This is due to the different perceived combination of needs and goods to be included in the portfolio in terms of the combinations of needs. A combination of 2 beers or 4 eggs that a person may want to include into the portfolio is preferred because of the combination of needs to be satisfied (e.g., to get drunk faster or more intensely, or the preference for a sweet cake over an omelet satisfaction of needs—Rothbard example). Whereas the law of diminishing marginal utility is applied to a marginal change of the portfolio thus created. Using these examples, it is also possible to explain the economization of some non-economic free goods that are included in the portfolio if they satisfy a special complex of needs (e.g., the air enabling us to survive underwater), and we remove these goods from the portfolio as soon as the actual complex of perceived needs changes (e.g., we will stop diving).

We can better express ourselves using a moral (not economic) example given in Hoppe (2005) about a mother who had two sons, Peter and Paul, whom she loves equally. When they are drowning, and she can save only one of them. According to Wysocki (2017), saving Peter only implies that it happened that way, and that, for whatever reason, the mother prefers the world with Peter and not with Paul. According to Wysocki, we know nothing else from the praxeological point of view. From our theory's point of view, we know that "whatever reason" is not enough. We know that it is always a combination of needs and a combination of means and circumstances that made the mother choose Peter and not Paul. From a moral, legal, and praxeological point of view, this knowledge about the combination of needs and means gives us a point of reference to assess what the mother has done. Whether she will be a heroine or a murderer, whether we will sympathize with her, or not, or whether we say that she did the best she could or not, and so on.

The proposed solution also shows that Machaj (2007) is correct with his focus. He is focusing on the evaluation as the main way of explaining the problem. In my opinion, what is interesting is that in this way, it is also possible to explain the neoclassical claims about indifference. A person can actually be indifferent to the good A vs. good B, or any multi-dimensional model of goods (an example of multi-dimensionality is used in Wysocki 2016) because the case of indifference implies no change of portfolio, i.e., a person prefers to have the present time portfolio in a time continuum, which they composed in the past and which currently suits them (present time) best (focused on the future elimination of uneasiness).[17] O'Neill's (2010) remarks that needs should be assessed in the context of "*no worse than*" changes the meaning within the context of the solution presented here; meaning the complex of needs can be met by different combinations of the goods within the portfolio. This does not imply a weak indifference among particular goods, it implies a *relative* grouping of goods in the portfolio that enables the satisfaction of a *relative* combination of needs.

The neoclassical mainstream must acknowledge that during the moment when a person is indifferent to good A and B, the person is actually in an optimal position; he/she is in his/her kind of equilibrium. Indeed, being indifferent to both A and B implies that the person is satisfied with what he/she has—some portfolio of goods that he/she anticipates will best respond to what the future will bring. For Austrians, it is possible to realize that the invariance of the portfolio is not necessarily an intentional choice for a person at any time-point in their life; e.g., while sleeping or doing nothing economically, or just performing certain actions automatically without the need to interact economically. It does not mean that he/she does not act. It means that a person does not act *economically* in the sense of a purposeful change of portfolio by which he/she satisfies his/her needs. This is understandable because a person can be ignorant of slight changes in his/her portfolio. This is because it is possible to meet a combination of needs by way of a portfolio over time. Only a significant marginal change to the portfolio or a different combination of needs causes a feeling of uneasiness after which an intentional action is taken to re-arrange the indifferent state of affairs—the asked portfolio.

---

[17]This knowledge has implications for the problem of equilibrium, the process of equilibrium, or the definition of the state of equilibrium at the individual level as we saw in Chapter 3.

Similarly, we can now see the freshness and relevance of the solution presented in Block (1980), where he shifted the state of indifference per se into the thymological field. Although it was necessary to make several adjustments to this assertion, in the thymological field the indifference remains. However, and this is a controversial piece of a consequence the argumentation presented is also found in the action (praxeological) area. Indifference is not only a psychological-historical conception, but it is also a conception of our actual actions, i.e., it is an action-thymological concept.[18] At this point, it can be argued that the decision for no change to the portfolio still means strict preference (action). In my opinion, this is a thymological state of the matter because the portfolio was compiled sometime in the past. This ambiguity exists because we deal with Nozick's objection as another layer of thinking—the sum of needs is satisfied by the portfolio in the future. Therefore, to me, it seems relevant to mention that the concept of indifference is precisely *action-thymological* in nature. This allows the Austrian School thinkers to understand what the neoclassic mainstream refers to when they talk about optimality in making decisions based on indifference.

4.3.2 Implications Within the Mainstream View of the Problem of Indifference

The solution as presented, also has some implications for the mainstream approach. As we have shown—indifference is a state that is *the result* of some intentional economic activity (action). We do not make decisions based on indifference but in the context of indifference (as our benchmark). We decide, act, and try to achieve the given state of affairs (indifference). The emphasis on describing the decision-making process is the point of the Austrian School. The choice and decision must always be specific. We cannot make decisions based on indifference. However, as we have shown, the choice and decision lead to some state of indifference. Let us illustrate from the point of view of this text how it is possible

[18]We will see how Block or Wysocki, whose opinion is that indifference is purely subject to thymology (the area of psychological-historical reasons for action), will potentially respond to this statement.

to look at this methodological twist. This description can be achieved by answering the following question[19]: "*Is the glass I have in the kitchen and the glass I have in my hand the same good? Is there an indifference?*"

There is no indifference at the level of choice associated with choosing some economic good. The indifference is only at the level of the overall situation. The overall situation is the satisfaction of some combination of needs by some combination of goods (the portfolio) that I have while I do not need to change this combination. The given overall situation is, of course, composed of some parts, but the combination of the given parts also creates an ontologically independent structure of its perception (Lawson 2012). We can perceive only heterogeneous choice at the level of specific goods. However, we can also perceive the homogeneous structure of some state of overall affairs at the level of the overall situation. By combining and creating relationships between individual parts, we strive for a given overall situation. Let us examine this closely.

Let's say I'm sitting in the living room watching TV and, on the table, next to me I have a glass of water[20]; I am thirsty. However, I go to the kitchen to get a glass of water from there and drink from it. Obviously, I have demonstrated that the glass of water in the kitchen is *the* good I chose. I was not indifferent to the glass next to me or the glass in the kitchen, a few meters from me. Why? Maybe because the combination of my needs implies going to the kitchen for a glass of water. The combination of needs can be such that when I drink water, I don't want to cut my lips and the cup next to me seems to be dangerous (maybe it's a little cracked, or I only think it is cracked). Or it may be that I need the exercise, and some steps to the kitchen and back are a suitable way to fulfill a given combination of needs—my exercise. The choice and subsequent action is always particular and depends on the combination of needs that I want to satisfy. The choice is not about meeting needs that I have already satisfied. It could still be that I will not drink at all, no matter how thirsty I am. Let's say that I keep watching TV and I'm

[19]I had received the question from an unknown reviewer. I think that it goes directly to the point, so I will use it to demonstrate the methodological point.

[20]I would like to slightly change the example in the question above; this is only a minor change from the original question, but it demonstrates the situation in a better way. However, if the cup is in hand, the same reasoning applies, in principle.

in a situation where I have been, 30 minutes or maybe an hour before. *This* is the description of the indifferent thymological-praxeological state of affairs. No matter how thirsty I feel I won't make a choice yet; the given perception of the overall situation is not sufficiently significant for me to make a choice. Only a marginal significant change in the perception of this whole state can cause me to decide to drink from the glass next to me or from the glass in the kitchen, depending on the current combination of needs.

This example shows the process of transition between choice, action, and indifference. The choice is an intentional decision and is made on the basis of an assessment of costs and expected revenue. Each action is associated with some cost and an expected achievement of a situation or the removal of some uneasiness connected with a situation that would be worse if I did not act. In other words, the expected achievement of some returns (which ex post can be assessed as a loss). This is also the reason for the bid-ask exchange phenomenon on the market, which indicates that I have to get rid of something in order to acquire something else. In a nonmonetary economy, it shows what I offer from my portfolio to someone else's portfolio, and what I expect to gain from the other person's portfolio. The same is true at the level of the individual. When choosing (alone; not in an exchange), I consider the cost (Is it worth getting up from the couch and going for a glass of water in the kitchen?) and what I get (a subjective gain such as training, quenching the thirst), while it is still true that I can stay in an indifferent position (I continue watching TV) without changing the overall state of my own affairs. If I remain in the unchanged state of affairs, this is not a third option or choice—nothing happens. I am merely sitting and watching TV; the decision was made an hour ago. This is true, despite the fact that I feel thirsty and that I also know that I have to walk to achieve fitness. It is a condition that has a thymological-praxeological character. Why is this so? The marginal change that is of course happening, i.e., the body is gradually increasing its state of thirst so I only slowly realize that I have been sitting too long and should start walking, is not significant enough for me to move out of this balanced state. Only a significant marginal change causes intentional choice. The significance of the change is related to either a change within the portfolio (I consume goods which I have so I have to act again) or a change in the perception of the combination of needs. Only this raises a reason to re-assess the situation, consider the costs and gains, conduct action, and potentially move toward a new state of indifference.

This means that a person judges what he/she spends and what he/she gets in the context of how the overall state of the portfolio changes. In this way the person can assess the ex post economic error as well. It may well be that I find out that that it was not particularly wise of me to get a glass of water from the kitchen, since I had one next to me and did not notice. In other words, I could have been in an equilibristic position, which I left due to my ignorance of the state of affairs, and later I regretted the action of going to the kitchen. The countermeasure may be that, in the future, I will buy multi-colored cups in order to be more attentive or binoculars because I discover that my vision had deteriorated. And the good (the binoculars or multi-colored cups) will once again begin to contribute to the puzzle-mosaic of the whole state of affairs for which I am striving.

This description indicates *what is* the indifference or the definition of indifference. We know that the theory presented here implies the existence of a mental concept in the form of a combination of needs and a combination of means (the portfolio of goods). We also know that the utility of goods is attributed to goods. The usefulness of goods is therefore derived from us; it is not an intrinsic given part of the goods. At the same time, choice directs us from one state of the portfolio structure (when we have to give up something) to another state of the portfolio structure (when we get something), while the overall combination of a given state implies the optimality of the achieved state of affairs. So, what is indifference, apart from the fact that it is a situation in which there is no choice and consumers have no preference?

The indifference state between A-good and B-good describes an *ideal idea of a part of the portfolio structure, which is connected with A and B-goods.* Until a person reaches some local state of indifference between A and B, they try to add A and B to the structure of the portfolio that completes the ideal structural state of the portfolio. This way, a person maximizes their intended utility at the overall level and once it is achieved, no additional combination of goods in question is needed.

The state of indifference is thus some *intended idea of the structure of the portfolio* first. Through action, we fulfill the idea. If the given structure is achieved, we maximize our intended utility of the overall state of affairs, which we transpose into realistically owned goods, combinations of real things that we actually own.

This interpretation implies that the current graphical representation of the indifference problem should be moved to 3D space graphs, leaving the classical representation in 2D space.[21] This is not entirely new knowledge; it is Sotelo and Block (2014, pp. 8–11) who show this kind of attempt to sketch curves in a multi-spatial way and also show the development in plotting indifferent curves through different economic literature. Sotelo and Block (2014, diagram nos. 32–34, pp. 36–38) conclude that sketches used by Vickery, or Boulding, or McClosky have the character of various landscape sketches that most faithfully depict the situation related to indifference analysis. The topological description of the problem should enable us to describe the process between choice and indifference as intended as well as the consequently achieved state of affairs. That is when the indifference (e.g., between goods A and B) is at the beginning of the process of achieving some intentional part of the structure of the portfolio we would like to achieve, based on some existing portfolio restrictions (or budget restrictions when we move into the monetary economy).

References

Bilo, Šimon. 2004. The Theory of Imputation: A Context of Value Spreads Between Means and Ends. WWW DOCUMENT. http://www2.gcc.edu/dept/econ/ASSC/Papers2004/Imputation_Bilo.pdf. Accessed on 9 Jan 2019.

Block, E. Walter. 1980. On Robert Nozick's On Austrian Methodology. *Inquiry* 23 (4, Fall): 397–444.

[21]The author is unable to describe the mathematical notation of the situation, given the fact that he is not trained in this area.

Block, E. Walter. 2009. Rejoinder to Hoppe on Indifference. *Quarterly Journal of Austrian Economics* 12 (1): 52–59. WWW DOCUMENT. https://mises.org/library/rejoinder-hoppe-indifference.

Block, E. Walter. 2012. Response to Ben O'Neill on Indifference. *Dialogue* (2): 76–93. WWW DOCUMENT. https://dlib.uni-svishtov.bg/handle/10610/2380.

Block, E. Walter, and Barnett II. William. 2010. Rejoinder to Hoppe on Indifference, Once Again. *Reason Papers* 32: 141–154. WWW DOCUMENT. https://philpapers.org/rec/BLORTH-5.

Engliš, Karel. 1930. *Teleologie jako forma vědeckého poznání* [The Teleology as a Form of Scientific Knowledge]. Praha: F. Topič Publisher.

Hoppe, H. Hans. 2005. "Must Austrians Embrace Indifference?" *Quarterly Journal of Austrian Economics* 8 (4): 87–91. WWW DOCUMENT. https://mises.org/library/must-austrians-embrace-indifference.

Hoppe, H. Hans. 2009. Further Notes on Preference and Indifference: Rejoinder to Block. *Quarterly Journal of Austrian Economics* 12 (1): 60–64. WWW DOCUMENT. https://mises.org/library/further-notes-preference-and-indifference-rejoinder-block.

Lachmann, Ludwig M. 2005. Expectations and the Meaning of Institutions: Essays in Economics, ed. Ch. Donald Lavoi. First published 1994 by Routledge. Taylor & Francis e-Library. WWW DOCUMENT. https://www.mises.at/static/literatur/Buch/lachmann-expectations-and-the-meaning-of-institutions.pdf.

Lawson, Tony. 2012. Ontology and the Study of Social Reality: Emergence, Organisation, Community, Power, Social Relations, Corporations, Artefacts and Money. In Lawson, Tony. 2019. *The Nature of Social Reality: Issues in Social Ontology* (Economics as Social Theory). New York, USA: Routledge.

Machaj, Mateusz. 2007. A Praxeological Case for Homogeneity and Indifference. *New Perspectives on Political Economy* 3 (2): 231–238. https://www.cevroinstitut.cz/upload/ck/files/NPPE/nppe3_2.pdf.

Mises, Ludwig. 1949, 1998. Human Action. Scholar Edition. Auburn, Ala. Ludwig Von Mises Institute. WWW DOCUMENT. https://mises.org/library/human-action-0/html/pp/663.

Nozick, Robert. 1977. On Austrian Methodology. *Synthese. Vol. 36, No. 3, Mathematical Methods of the Social Sciences, Part II (Nov. 1977)*, 353–392. WWW DOCUMENT. https://www.jstor.org/stable/20115233.

O'Neill, Ben. 2010. Choice and Indifference: A Critique of the Strict Preference Approach. *The Quarterly Journal of Austrian Economics* 13 (1, Spring 2010): 71–98.

Pavlík, Ján. 2004. *F.A. Hayek a teorie spontánniho řádu* [F.A. Hayek and the Theory of Spontaneous Order]. Praha: Profesional Publishing.

Pavlík, Ján. 2006. Austrian Economics and the Problems of Apriorism. *E-Logos—Electronic Journal for Philosophy* 13: 1–73. ISSN 1211-0442. WWW DOCUMENT. http://nb.vse.cz/kfil/elogos/science/pavl106.pdf.

Pošvanc, Matúš. 2019a. Evolutionary Possibilities of the Emergence of Economic Calculation and Money: The Problem of the Impossibility of Socialism. Working Paper. WWW DOCUMENT. https://www.researchgate.net/publication/334084336_Evolutionary_possibilities_of_the_emergence_of_economic_calculation_and_money_The_problem_of_the_impossibility_of_socialism.

Pošvanc, Matúš. 2019b. Why I Am Not Mises' Adherent. Working Paper. WWW DOCUMENT. https://www.researchgate.net/publication/333774098_Why_I_am_not_Mises'_Adherent.

Rothbard, N. Murray. 1997, 1956. Toward a Reconstruction of Utility and Welfare Economics. In *The Logic of Action One* (pp. 211–254). UK: Edward Elgar Publishing Limited. WWW DOCUMENT. https://mises.org/library/toward-reconstruction-utility-and-welfare-economics-1.

Rothbard, N. Murray. 2004. 1962, 1970. Man, Economy, and State. Auburn, Ala. Mises Institute. WWW DOCUMENT. https://mises.org/library/man-economy-and-state-power-and-market.

Sotelo, Jose Antonio Manuel Aguirre, and Walter E. Block. 2014. Indifference Curve Analysis: The Correct and the Incorrect. *Oeconomia Copernicana* 5 (4): 7–43. https://doi.org/10.12775/OeC.2014.025.

Stroukal, Dominik. 2014. Inkorporace metodologického singularismu do metodologie ekonomie [Incorporation of the Methodological Singularism into the Methodology of Economy]. *E-Logos—Electronic Journal for Philosophy* 21 (1): 1–15. WWW DOCUMENT. https://nb.vse.cz/kfil/elogos/science/stroukal14.pdf.

Wysocki, Igor. 2016. Indifference—In Defense of Orthodoxy. *Societas et Ius* 5: 15–30.

Wysocki, Igor. 2017. A Note on Block-Hoppe Debate on Indifference. *Quarterly Journal of Austrian Economics* 20 (4): 360–365. WWW DOCUMENT. https://mises.org/library/note-block-hoppe-debate-indifference.

Wysocki, Igor, and E. Walter Block. 2018a. An Analysis of the Supply Curve: Does It Depict Homogeneity Among Its Constituent Elements? Another Rejoinder to Nozick. *MEST Journal* 6: 132–143. https://doi.org/10.12709/mest.06.06.01.14.

Wysocki, Igor, and, E. Walter Block. 2018b. Homogeneity, Heterogeneity, the Supply Curve, and Consumer Theory. *Quarterly Journal of Austrian Economics* 21 (4, Winter 2018): 398–416.

5
Conclusion

At the beginning we set out to answer two basic questions: "*Why are we successful? And how do we know we have made an economic error?*" These were not trivial questions. They are necessarily related to the problem of estimating the future, the question of the rationality of our actions, the problem of the concept of economic profit/loss and costs, or the problem of the coordination of several individuals in the economic community. The direction of the solution presented here has a conceptual character, its *modus operandi* lies in the form of a modified theory of subjective value. It was shown that a slight modification of the theory enables us to deal with the above-mentioned questions, however, only with reference to Hayek–Pavlík's method of evolutionary apriorism based on: the so-called "germ cell" as a basic concept, the interconnections between simple phenomena causing the borders of complexity and the crossing of the boundaries of complexity by new emergent "more abstract" phenomena, creating new simplicity. We claimed that we estimate the future on an individual level by relativizing its *specific* meaning. We prepare for several eventualities concerning some composition of needs that may occur, by building suitable portfolios of economic goods.

M. Pošvanc, *The Evolutionary Invisible Hand*,
Palgrave Studies in Classical Liberalism,
https://doi.org/10.1007/978-3-030-71800-8_5

It can be said that we do not strictly predict the future state of our needs, which we prepare to meet via some collections of goods (the portfolio); we relativize its specific meaning because we compose needs as some combination of ideas of what something should be like. It is some kind of combination of goods and some kind of combination of the features of goods which we try to achieve in order to meet some relative and uncertain composition of our needs. This process is taking place, as well as an evolutionary development of new forms of the combination of needs and new combinations of the features of goods.

Although we are faced with the presented theory of some kind of subjective relativism, it is not finally so. Yes, it is still correct that what is appropriate for one human subject may not be appropriate for another. However, given that we grasp *economic reality* through the relativization of the future in its concrete form, as well as in the mutual interaction of individuals in the community, it was never a problem for our predecessors to implement cooperation in principle. It was not a matter of attaining *exactly* what the other one wanted. It was enough to arrive at this estimation in relative terms of accuracy. If, on the other hand, we grasped the reality, the future, and the needs of others in a mode of strict concreteness, we would inevitably get into the dilemma defined by Hayek (1937), meaning here how it is possible for the individual perception of goods to be transmitted as objective information to another individual, while at the same time not knowing everything about his subjective point of view. By modifying the theory of subjective value in terms of the concept of the sum of needs satisfied by the sum of economic goods at the level of the individual concepts of the perception of economic reality, a very large space for explaining the mutual coordination of individuals is initiated. We have to realize that the compositional and relational character of the concept of needs and portfolio enable us to also use some time-invariant mental concepts based on which we are able to construct our own tools to compare two points or state of affairs over time as well as, and this is thrilling knowledge, we are able to construct intersubjective tools which enable us to communicate with each other the inner conditions we are trying to achieve. It enables us realistically to define tools for the economic concepts of success/error, costs, the economic calculation unit, to explain how coordination takes place on the level of ideas and plans. It shows us that there are two kinds of concepts—subjective and intersubjective. They have their own characters and they are phenomena per se. Some of them exist on subjective as well as intersubjective levels; such as on the level of subjective success/error, costs, our own calculation unit, profit, and loss. However, there are some phenomena which have an exclusively intersubjective character such as prices spreads, interest, and money which we subsequently use to recognize the success/error, costs, profit and loss. As was shown these are used concerning our knowledge about meeting the needs of others members of an economic community. All intersubjective phenomena are here described as emergent; they emerge based on the interactions of individuals.

The fact is that subjective relativism inevitably leads to problems of connotation. But as was shown, these problems were eliminated. How? Individual economic relativism was overcome through intersubjectively created standards in order to understand each other. Our *modus operandi* was thus a description of how new, intersubjective concepts are emerging from the individual concept of grasping the economic reality (the portfolio). It was argued that these standards enabled us to rationally communicate our individual ideas about economic reality with each other. This is so that the given standards became valid coordination mechanisms of human activity during the socio-cultural evolution. These intersubjective concepts did not occur consciously. As we have shown, they arose first spontaneously against the backdrop of the not yet fully conscious activities of our predecessors, i.e., in the sense of Hayek–Pavlík's theory of evolutionary (intersubjective) apriorism, as a sedimentary history, which is then used by already conscious minds in an economic interaction with others. However, once the rational mind emerged in its full consciousness, it was a kind of forever-present interaction: the very notion of the conscious differentiation of human subjects' activities and the background natural selection of abstract general or apriori principles which are transformed not only into the particular forms of normative orders but also into the particular forms of teleological—economic—tools to enable us to recognize our successful or erroneous economic activities. From this vantage point, they are emerging elements of the economic interaction of individuals. The standardization of economic communication thus takes place at the level of interaction of more individuals. The standardization, i.e., the "spontaneous agreement" of more people transmitted through economic interactions and normative social ties to other members of the community, subsequently allows for the emergence of what we are able to call (mutual) intersubjectively created coordinates of individual economic action. Individual economic relativism, which would inevitably lead to chaos and make life impossible within the community, was actually eliminated by evolutionary economic-normative standardization. This process is still alive and will continue to be alive.

In the second part, the introduced concept led us to related conclusions regarding the definition of the concept of equilibration at the individual as well as at the social level. It allowed us to define, I believe, a realistic teleological idea of the individual state of equilibrium. The concept also allows us to define a static-dynamic mode, respectively a thymological-praxeological mode of individual equilibrium. The above concept allows us to identify the teleological causes behind the equilibrium efforts as well as the teleological causes that lead to disequilibrium—on the level of the individual as well as within the market process. We left the domain of prices and focused on the domain of spreads—individual as well as market present ones. This enabled us to shift the coordination process with regard to the level of plans, ideas, and expectations; and left behind static states of outcomes defined by prices or defined by outcomes of plans, ideas, and expectations. We have tried to show why it seems to us that an "invisible hand" of the market coordinates us and why it seems to us that some invisible hand "leads" market participants to some form of coordination. In my opinion, this section can also be presented as an attempt to link Mises's concept of equilibration (after its modifications) with Hayek's theory of social ordering. This concept also allows us to construct model economic situations for the purposes of social scientists in order to elaborate the complexity of market phenomena and the importance of the phenomenon of entrepreneurship, which can under no circumstances be removed from any theory of equilibration. Any model situation should also be a description of some result of human activities and thus the phenomenon of entrepreneurship. It should be clear from what has been presented that any attempts at the central planning of the economic community must be less effective than market-based solutions.

The last part looked at the problem of individual equilibration and the related topic of indifference. The topic of indifference is often considered redundant in the circles of the Austrian school, respectively non-existent. However, as Nozick (1977) rightly states, if the Austrians did not recognize the existence of the phenomenon of indifference, one of the basic pillars of the marginalist concept, the law of diminishing marginal utility could not be valid. It is therefore important to address the challenge addressed by Nozick. In the text, we have shown once again the vital use of the presented concept. Similarly, the proposed solution allows us to link the Austrian School with the neoclassical approach to the problem of indifference and choice. The solution indicates that the proposed modification of the theory of subjective value has a vital character. The solution suggests that indifference analysis describes the search for the optimal setting of the individual portfolio—the state of goods in the broadest sense of the term. The solution is also compatible with the above-presented theory of equilibration.

The conclusions of this work imply the need to differentiate between individual economic phenomena and social (intersubjective) economic phenomena, but they also require a description of their interdependence and influence. Many of the economic problems of the Austrian school today are seen only from the point of view of the individual. I think it is necessary to admit the existence of intersubjective economic phenomena, which have their emergent nature. This will allow us to better understand phenomena such as interest, money, the banking system, and it will allow us to more accurately describe related areas such as capital theory or the economic cycle theory. Differentiation will also make it possible to better identify and understand e.g., political influences on the economic community, or to show the mutual influence of the free market and political phenomena. From a practical point of view, differentiation could provide useful information for the behavior of political elites in decision-making and interfering with the economic freedoms of individuals.

My final remarks are connected with my personal persuasion that the presented theoretical solution is still far from a fully fledged description of social and economic phenomena. Although I tried to use a high degree of abstraction in order to provide as general a principle as possible, it is necessary to state that the proposed solutions will need to be further elaborated upon. I therefore see this text as an invitation to further research and, of course, as a critical evaluation of the proposed solutions. The problem we face is one of the most impressive in terms of its complexity; and only this can be stated without exaggeration.

If the vitality of the presented approach is proven, we are faced with the need to explain the origin and character of the described phenomena in an evolutionary way. It seems that we are looking at various economic intersubjectively formed (mind) structures which materialize in the societal phenomena (such as laws, institutions, capital structures, economic plans, accounting and economic standards, interest, money, etc.). They arise in an emergent way—their characteristic feature is that they seem to be as if "quietly formed" against the background of the individual activities of people and their mutual interactions. They affect people's intuitive and rational decisions. The mutual interactions created among people subsequently cause the limits of their mutual coexistence, in terms of being reached. The limits of coexistence are subsequently exceeded—precisely by using those structures that seem to appear suddenly and begin to be used as better abstractions for the grasping of economic phenomena.

It is interesting from my point of view that, in principle, these are mind structures. First, they were vague, unspoken, and intuitive; the products of the natural evolution of our predecessors living in some prehistoric groups. However, how differentiation of the mind started to create more aware humans, the formulation of these structures appeared in the forms of the first primitive ideas, plans and intentions based on an interaction with others. It is evident that subjective and intersubjective phenomena influence each other and enable the further development of self-awareness and the development of the materialization of these structures in the form of different normative institutions and concepts. To claim, therefore, that we are looking at one of the most impressive complexes of reality is not an exaggeration.

The program that Hayek indicated within the Austrian school is therefore the vital path we should take and explore. The program outlined here contains this ambition. From my personal perspective, I plan to go further and evolve these directions. The theory presented here with regard to how we estimate the future, how we learn and how we can assess economic success and error, and what tools we have created to do so in order that we can coexist as individuals with individual goals and needs is one of the gradual and necessary steps needed to modify the Austrian theory of capital and the economic cycle. However, the presentation of this modification is subject to another modification. I think it is necessary to modify some of the premises of Hayek's theory of cultural evolution and to try to think about the possibilities of connecting cultural and biological evolution. It will probably be necessary to show how cultural evolution is based on the mutual interaction of human rationality and what we call "natural selection." It will be necessary to demonstrate the principles of this interaction and to focus on how the intended actions of human beings and the unintended consequences of these actions are affected. I think that there are many interesting questions in before us which are worth exploring.

References

Hayek, A. Friedrich. 1937. Economics and Knowledge. *Economica*. New Series 4 (13): 33–54. Online Version on WWW DOCUMENT. https://mises.org/library/economics-and-knowledge. Accessed on 22 Jan 2021.

Nozick, Robert. 1977. On Austrian Methodology. *Synthese. Vol. 36, No. 3, Mathematical Methods of the Social Sciences, Part II (Nov. 1977)*, 353–392. WWW DOCUMENT. https://www.jstor.org/stable/20115233.

References

Block, J.H., C.O. Fisch, and M. Van Praag. 2017. The Schumpeterian Entrepreneur: A Review of the Empirical Evidence on the Antecedents, Behaviour and Consequences of Innovative Entrepreneurship. *Industry and Innovation* 24 (1): 61–95. https://doi.org/10.1080/13662716.2016.1216397.

Caplan, Bryan. 2001. Probability, Common Sense, and Realism: A Reply to Hülsmann and Block. *The Quarterly Journal of Austrian Economics* 4 (2): 69–86. WWW DOCUMENT. https://mises-media.s3.amazonaws.com/qjae4_2_6_6.pdf.

Gunning, J. Patrick. 1989. Mises on the Evenly Rotating Economy. *Review of Austrian Economics* 3: 123–122. WWW DOCUMENT. https://mises.org/library/mises-evenly-rotating-economy.

Hayek, A. Friedrich. 1952, 1976. *The Sensory Order*. Chicago, IL, USA: University of Chicago Press.

Hoppe, H. Hans. 2009. Further Notes on Preference and Indifference: Rejoinder to Block. *Quarterly Journal of Austrian Economics* 12 (1): 60–64. WWW DOCUMENT. https://mises.org/library/further-notes-preference-and-indifference-rejoinder-block.

M. Pošvanc, *The Evolutionary Invisible Hand*, Palgrave Studies in Classical Liberalism, https://doi.org/10.1007/978-3-030-71800-8

Kirzner, M. Israel. 1960. *Economic Point of View*. Kansas City: Sheed and Ward. WWW DOCUMENT. https://mises.org/library/economic-point-view-essay-history-economic-thought.

Klein, G. Peter, and K. Sandra Klein. 2001. Do Entrepreneurs Make Profitable Mistakes? Evidence from Corporate Divestitures. *The Quarterly Journal of Austrian Economics* 4 (2): 3–23.

Knight, H. Frank. 1964. *Risk Uncertainty and Profit*. New York: Augustus M. Kelley. WWW DOCUMENT. https://mises.org/library/risk-uncertainty-and-profit.

Lachmann, M. Ludwig. 1977. *Capital, Expectations, and the Market Process: Essays on the Theory of the Market Economy*, ed. with an Introduction by Walter E. Grinder. Kansas City: Sheed Andrews and McMeel. WWW DOCUMENT. https://oll.libertyfund.org/title/lachmann-capital-expectations-and-the-market-process.

Luther, J. William. 2014. Evenly Rotating Economy: A New Modeling Technique for an Old Equilibrium Construct. *The Review of Austrian Economics* 27: 403–417. https://doi.org/10.1007/s11138-013-0242-8.

Packard, D. Mark, B. Brent Clark, and Peter G. Klein. 2017. Uncertainty Types and Transitions in the Entrepreneurial Process. *Organization Science* 28 (5): 840–856. https://doi.org/10.1287/orsc.2017.1143.

Potužák, Pavel. 2013. Hayekova teorie lidské mysli [Hayek's Theory of Human Mind]. *E-logos: Electronic Journal for Philosophy*. WWW DOCUMENT. https://nb.vse.cz/kfil/elogos/mind/potuzak13.pdf.

Ricketts, M., and I.M. Kirzner. 1992. Kirzner's Theory of Entrepreneurship-A Critique. In *Austrian Economics: Tensions and New Directions*. Recent Economic Thought Series, vol. 30, ed. Bruce J. Caldwell and Stephan Boehm. Dordrecht: Springer. https://doi.org/10.1007/978-94-011-2186-6_3.

Schumpeter, A. Joseph, and Redvers Oppie. 1934. *The Theory of Economic Development: An Inquiry into Profits, Capital, Credit, Interest, and the Business Cycle*. Cambridge, MA: Harvard University Press.

Wang, Mei, Marc Rieger, and Thorsten Hens. 2011. How Time Preferences Differ: Evidence from 45 Countries. Discussion Papers 2011/18, Norwegian School of Economics, Department of Business and Management Science.

Index

M. Pošvanc, *The Evolutionary Invisible Hand*,
Palgrave Studies in Classical Liberalism,
https://doi.org/10.1007/978-3-030-71800-8

The manufacturer's authorised representative in the EU is Springer Nature Customer Service Centre GmbH, Europaplatz 3, 69115 Heidelberg, Germany. If you have any concerns regarding our products, please contact ProductSafety@springernature.com

Printed and bound by CPI Group (UK) Ltd, Croydon, CR0 4YY
30/09/2026
02225702-0015